Oakton Community College

Morton Grove, Illinois

LAWRENCE L. LANGER

the
age
of
atrocity

Death in Modern Literature

Beacon Press: Boston

(hardcover) 9 8 7 6 5 4 3 2 1

Nelly Sachs: excerpted from *Fahrt ins Staub lose,* © Suhrkamp Verlag, Frank-
furt am Main, 1967; and from "Chorus of Clouds" from *The Seeker and Other
Poems* by Nelly Sachs, translated by Ruth and Matthew Mead. Copyright © 1970
by Farrar, Straus & Giroux, Inc. Reprinted with the permission of Suhrkamp
Verlag and Farrar, Straus & Giroux, Inc.

Thomas Mann: excerpts from *The Magic Mountain,* translated by H.T. Lowe-
Porter, copyright 1927 by Alfred A. Knopf, Inc.; copyright 1952 by Thomas
Mann. Reprinted with the permission of Alfred A. Knopf, Inc.

Albert Camus: excerpts from *The Plague,* copyright 1948 by Stuart Gilbert;
and from *Lyrical and Critical Essays,* copyright 1968 by Alfred A. Knopf, Inc.,
© copyright 1967 by Hamish Hamilton, Ltd. and Alfred A. Knopf, Inc. Reprinted
with the permission of Alfred A. Knopf, Inc.

Alexander Solzhenitsyn: excerpts from *Cancer Ward* by Alexander Solzhenitsyn,
translated from the Russian by Nicholas Bethell and David Burg. English translation © The Bodley Head Ltd., 1968, 1969. Front and back matter of American
edition © 1969 by Farrar, Straus & Giroux, Inc. Reprinted with the permission
of Farrar, Straus & Giroux, Inc. and the Bodley Head Ltd.

Charlotte Delbo: excerpts from *Une Connaissance Inutile,* © 1970 by Les
Éditions de Minuit. Reprinted with the permission of Les Éditions de Minuit.

Library of Congress Cataloging in Publication Data

Langer, Lawrence L.
    The age of atrocity.
    Includes bibliographical references and index.
    1. Death in literature. 2. Atrocities in literature.
2. Literature, Modern—20th century—History and criticism.
    I. Title.
PN56.D413   809'933'54   77-88335
ISBN 0-8070-6368-1

For Sandy

Andy and Ellen

Sterbespieler sind wir
Gewöhnen euch sanft an den Tod.
Ihr Ungeübten, die in den Nächten
    nichts lernen.
Viele Engel sind euch gegeben
Aber ihr seht sie nicht.

We play at dying,
Accustom you gently to death.
You, the inexperienced, who learn
    nothing in the nights.
Many angels are given you
But you do not see them.

—Nelly Sachs

CONTENTS

PREFACE

Recently an acquaintance told me a story that does much to
illuminate the main theme of this study. She recalled her
childhood years in eastern Europe during the Hitler era, flee-
ing from one sanctuary to another with her parents to escape
the Nazi Holocaust. Occasionally, from her place of concealment, she witnessed mass executions of Jews. Even more
often, she heard whispered tales about such bizarre episodes.
They were engraved on her imagination. She survived, and
after the war she made her way with her parents to Israel.
Shortly after their arrival, a close friend of the family died,
and her mother took her to the funeral—the first she had ever
attended. She remembers the coffin being lowered into the
grave, and her own confusion when some men began shovel-
ling in the earth. Turning to her mother in distress and per-
plexity, she asked: "But where are the *other* dead people?"

The notion in a child's mind that men and women no longer
die alone but en masse, that the grave is not "a fine and private place" but a dumping ground for innumerable anonymous
corpses, is a pure example of how atrocity may transform our
view of human destiny. To be sure, the example is extreme,
since unlike most of us this child lacked the opportunity to
develop an inner imagery adequate to the experience of dying,
an imagery confirmed by the ceremony of burial and mourning that normally eases the passage from life to death. Her
own recollection of death as violent, "communal," and pre-

mature clashed with the solemn tone of the funeral. The memory of atrocity was her heritage, and the traditional imagery of dying did nothing to validate it.

This book is concerned with the evolution of the idea of atrocity in the twentieth century, and the attempt of a few significant writers to assess its influence on our conception of the human image. The shadow of atrocity haunts that image, diminishes its stature, without quite effacing it—at least this is a theme that links the works considered in this volume. But the sheer quantity of lives wasted by atrocity has corrupted the redeeming power of tragic insight, which once enabled the imagination to leap beyond physical death to the consolations of a noble moral or spiritual destiny. "Almost invariably," observes Frederick Hoffman in *The Mortal No: Death and the Modern Imagination,* "tragedy requires a controlled view and estimate of corpses. It also demands a clear line of progress in the analysis of events leading to death. Death as total surprise loses much of its tragic value." Death as a sudden and discontinuous experience—death as atrocity—threatens to reduce life to a cruel and random event, unless the imagination can learn to survive on a leaner diet. The facts of recent history have destroyed much of the sustenance that once fed our conceptions of human dignity. This book explores some of the implications of an age that has imposed on the traditional idea of death the prospect of atrocity; it records and hopes to illuminate a shift from the habit of satisfying spiritual appetites to the more urgent predicament of avoiding psychological starvation.

It would be naive, however, to argue that the idea of atrocity was born with Freud, World War I, or any single crisis of the twentieth century. Goya knew it well, as his *Disasters of War* testify, and many others, like de Sade, Daumier, and the Voltaire of *Candide,* share with him the sense of the body's dehumanization which atrocity can inflict on its victims. But this study is not a survey of the experience of atrocity in history and art. Its intentions are more limited, its scope less ambitious. I am primarily concerned with the gradual erosion of the human image in selected works by four authors as they respond to major traumas of our time: Mann to World War I, Camus to World War II, Solzhenitsyn to the Soviet labor camps, and Charlotte Delbo to the Nazi extermination camps. The progress from death to atrocity in these works may be described as a momentum from man dying to men dying to mass death to mass annihilation; and as the artist struggles to invent images equal to the horror of the historical events, we encounter the dilemma of a culture imaginatively unequipped to respond to the reality in which it is enmeshed.

To be in touch with the intolerable, and to remain psychologically whole, is the vexing challenge that confronts us. To ignore the intolerable, as if death by atrocity were an aberration and not a crucial fact of our mental life, is to pretend an innocence that history discredits and statistics defame. But it is easier to formulate this challenge than to face it. To embrace the possibility of inappropriate death is to admit the possibility of inappropriate life, of a precarious existence which may be snuffed out without warning, leaving the survivors oblivious to any discernible relationship between cause and effect. For the imagination distilled in the crucible of such perception, the frontiers of self shrink and survival requires that self to consider, like Kostoglotov in Solzhenitsyn's *Cancer Ward,* not what men live by, but what men die by. After this consideration, men may have little left but "knowledge and memories," like Dr. Rieux in *The Plague,* or Charlotte Delbo's narrator as she returns from the death camps to civilization only to discover that the dead she has left behind are more vivid than the living men and women she now encounters. Like the child who imagined dying as mass execution, these characters gradually realize that the new forms of death create a psychological vacuum in the mind. They find themselves in a situation described by Robert Jay Lifton in *The Life of the Self:* "One comes to feel the self disintegrating at moments when one's inner forms and images become inadequate representations of the self-world relationship and inadequate bases for action." Lifton recognizes the need for a new kind of transcendence, but the authors I examine in this study are far more hesitant than he about the ease of achieving it: between the need and its realization lies the painful experience of atrocity, which stubbornly opposes the longing for reintegration and mutes the appeal of a future if limited hope.

Although this study is essentially a criticism of literature, it grows out of historical conditions which have encouraged some men and nations to consider torture and inappropriate death as acceptable features of contemporary political reality. This book is not a direct protest against that reality. But if criticism can in any way illuminate the melancholy shadows of modern history, it may contribute to the awareness that, in losing reverence for the human image, we are accelerating our own doom. In my more cheerful moments, I share Thomas Mann's hope that reverence for life will finally triumph over the blood-sacrifices on which that life seems to thrive—or at least, to depend. But as those sacrifices mount, as they have incalculably since the appearance of *The Magic Mountain,* I wonder whether this literature can do any more than bear witness to our pain, and to the fragile moments of love that briefly relieve it.

Once more I am grateful to the Simmons College Fund for Research for a travel grant that supported the preparation of this book. I would also like to express my appreciation to William Blythe of Veneux-les-Sablons, France, for help in translating passages, and particularly poems, from the works of Charlotte Delbo; and to Ray Bentley, my editor at Beacon Press, for the many suggestions that have helped to improve the manuscript. To the three persons named in the dedication who sustain my reverence for life, and especially to the oldest among them, I owe thanks of a different sort, for the fulfillment of a love neither fragile nor brief, more durable than death, more vital than the triumph of survival.

The Age of Atrocity

> To endure life remains, when all is
> said, the first duty of all living
> beings. . . . If you would endure
> life, be prepared for death.
> —Sigmund Freud

1

THE EXAMINED DEATH

If the intellectuals in the plays of Chekhov who spent all their time guessing what would happen in twenty, thirty, or forty years had been told that in forty years interrogation by torture would be practiced in Russia; that prisoners would have their skulls squeezed within iron rings; that a human being would be lowered into an acid bath; that they would be trussed up naked to be bitten by ants and bedbugs; that a ramrod heated over a primus stove would be thrust up their anal canal (the "secret brand"); that a man's genitals would be slowly crushed beneath the toe of a jackboot; and that, in the luckiest possible circumstances, prisoners would be tortured by being kept from sleeping for a week, by thirst, and by being beaten to a bloody pulp, not one of Chekhov's plays would have gotten to its end because all the heroes would have gone off to insane asylums.[1]

This catalogue of medieval atrocities from Solzhenitsyn's *Gulag Archipelago* may have deranged intellectuals in literature, but intellectuals in contemporary life have learned to live with it as part of their twentieth-century heritage. Nor need we confine ourselves, when contemplating it, to the excesses of a single nation. Indeed, such a catalogue may defame medieval indulgence in similar excesses, since these often had the welfare of the soul as a "justification." But the modern spirit of atrocity seems gratuitous, the fruit of a contempt for the body and a scorn for the human image that discount the value of a single life. Such scorn and contempt are contrary to all the ideas and feelings we have inherited from classical and Judaeo-Christian traditions. But they exist, and we ignore them at our peril.

Their source is a matter for another investigation. I am more concerned with their effect on the literary imagination. Mere catalogues of atrocities make dreary reading; a literature that failed to uncover traces of the human amidst the inhuman debris of our recent history would quickly lose its audience and might in fact be guilty of exploiting atrocity for questionable reasons. But confronting the implications of the horrors Solzhenitsyn describes involves other risks: the writer must accept inappropriate death as a condition of existence, and portray humiliated man dying in ways he would *never* choose for himself, had he the option. This immediately excludes the vision of tragedy as we know it, leaving the alternatives of discarding it as a viable literary form or creating a new idea of tragedy, anchored in chaos rather than order and granting to the humiliation of the body a priority once reserved for the dignity of man's moral nature.

In his Nobel prize acceptance speech Albert Camus alluded to the dilemma facing writers who had survived the convulsions Solzhenitsyn described, not only a Europe of torture and prisons, but a world threatened with nuclear destruction: "We had to fashion for ourselves an art of living in times of catastrophe in order to be reborn before fighting openly against the death instinct at work in our history." Living in times of catastrophe shifts the rhythm of our imaginative efforts from creating the future—the challenge for our ancestors—to fighting a rearguard action against forces which menace us with annihilation. In such a world, as Camus describes it, "threatened with disintegration, in which our grand inquisitors may set up once and for all the kingdoms of death," survival itself is a form of rebirth, but it is less like a new flowering than the last petals clinging valiantly to a frost-blasted rose to remind the world of its diminished splendor.

The age of heroism is over, and Camus acknowledges its passing with a chastened view of the writer that in turn reflects the faded glory of man struggling for legitimacy in an era that questions man's worth: "Vulnerable but stubborn, unjust and eager for justice . . . constantly torn between pain and beauty, and devoted to extracting from his dual nature the creations he obstinately strives to raise up in the destructive fluctuation of history."[2]

Such fluctuations recur in all historical periods; yet Solzhenitsyn believed that their appearance in his own would have driven Chekhov's intellectuals mad. Is it because atrocity seems more at the heart than the edge of contemporary darkness, not an aberration, as past generations might have regarded it, but central to our civilization, an expression of history's energy in behalf of violent, arbitrary death? Only the most courageous cynic could answer such a question with a confident "yes," but a negative response would betray an even grosser ignorance of the human condition in our time. For the chaos of modern history has wasted individuals, racial identities, national minorities and general populations in staggering numbers, as if dying in extremity were the natural aim of creation and the ability to tolerate its necessity the sign of a civilized man. Of course no one believes this, though relatively few voices protest against the abuse of life that gave it birth, and fewer analyze with scientific precision what such dying is really like, how it affects our image of ourselves and the prospects for human survival in the twentieth century.

A. Alvarez ends his sensitive study of suicide and literature with a bold challenge to the contemporary mind: "The real resistance now is to an art which forces its audience to recognize and accept imaginatively, in their nerve ends, not the facts of life but the facts of death and violence: absurd, random, gratuitous, unjustified, and inescapably part of the society we have created."[3] As we shall see, this is a derivative cry rather than an original one; but the very fact that it is still being made in 1970—after Verdun, after the Marne, after Bataan, Stalinism, Auschwitz, Hiroshima, nearly ten years of Vietnam and who knows how many unrecorded or ignored atrocities in our century—proves how slowly images of death in the shadow of atrocity infiltrate human consciousness. The paintings of Hyman Bloom and Francis Bacon, the woodcuts of Leonard Baskin are only a few examples depicting flayed and mutilated bodies that now are "inescapably part of the society we have created." Together with the literature that forms part of this study, they are aesthetic corollaries to the physical disfiguration that is one price we pay for the random death Alvarez speaks of. Like all art, this literature holds a mirror of possibility up to life, but this time it is a mirror for the fun house of death rather than for the boudoir. The distorted image it reflects must be set beside the noble figure that has inspired man's dreams—and his art—for centuries.

Distortion does not cancel out nobility—but it unsettles our confidence in the uniqueness and distinction of our vitality. Alvarez quotes from the famous Kafka letter ending "a book should serve as the axe for the frozen sea within us." Beneath that layer of inner ice, one might suggest, lies the fear of inappropriate death. "The books we need," Kafka wrote, "are the kind that act upon us like a misfortune."[4] But since the ultimate misfortune is death, they must be saturated with a sense of personal disaster that attracts the emotional and intellectual curiosity of the reader without alienating him. Just as Dante's pilgrim undergoes a baptism in sin before earning a vision of immortal bliss, so contemporary man must suffer an imaginative baptism in random death if survival—not bliss—is to reach the status that Camus set for it: "an art of living in times of catastrophe." The artist shares with psychologist and historian the task of describing that catastrophe for us. It is a ponderous, unappealing responsibility since it shifts our focus from renewal to decay; but the alternative is a blind insistence on the continuity of culture that contradicts the rhythm of mutual destruction which history has imposed on our time.

Alvarez's ambivalent response to this need underscores the difficulty of the challenge. He calls for an art "which forces its audience to recognize and accept imaginatively, in their nerve ends, not the facts of life but the facts of death and violence"; but he also believes that police terror and the concentration camps (our most potent images of absurd, random, gratuitous, and unjustified death) are more or less impossible subjects for the artist. His protest is a familiar but not necessarily accurate statement on the limits of art: "Since what happened in [the camps] was beyond the imagination, it was therefore also beyond art and all those human values on which art is traditionally based."[5] This position bears scrutiny, since a literature which moves beyond the unimaginable, beyond atrocity, which chooses as its subject inappropriate death, must find ways of reaching the nerve ends of the imagination with a subject more or less impossible to depict.

What does it mean to say that an event is beyond the imagination? It was not beyond the imagination of the men who authorized it; or those who executed it; or those who suffered it. Once an event occurs, can it any longer be said to be "beyond the imagination"? Inaccessible, yes; unthinkable in its horror, certainly; contrary to "all those human values on which art is traditionally based," of course. But this is a comment on those values, not the imagination's capacity to absorb atrocity. Resistance, as Alvarez himself implies in the passage quoted earlier, is not the same as impenetrability. Is Solzhenitsyn's catalogue of atrocities in the twentieth century beyond the imagination? Of Chekhov's intellectuals, who had not seen the death instinct at work in history as we have, perhaps. What we confront is not the unimaginable, but the intolerable, a condition of existence that so diminishes our own humanity that we prefer to assign it to an alien realm. The literature I am concerned with in this study accepts as a common goal the urgency of bringing the intolerable back to earth, at the risk of sacrificing some of those traditional human values on which not only art but all civilized life has been based. It strips death of its romantic dress and finds that this leaves man more naked too. It refuses to pretend that we have not paid a price for atrocity.

But even Alvarez admits that the subject is *more* or *less* impossible, not totally so, and one can have no quarrel with this view. His reservations point to one of the most difficult problems for contemporary artists—his own catalogue of suicides among them is mournful evidence—a problem already raised by the passage from Solzhenitsyn: the pressures of modern history on the imagination. His "honor roll" of those victims of self-destruction may also be seen as a list of those who felt themselves so dishonored as human beings by the reality about them that they decided life was not worth the price. Death has a dominion over the modern sensibility that we are finally beginning to examine in detail. Suicide, rejected by Camus as an answer to the death instinct in history and the atmosphere around us, has been accepted by others as the only human response to an unendurable life. New versions of inappropriate deaths breed fresh interpretations of appropriate ones, with a resulting process of redefinition that is one source of the confusion about death that we face today.

Thanatologist Edwin Schneidman defines an appropriate death as one "which a person might choose for himself had he an option."[6] History has eliminated this option for so many millions since Chekhov's intellectuals played at divining the future that it sometimes seems an exception to the "logic" determining our destiny. For in an age of private violence and public slaughter, which threatens to make atrocity socially respectable, inappropriate death has become an issue which we can no longer consider an aberration from the normal rhythms of experience. Sudden violent death is now a fact of our imaginative existence, crowding out the serene metaphors about a golden age that once dwelt there and assaulting our psychological life with a latent apprehension that must be acknowledged if we are to survive the tensions it creates. Shortly after World War II the generalized metaphor of the mushroom cloud entered our vocabulary as well as our imagination, and for a time the fallout shelter became the figurative (and in some affluent instances the literal) refuge for these tensions. More recently the mushroom cloud has been displaced in our national consciousness by a personal act of aggression gradually approaching the status of metaphor—assassination. Is it fanciful to suggest that one consequence has been a radical shift in the cultural formula governing our thinking about ourselves at least since the time of Socrates? Western humanism has evolved from the principle that the unexamined life is not worth living. The future of that humanism may depend on our acceptance and understanding of the corollary principle that the unexamined death is not worth dying.

As so often in our century, the origin of this inquiry goes back to some intuitive perceptions of Freud. In an essay unpretentiously called "Thoughts for the Times on War and Death," published in 1915 shortly after the outbreak of World War I, he recognized that a conflict of such dimensions would disfigure conventional assumptions about dying; he sought to prepare his readers for the ensuing dilemma. Modern survivors of atrocities far more barbaric than this conflict might find a Victorian quaintness in Freud's restrained language when he asserts that "never has any event been destructive of so much that is valuable in the common wealth of humanity, nor so misleading to many of the clearest intelligences, nor so debasing to the highest that we know."[7] But his vocabulary later in this essay laid the foundation for our own confrontation with the problem: "inchoate future," "disorientation," "mental distress," "disillusionment." All wars, Freud argued, affect our view of death; but the rapacity, duplicity, and cruelty of the contending powers in this one, when joined with the magnitude of the fatalities—sometimes 10,000 in a single day!—imposed on the imagination strains that it had never had to contend with before. If the war had taught his contemporaries to be dismayed no longer by the treachery of states or even the brutality of men, they still needed a center of moral focus to enable them to endure the fragmentation of self which followed from such depressing knowledge. Freud intensified the dilemma when he pointed out that much of the disillusionment with the barbaric behavior of the warring nations was unfounded, since the notion that this betrayed an ideal of civilized conduct was itself an illusion: "In reality our fellow-citizens have not sunk so low as we feared, because they had never risen so high as we believed." The initial revision in men's attitudes would be to accept the instinct for killing as normal under certain conditions. But we can imagine how unconsoling Freud's readers must have found his reassurance that in times of peace the concurrent civilized instincts would reassert themselves.

History and heritage thus confronted each other with contradictory testimony, and the once solid image of man's sufficiency for the death encounter began to shudder and crumble. The dignity of dying was incompatible with the atrocity of killing: men could not preserve one while practicing the other. The language and psychology of heroism, which made previous wars "tolerable," soon ceased to fool the more sensitive victims of this one. For Freud, the only way to rescue the individual from his sense of estrangement "in this once lovely and congenial world"[8] was to reshape his attitude toward death, which was so inadequate to the events then transpiring. In a phrase itself quoted to death by his successors, Freud outlined the basis of the difficulty, rooted in the fundamental psychological principle that "at bottom no one believes in his own death, or to put the same thing in another way, in the unconscious every one of us is convinced of his own immortality." Freud did not regard this as a healthy condition, since the war had intensified the strain of being trapped between intellectual assent to and psychological denial of the fact of death. We "cannot maintain our former attitude towards death," he insisted in a crucial observation, "and have not yet discovered a new one." A tradition of evasion (in civilized society) faced a drama of encounter (on the battlefields of Europe). Until men recognized the truth implicit in the confrontation, they would continue to live psychologically beyond their means. Beyond their means, not within—or with them; Freud is not entirely lucid here, but he seems to imply that obscuring the vision of dying blocks the impulse toward living. "Life is impoverished," he had asserted earlier in the essay, sounding much like a modern existentialist, "it loses in interest, when the highest stake in the game of living, life itself, may not be risked."[9]

Freud's later investigations and revisions of the power of Thanatos and Eros in our lives do not concern us here; but he appears to have had a glimpse of the limitations of the clinical approach for a full evocation of the problem he touched on in this seminal essay. He often drew sustenance from the literary imagination for inspiration in his own work, so it is not surprising that he should celebrate literature as a primary source of insight into the dilemma:

> It is an inevitable result of all this that we should seek in the world of fiction, of general literature and of the theatre compensation for the impoverishment of life. There we still find people who know how to die, indeed, who are even capable of killing someone else. There alone too we can enjoy the condition which makes it possible for us to reconcile ourselves with death—namely, that behind all the vicissitudes of life we preserve our existence intact. . . .[10]

I shall explore later why the world of fiction should provide us with the possibility of integration denied us by the world of men, why in art we should often find people who "know how to die" while in life we so rarely do. Freud offers us no clue here beyond the force of his conviction. Part of the mystery lies in the ability of art to illuminate the human condition with an intensity that surpasses the spontaneous power of intellect. In recent years we have been buried beneath an avalanche of writing about death, but unless it gives us fresh insight into the human condition—and much of it does not—it represents a dismal waste of human effort.

One of those who continues to provide insight into the contemporary problem of facing death is Robert Jay Lifton, a psychologist who has devoted much of his career to understanding the implications of living in an age of threatened nuclear holocaust. Freud wrote his essay when the carnage of the First World War was just beginning; Lifton inherited as his "material" the slaughter of both wars, and in his more recent work, the equally senseless and bloody devastation of Vietnam. Such a heritage, he argues, has destroyed the sense of continuity in life which previous generations enjoyed, and its absence has made inappropriate death, or as Lifton calls it, borrowing from Camus, absurd death, an omnipresent possibility in our mental experience. The consequences are grave:

Without a cultural context in which life has continuity and boundaries, death seems premature whenever it comes. Whatever the age and circumstances, it is always "untimely." But when individual life appears to lack significance beyond itself, death becomes profoundly threatening, unacceptable.

And life becomes profoundly confusing and void of significance. Lifton (and, in this instance, his collaborator) extend Freud's preliminary remarks by suggesting that a psychological crisis regarding death occurs "when historical events are too large or absurd or terrifying to be given meaningful expression through the culture's available symbols."[11] How such a crisis maimed many of the post–World War I writers is now literary history. But their disillusionment represented only an overture to the despair that oppresses the sensibilities of men in the age of Hiroshima.

"The ultimate threat posed by nuclear weapons," says Lifton, "is not only death but meaninglessness: an unknown death by an unimaginable weapon."[12] Human associations seem pointless because all men must face the prospect of such an irrational end. Lifton probably exaggerates the importance of the mushroom cloud as a symbol for the generation growing up in the sixties and seventies, but the image of assassination represents an equally irrational end, and the anxiety about dying remains valid, even when the weapon becomes imaginable. Lacking the power—and the resources—to translate its apprehensions into culturally acceptable symbols, this generation, like its predecessor, must face the challenge of absorbing the fact that inappropriate death is now part of our individual fate. If this gloomy truth is less comprehensive than the reality that possible nuclear holocaust forces us to contemplate the death of everyone, it is no less threatening. For who can comfortably imagine dying for no reason?

Yet our age has thrust this responsibility upon us. As Freud foresaw, and as Lifton has confirmed in his research with Hiroshima survivors and Vietnam veterans, it has left us groping for a response, where we have not simply avoided one. If, as Lifton maintains, "we have no images adequate to the possibility of total extinction," we have equally few adequate to the possibility of the kind of irrational individual death which many of Lifton's Vietnam veterans faced—or inflicted on others. They too need to reconcile their lives with a tradition of normalcy; they grope, Lifton declares, "toward a way to express and give meaning to their experience." The language Lifton uses to describe their dilemma reminds one of Freud's reliance on the world of fiction to offer a fully integrated picture of man's altered vision of death:

In this effort to give form to their feelings, they show the survivor's need to achieve a new sense of self and world. They take on the survivor mission of telling their tale, and they tell it with rare intensity and moral force. Their truth must be shared; others must be enabled to participate in their survivor experience and, above all, to share the guilt and responsibility. Telling the tale is a political act. . . .[13]

But one doubts the sufficiency of telling the tale as a political act; Vietnam has not yet inspired its *Farewell to Arms* or *The Naked and the Dead,* though assuredly it will. But until then, the impact of that historical event on man's imagination, the magnitude of its contribution to our obsession with inappropriate death, must remain obscure.

For if men are guilty, art is not; if Thomas Mann is correct, art has more to do with consolation than reminding men of their responsibility for moral conduct. Certain artists in our time, whose work forms the main subject of this study, have recognized the need to give form to the feelings of "death-survivors," all those human creatures in the twentieth century who, from the time of World War I with an increasing sense of inner dislocation, have been forced to live psychologically beyond their means, unable to reconcile their lives with the death-anxiety that haunts the modern imagination. Transcending the political (though not heedless of it), these artists acknowledge the urgency of wondering how, following Freud's vision, "behind all the vicissitudes of life" we may "preserve our existence intact."

Like Lifton's Vietnam veterans, like his survivors of Hiroshima, authors like Mann and Camus, Solzhenitsyn and

Charlotte Delbo, "have been to the far reaches of what this culture is capable of creating (a land of death)," some of them more literally than others, and if they have not all returned, like the actual veterans, "with grim but potentially revitalizing truths,"[14] it may be because the aspirations of art are more modest than those of life. It is no longer original to assert that the experience of our century has left the imaginative vision little to invent in the realm of atrocity; but experience does not automatically bequeath its own insights, and here the artist's vision may have something to add that political and even psychological truth illuminates with only a shadowy light. As for the rebirth that Lifton calls for, that may merely be a necessary hope to replace the illusions that our altered view of death has compelled us to abandon. We must let each author speak for himself.

Lifton's reasoning, however, is immensely useful, since it pinpoints a crucial problem facing each of these authors. For if the idea of inappropriate death has grown out of the images of holocaust and annihilation that surround us, we can restore the balance between life and death only by "the continuous creation and re-creation of images and symbols" that permit the reader to value his survival as well as to mourn his fate. Such a process, Lifton declares, is essential to human mental life: "A sense of vitality can proceed only so long as the symbolizing process provides forms and images adequate to guide behavior and render it meaningful." The didactic tone of the psychologist should not discredit the acuteness of his perception, for, as he says, the present historical moment reminds us that "we need the theme of death to reconstitute our lives." Concern with death is not only not morbid; it is crucial. In quoting E.M. Forster's paradox, Lifton affirms the challenge before us: "Death destroys a man; the idea of Death saves him."[15]

Thinking about death has infiltrated our lives, if not yet our thinking about life. Our task, as Lifton points out, is to develop an "inner imagery" sufficient to give significance to our experience. Men have always tried to do so, to make their lives tolerable, but never before has their external reality so cruelly contradicted traditional internal sanctuaries against death. In addition, they have had to contend with current controversies over the clinical redefinition of death itself, and though no one has studied the fears such activities add to our death-anxiety, they must be considerable. The debates over what constitutes an appropriate death for terminally ill patients introduce an external image of man as helpless victim depending on machines and (in some instances) judicial review for his survival—thrusting even further into the background Schneidman's notion of the relationship between human choice and appropriate death. The clinical approach to the question of death and dying, so popular in recent literature, offers little in its attitude and its medical rhetoric to that growth of inner imagery Lifton finds vital, and may indeed interfere with its development. Clinical clarifications of the issue paradoxically diminish awareness of the more urgent need for an imaginative response to death, as once again the humanistic vision—its fate in the twentieth century—defers to the technological view.

This is not to say, of course, that the clinical approach willfully obscures men's needs. In her widely-acclaimed work, *On Death and Dying*, Elisabeth Kübler-Ross tries to confront the issue squarely, even suggesting that the recent emphasis on machines and definitions represents a new sanctuary for physicians unable to contend with the mortality of their patients:

Is the reason for this increasingly mechanical, depersonalized approach our own defensiveness? Is this approach our own way to cope with and repress the anxieties that a terminally or critically ill patient evokes in us? Is our concentration on equipment, on blood pressure our desperate attempt to deny the impending death which is so frightening and discomforting to us that we displace all our knowledge onto machines, since they are less close to us than the suffering face of another human being which would remind us once more of our lack of omnipotence, our own limits and failures, and last but not least perhaps our own mortality?[16]

If research is replacing rather than increasing insights into the human condition, then we have to contend with a new form of refuge from our fate; if computer diagnosis of disease assures greater accuracy, it may also symbolize the ultimate flight from personal responsibility for acknowledging that we all share a common destiny. Medical progress paradoxically offers us another form of denial, and as Kübler-Ross implies, encourages us to live even more psychologically beyond our means than Freud predicted a half-century ago.

But even Kübler-Ross's cautions have their limitations. The conclusion that "if all of us could make a start by contemplating the possibility of our own personal death, we may effect many things"[17] says little new and indeed verges on platitude, for as Freud recognized, the fear of death resides not merely in men's contemplative powers but in their unconscious desires and apprehensions. We cannot close Lifton's symbolic gap between denying and facing inappropriate death with the neutral phraseology of direct statement; language unadorned by image tantalizes without satisfying—and certainly without altering—the imagination. Hence most of the interviews with terminal patients or members of their families recorded in Kübler-Ross's book and numerous others like it are oddly disappointing, perhaps because we expect so much more, though we should not be surprised to learn that ordinary intelligences dying differ little from ordinary intelligences living. The testimony has professional value for those who work with the terminally ill and family members (and of course this was the audience Kübler-Ross and her colleagues had in mind); but it provides little material for the metaphors or inner imagery Lifton calls for to give significance to our experience of dying in an age of atrocity.

In an era when few of us are witnesses to actual dying, our impressions of the event are inspired by written or verbal accounts and whatever psychological responses we may have inherited as human beings. Language plays a vital role in shaping these responses, so it is not surprising to find Avery Weisman, in *On Dying and Denying,* suggesting that men are reluctant to speak about death because "words have a primitive equivalence with the underlying reality to which they allude." To speak about real death, therefore, as opposed to death in the abstract, "puts us in the role of someone who violates a taboo. . . ." But the examined death requires us to violate that taboo, if we are to furnish any fresh insight into the role of death in modern reality. Indeed, we must find a way of doing it that will shock the heart into an act of recognition, so that perceptions like Weisman's "the wish to die can be more readily understood as equivalent to a wish to destroy or be destroyed, rather than as the antithesis of the will to live,"[18] can be translated into emotionally accessible imagined experience. In its present form the idea beckons from the printed page, but does not leap forth to assault and finally penetrate the resistant vision of the reader. Like Lifton, like Kübler-Ross, Weisman concedes that the most urgent quest of our time is the search for a purposeful death, in an environment increasingly barren of meaning. He shares with them too the premise and conviction that the way to this goal, though tangled with dense intellectual and psychological undergrowth, is not impenetrable. If, as Weisman argues, the will to live and the wish to die are two versions of hope, the same may be said for denying and confronting death, even in our melancholy time. The human imagination seems unable to exist without hope for a purposeful death.

My concern in this book is with the fate of that hope, and particularly with the imaginative strategies some of our writers have devised to illuminate the darkness that shrouds it. If in the end the journey turns out to be more meaningful than the arrival, this may merely reflect the limitation of man's obsession with eschatology, more secular today than divine, in a posteschatological age. In fact, despite all the talk of purpose and goal, most intellectual energy has been devoted to the journey anyway, to the psychological and symbolic equipment the traveler requires for the ordeal, and the prowess he needs to develop along the way. "Significant survival," to use Weisman's phrase, or more precisely, "significant surviving," is a piece of smooth rhetoric until a personal vision endows it with contours and some rough surfaces for the imagination to cling to. But when that happens, chameleon-like, it begins to shift colors, and we are confronted with multiple points of view depending on the perspective of the artist.

Every idea about death, then, is a version of life. But once we enter the realm of the imagination, we find versions of life that are *more* or *less* challenging, rather than "true" or "false." If we can accept Freud's idea that the first duty of all living beings is to endure, then there is much to be learned from the contemporary artist's vision of modern man's response to the prospect of inappropriate death. Not in order to discover how to live, since the highest art is never so simply didactic; perhaps only to derive consolation from the inconsistency in artistic points of view, which supports man's hope that he will never be reduced to a common, indistinguishable cipher; but chiefly to seek sustenance for the "inner imagery" which permits the individual to endure.

How to translate abstract notions about inappropriate death into concrete imagery that can appeal to the mind and emotions challenges the imagination of any writer who believes in the power of language to shock the heart. One example will have to suffice here. Albert Camus devoted his career to fighting the death penalty in all its forms, including capital punishment. But he knew that intellectual arguments against it, most of which had been used before, were useless to convince men of the essential human horror of the deed. Persuaded that society tolerated the barbarous procedure because it had been sheltered from its visceral impact, he shrewdly tried to close the symbolic gap between idea and response by quoting from a vivid medical report written by two doctors assigned to examine the bodies of guillotined victims after their execution:

If we may be permitted to give our opinion, such sights are frightfully painful. The blood flows from the blood vessels at the speed of the severed carotids, then it coagulates. The muscles contract and their fibrillation is stupefying; the intestines ripple and the heart moves irregularly, incompletely, fascinatingly. The mouth puckers at certain moments in a terrible pout. It is true that in the severed head the eyes are motionless with dilated pupils; fortunately they look at nothing, and, if they are devoid of the cloudiness and opalescence of the corpse, they have no motion; their transparence belongs to life, but their fixity belongs to death. All this can last minutes, even hours, in sound specimens; death is not immediate. . . . Thus every vital element survives decapitation. The doctor is left with this impression of a horrible experience, of a murderous vivisection, followed by a premature burial.[19]

Camus praises the visual energy of these lines: "It would become harder to execute men one after another, as is done in our country today, if those executions were translated into vivid images in the popular imagination." He may be more hopeful than accurate here, since those authorizing executions of any sort, ostensibly depending on legal sanctions rather than the popular will (when it is not simply a case of tyranny), usually lack squeamishness. Nevertheless, the passage he cites strips the veil from one visage of inappropriate death. "I doubt that there are many readers who can read that terrifying report without blanching," declares Camus. "Consequently, its exemplary power and its capacity to intimidate can be counted on."[20]

Unfortunately, the power of writing that presumes to confront inappropriate death honestly is not always intimidating—nor, in fact, exemplary. Very few prose writers possess the imaginative vigor, visual clarity, and stylistic precision that Camus's doctors display in their brief but forceful paragraph. The abundance of volumes in recent years by and about the terminally ill is deceptive; such works mislead us into believing that we are confronted with a surge of interest in inappropriate death and dying, and a fresh determination to heed Freud's counsel that in an age of mass slaughter we must learn to live psychologically within our means—that is, to face the possibility of absurd death. But whereas a hundred years after his birth and a half-century after its appearance we virtually ignore Thomas Mann's post–World War I masterpiece, *The Magic Mountain,* dedicated to easing that task for a war-shocked public, we greedily absorb memoirs that provide similar nourishment to our nuclear-shocked generation on a more manageable personal level.

Such memoirs probably shape our responses to death more powerfully than we realize. But it is questionable whether they add to our insights into the *significance* of the experience. For such memoirs usually serve a celebratory or informative purpose; only rarely, with their limited point of view, can they present their subjects as victims of absurd death, and even more rarely relate them to the contemporary climate of atrocity. John Gunther's *Death Be Not Proud,* for example, an account of his seventeen-year-old son's death from a brain tumor, has become a minor classic in the literature: for many, the book is to death what *Anne Frank: The Diary of a Young Girl* is to the Holocaust. It circumspectly skirts the horror implicit in the theme but leaves the reader with the mournful if psychologically unburdened feeling that he has had a genuine encounter with inappropriate death. The popularity of Gunther's book is a commentary on the needs of readers, not the talent of its author. One hesitates to trespass on the grief of a bereaved father, but Gunther was a professional journalist, and in telling the story he must have been prepared for critical as well as sympathetic responses. His memorial to—really encomium of—his son is symptomatic of a time when the total absence of a usable cultural context for inappropriate death (even though the book appeared in 1949, four years after Hiroshima and the Holocaust) left Gunther psychologically helpless except for the tradition of sentimentalism and denial to heal his dislocated sensibilities. What is announced as the account of a child's courageous struggle with death is really the story of a father's futile encounter with the fact that his son is dying, and of the father's inability to make of it a significant experience in a personal or universal sense.[21] It is a drama of concealment and pretense in which all actors know the truth but refuse to admit it to each other or themselves. Its chief interest, other than its compassionate narration of the pathetic early death of an unusually talented child, is the unexpressed psychological tensions and motivations of its "characters"—the Victim, the Father, the Mother, and the Doctors.

Far more important than what *Death Be Not Proud* reveals

about its characters is what it *doesn't*—how they actually faced the irreversible fact that Johnny Gunther was dying of a brain tumor in the prime of his youth and for no reason other than physiological chance. In a curiously unconscious shift of focus, Gunther makes of his book a partial celebration of his own unflagging efforts to alter the inevitable. Paradoxically, one way of confronting the death of those we love is to justify *ourselves*, not as a selfish act but a necessary one, confirming in our own eyes and those of the world that we are not in any way responsible for the other's death. The principle of a common fate, sometimes unredeemably harsh, scarcely intrudes on Gunther's thoughts because this *might* imply that the significance of his son's suffering was its meaninglessness, and this the father was unwilling (and psychologically unable) to accept.

The symbolic gap between meaningful life and insignificant death is lucidly corroborated (unintentionally, of course) by Gunther in his certainty that "we had to shield [Johnny] from definite, explicit knowledge, since his greatest asset by far—his only asset aside from his youth—was his will to live."[22] Gunther would have been utterly baffled by Weisman's complex idea that the will to live and the wish to die may be two versions of hope; he would have been equally perplexed by Freud's belief that to endure life men must be prepared for death. Although he confessed that deep down his son had a pretty complete awareness of what was going on, Gunther had no concept at all of how his encouraging this awareness might have enriched the remaining months of his son's life.

Of course Gunther's own intelligence was not immune to the philosophical stakes in the struggle for his son's life. But there is more melodrama than drama in his description of the contending forces, which sets the human self against a hostile universe, like Melville's Ahab threatening to strike the sun if it insulted him:

It was, we felt, as if reason itself were being ravaged away by unreason, as if the pattern of Johnny's illness were symbolic of so much of the conflict and torture of the external world. A primitive to-the-death struggle of reason against violence, reason against disruption, reason against brute unthinking force—this was what went on in Johnny's head. What he was fighting against was the ruthless assault of chaos. What he was fighting for was, as it were, the life of the human mind.[23]

The terms of the battle duplicate the heroic posture of much nineteenth-century romanticism, merely confirming how easy it is for the imagination to sidestep the darker vision of Freud in order to retain the more consoling heritage that preceded him. Of the many illusions about human nature that history has peeled from the eyes of men in the twentieth century, the value of the heroic stance has been one of the last to go.

Perhaps the most difficult and painful task of the healthy is to listen to the voice of the dying—indeed, to permit the dying to have a voice at all. Gunther scrupulously silences his son throughout his book, so that we never get even a glimpse of what consciousness of his mortality might have meant to Johnny Gunther. It would have been too much for his father to bear—understandably. But the result is that the reader is denied any insight into the significance of the experience, except to have repeated what he already knows—that the living possess strategies for dealing with their distress that have little to do with the dilemma of inappropriate death.

Clinical studies have demonstrated that maintaining an attitude of hope serves the psychological needs of the survivor more than the patient. It was impossible not to support his son's optimism, Gunther insists, though one need not probe far to discover the real subject of his words: "Any discouragement would have been a crushing blow. All he had now was his will to live. We had to keep that up at any cost." Gunther is hardly to be blamed for his desperate dependence on hope, since the world about him seemed to enter into a conspiracy of silence when the issue was the untimely death of a young child: "We tried to face asking the questions we could not bear to ask, since little by little new horriblenesses, new dreadfulnesses, were being hinted to us—about blindness, about paralysis. Several doctors seemed to be avoiding us. . . ." As a journalist during World War II, he must have participated imaginatively in the unprecedented horror and dread of those years, but 1947, when his son died, was apparently too soon for the implications to have penetrated the lower layers of being. Nothing else could explain his serene conclusion about such an inappropriate death: "He died absolutely without fear, and without pain, and without knowing that he was going to die."[24] If the atrocities of our time have taught us anything, it is that the moment of death is less important than the prospect of dying, and that the process, with the fear and pain and insights it induces, represents the period of significant experience for men. Measured against it, the moment of death is only a tiny, final station in an inward journey that can endure for many years.

Death Be Not Proud has importance for our purposes only because it testifies to the exhaustion of a tradition, one whose conventions served the imagination adequately prior to the age of atrocity. Medical rituals—changing bandages, getting x-ray reports, discussing Johnny's physical condition in technical language—fill up time and make it easier to avoid human confrontation. Even the ideas of Donne's sonnet, from which the title is taken, play a vital role; for in the end we get the portrait of a living memory, not a dying boy. Each reader will have to decide for himself how much this betrays a falsification of reality; certainly it does not illustrate the living psychologically within our means that Freud had in mind. Gunther's eulogy for his son—"Johnny transmits permanently something of what he was, since the fabric of the universe is continuous and eternal"—attempts to transform inappropriate death into a version of appropriate immortality. But in doing this Gunther pays a price: In making his account a tribute "to the power, the wealth, the unconquerable beauty of the human spirit, will, and soul,"[25] he substitutes the consolations of sentimental rhetoric for the challenge of genuine insight.

The examined death, then, requires much more than a narrative about the course of a terminal disease, even when the narration is "humanized" by the emotional tie of the narrator to the victim. Indeed, as we have seen, such a tie can often be a main reason for obscuring details of the account and avoiding opportunities to explore implications more complex than the temporal sequence of external events. More frank in its revelations is Lael Wertenbaker's story of her husband's death from cancer, *Death of a Man,* because the victim is told immediately (though the surgeon finds the fatal diagnosis almost as painful for himself as for the patient, and counsels concealment). In addition, Wertenbaker has a chance to readjust (as Johnny Gunther did not) to a crucial force in his life—time— and this single detail adds a philosophical dimension to the report that was totally lacking in the previous one. Mann, Camus, Solzhenitsyn, and Delbo will devote considerable energy, as we shall see, to the relation between mortality and time inspired by inappropriate death. For atrocity attacks the future, forcing the frontiers of time back toward the present and past, and shifting the long-range expectations of the imagination to a more urgent confrontation with immediate experience.

Charles Wertenbaker's ordeal begins the moment his wife announces his death sentence to him. As a shared experience, it requires a more complex level of involvement from the reader, who cannot retreat behind the barrier that Gunther erects between truth and hope. The author sets the tone for a narrative without illusions when she speaks of "the two loneliest acts of all, dying and being left living."[26] She presents a man midway between inappropriate and appropriate death, that is, acquiescing to his death sentence without seeking a heroic pose to "justify" it, but adhering firmly to Schneidman's principle (though giving it a personal twist) that an appropriate death "is one that a person might choose for himself had he the option." Others are awed and stunned by his willingness to live with the knowledge of his terminal condition and his resolution to decide the moment of his own death through an overdose of morphine when the pain becomes unbearable or, failing this—as indeed becomes the case—suicide by cutting his own wrists.

Janet Flanner, *New Yorker* columnist and friend of the family, affirmed in a letter the value of Wertenbaker's attitude and of his wife's response to it as if she were assessing a work of fiction, implying how rich this biography might be as a source for the more complex vision of literary art:

You made a new kind of acceptance of death in terms of still being alive, of consciousness, of conscience, of reality; it was a new kind of drama of domesticity, in the highest terms that drama can be used, as conflict with an ending, dependent upon characters in movement. . . .

Accepting death in terms of still being alive is a lucid description of Lael Wertenbaker's portrait of a man dying, for she stubbornly refuses to divide life from death as if they represented discrete categories. Death for her is the *end,* not the story; except for a brief paragraph, her narrative concludes with Wertenbaker's suicide. Its finality requires no postscript to justify his existence, which has been justified by his own prior recognition that "nothing is ever lost that has been experienced and it can all be there at the moment of death—if you don't wait too long."[27]

It may be that in an age of atrocity we need to reexamine the role of hope in our lives to see whether it contributes to our living psychologically beyond our means. The optimism implicit in hope may be a value inherited from a previous era that is no longer supported by the conditions of our existence, and our reluctance to discard it may be one reason why an inner imagery more consonant with an age of atrocity is so slow in developing. When Wertenbaker and his wife admit that "death had moved into the middle-foreground of our lives, like a mountain, as a fact," they acknowledge that there is no way to celebrate the value of the abstraction we call life without simultaneously conceding that it shares the stage with an omnipresent death. For them it is literally present, its concrete assault on the body a constant reminder to both of the futility of evasion, and from this mountainous fact they develop a strategy. If its vivid autobiographical actuality still fails to reflect metaphorically the larger reality of the human condition, it nevertheless furnishes some clues about perceiving that reality more accurately.

Wertenbaker learns how rare simple acceptance is to an imagination trained by its culture to delude itself with heroic postures. "It is easier perhaps," writes his wife, "to be noble than natural in the face of death."[28] He also discovers the value of cutting oneself off from the rituals and institutions that support such deception. Among the least consistent "characters" in these studies of human mortality are the medical figures, who are so confused and distressed by their dual roles as professional and private persons that they have difficulty developing a center of being. They are dedicated to the science of healing, but terminal illness contradicts the purpose of their careers; Wertenbaker's American surgeon feels defeated when both patient and wife insist on knowing the full truth. And his doctor in France, where he retires to die, is simply incredulous when he learns that Wertenbaker has been told that his condition is hopeless; he attributes it to the eccentricity of Americans. Thus it is not surprising that one of the images to have crept into the modern literary consciousness as metaphor of an official contender with death is the doctor; nor can it be coincidence that leading characters in several of the works considered in this study are physicians, or that hospitals are major settings for the action.

Wertenbaker is relieved to learn that he can dispense with all institutionalized medical attention once he discovers the gravity of his condition; and when his French physician urges an operation to relieve some of the pressure on the intestine (though in no way diminishing the certainty of death), Wertenbaker firmly refuses. The physician is appalled, but the patient feels liberated: "Since he had only to die, he preferred his own authority on how to do so."[29] Wertenbaker realized that this freedom was a privilege for him, not an option available to everyone. Indeed, his quest for an appropriate death gains perspective from his awareness—at least his wife presents it this way—that his personal ordeal was a pale but valid reflection of the general torment men have suffered in an age of atrocity.

One clue to help explain Wertenbaker's personal fortitude in the face of death emerges when we learn that he had been present at the liberation of Buchenwald concentration camp. We cannot know how this affected his own "inner imagery" for dealing with public atrocity, but we have his wife's testimony that it had "stayed always vivid in his consciousness as the terrible proof that prolonged and sufficient suffering could destroy the humanity of even very good and very strong men."[30] This enabled him to distinguish between the impersonal (and "natural") torture of cancer and the unnatural pain which men are capable of inflicting on each other. But his consciousness of what the agony of the latter can do to the unarmed sensibilities of the victim seems to have played an undefined role in strengthening his capacity to resist the illusions spawned by conventional modes of consolation. Despite the human difficulty of bearing pain under torture, he had borne his own and survived, not through heroic resistance but through an effort of will to tolerate the conditions of his moral (and physical) existence. Part of the pain which the modern imagination must bear is the agony that *other* men have suffered in our age of atrocity; and there is some evidence that accepting this metaphorical heritage gave Wertenbaker the strength to live out his personal fate as an expression of the destiny of his time. His refusal to see himself as a special case—his wife's refusal too—makes the portrait of his dying a grim illustration of the qualities necessary to make inappropriate death tolerable.

Another of these qualities is recognition of the fact that death in an age of atrocity introduces a new emphasis on loneliness. Once we dismiss the platitudes we arm ourselves with when we confront the dying, we find little left to say. As a healthy man in his fifties, Wertenbaker had planned eagerly to make his final years as fulfilling as his early ones; after his death sentence has been announced, his wife wonders whether this had been a final act of *hubris:* "Must he learn at the end that every man is wholly alone?" During his cries of intolerable pain, she discovers how futile her compassion is, and adjusts herself to the necessary alienation that such suffering imposes, by training herself to "go away inside myself, sit there or sleep at night, not to try to *be* there with Wert during them. I could neither share nor ease his pain by sympathetic suffering. My sympathy only twisted me so that I could not emerge from sympathy in time to share the free time with him."[31]

Implicit in Lael Wertenbaker's evocation of the loneliness in death is the possibility for a fresh view of the shared *and* isolated nature of the experience. Except for his wife's constant presence and unflagging support for his position—she even holds him while his lifeblood pours into a casserole after he has slashed his wrists—Wertenbaker faces his death alone. The community of human pain turns out to be another myth inherited from the past, discredited by the clarity of his perception. He seeks no solace because he knows that any consolation would be an attempt to divert his attention. If his death lacks more emblematic resonance, it is because this special kind of biography offers few opportunities for the kind of imaginative identification with character that fiction makes accessible. Our glimpses of his past have been brief and fragmentary, their presentation creating no rhythm or pattern in the narrative, furnishing information rather than insight. When he dies, we share the death of another human being, but one who remains essentially a stranger.

In one sense, Lael Wertenbaker's restraint in *Death of a Man* is admirable; the absence of melodrama adds dignity to herself and her husband. But the closing words of her volume— "Then there was time to mourn the death of a man"—reveal an important omission: if dying is a process enacted while one is living, mourning is too, and suppressing it (or the account of it) until after death has occurred introduces an artificial division between compassion and grief similar to one that conventionally separates life from death. The ultimate revelation—at least in a personal memoir—would include an honest presentation of another's dying together with one's own response to this "mountain" of a fact. The psychological complexity of the experience demands of one the effort to penetrate the mist of which Lael Wertenbaker so movingly wrote, to interpret the distorted visions, blurred sounds, silent screams, and unexpressed terrors that inhabit the unconscious and conceal our deepest feelings about ourselves and others, especially when that mist intervenes between the living and the dying.

Simone de Beauvoir's *A Very Easy Death* does not qualify as the "ultimate revelation," but it comes far closer than the previous two works to a confrontation with the inappropriate death of a loved one, in this instance her mother. But even in this narrative, disclosure is balanced by unconscious suppression, as we witness how a sensitive literary intelligence (when writing from her own point of view) has difficulty exploring all the implications of mortality. One is tempted to conclude that art alone liberates the imagination to probe the darkest corners of the arena where man contends with the experience of dying—his own and others'. It seems that de Beauvoir's literary intuition taught her this, because she organizes the chronicle of her mother's death around an alternating pattern of present scene and past recall so that the two time sequences flow into each other and memory becomes an important means of confronting death. The patient has a social existence as a mother, a daughter, a wife, a good Catholic, a friend—and these roles sometimes contradict, sometimes reinforce each other. Simultaneously, the author has a multiple existence as daughter, sister, companion of Jean-Paul Sartre (whom she mentions only occasionally, but whose influence as a spokesman for the postwar French intellectual tradition shines through in the book's closing lines), and—vitally important—as the narrator of the events.

Simone de Beauvoir recognizes what John Gunther and Lael Wertenbaker fail or refuse to see: that when an "other" voice intervenes between the dying and their death, we can never obtain a fully objective portrait, but only an interpretation tempered by the insight and psychological courage of the observer. *A Very Easy Death,* more openly than the others, is a *dual* account—of how the mother died, and how the daughter adjusted to the fact. For every death necessitates at least two responses, from the victim and from the survivor(s); moreover, these responses often interact, modifying each other. The reaction is further complicated by the survivor's memory: in Simone de Beauvoir's case, the earlier deaths of her father and of an uncle interfere with a "pure" confrontation with her mother's suffering. Indeed, one is led to believe that no confrontation is ever "pure" in the sense of a totally selfless concern for the dying.

In a thinly fictionalized narrative of his early years, *Childhood,* Tolstoy presents a version of his mother's death and funeral. Along with the expected grief, his young protagonist feels a sudden self-importance, enjoying the sense of his own sorrow. His emotions are bathed with pleasure, and for a moment gratitude wars with grief as he struggles to achieve a single "natural" response to his mother's death.[32] Tolstoy does not plunge into the darker realm of the death wish; neither does de Beauvoir, but she approaches this difficult issue when she rehearses, in an early section, all the reasons why she feels hostile to her mother, as if she were preparing her own sensibilities for the instant when she loses her. "She was possessive," she recalls; "she was overbearing; she would have liked to have us completely in her power." And later: "With regard to us [de Beauvoir and her sister], she often displayed a cruel unkindness that was more thoughtless than sadistic: her desire was not to cause us unhappiness but to prove her own power to herself."[33] Thus a new strategy appears, though one hesitates to call it more honest than merely celebrating the virtues of the dying. Although listing the victim's limitations may assuage the survivor's guilt, it cannot brighten the gloom of inappropriate death which the cancerous disease reminds us of, or satisfy the unappeased will to live which inspires both victim and reader. Simone de Beauvoir gradually discovers this, which makes her own ordeal the subterranean drama of the narrative.

During the initial stages of her mother's illness, de Beauvoir verifies through personal experience what as a novelist she must have known all along: the insufficiency *and* necessity of language as consolation to the dying and the survivors. Racked by pain, her mother still utters ready-made phrases about the motives of nurses or how badly "the lower classes" bear adversity: "The contrast between the truth of her suffering body and the nonsense that her head was stuffed with saddened me," the daughter reflects. But Simone de Beauvoir is guilty of seeking similar refuge in words, as she instinctively turns to the platitude that at seventy-eight her mother "is of an age to die," then recognizes that "the words were devoid of meaning, as so many words are. For the first time I saw her as a dead body under suspended sentence." And her heart is wrenched with compassion at the vision of a woman bereft of means to rationalize her situation—only words to extend the deception: "A full-blooded, spirited woman lived on inside her, but a stranger to herself, deformed and mutilated."[34]

What is the measure for determining the adequacy of the means the dying employ to rationalize their situation? To say nothing of the means survivors employ to rationalize theirs? "When someone you love dies," Simone de Beauvoir concludes, "you pay for the sin of outliving her with a thousand piercing regrets." Sin? The very words we choose to meet the fact that silence is not enough become a form of rationalization. But we exist in an age when "outliving others" has left an unavoidable patina of guilt on the collective memory of men, and de Beauvoir's sense of regret may be more resonant for the reader than she intends. In an age of atrocity, the terms of the struggle have shifted: it is no longer a contest between dying or living, but, as Simone de Beauvoir shrewdly indicates, between death and torture. If regret is a wasted emotion for those who have died in our century after intolerable suffering beyond our power to alleviate, it intensifies for those like Simone de Beauvoir who witnessed her mother's torment but lacked the will or the means of ending it. In this respect, Wertenbaker and his wife were far more in control of his destiny. Simone de Beauvoir assumes that she has been beaten by the ethics of society, but Sartre, with keener insight, declares that she was beaten by technique, and she finally realizes how accurate he is: "One is caught up in the wheels and dragged along, powerless in the face of specialists' diagnoses, their forecasts, their decisions. The patient becomes their property: get him away from them if you can!"[35]

Suicide or euthanasia may be one way of rebelling against this threatened loss of control over one's fate; vision or perception, or what Camus will call "lucidity," is another.

All human beings require a strategy, in Simone de Beauvoir's delicate phrase, for taming "the transition between presence and the void." Her own was her superior consciousness, a somber, unassuming attitude which carefully avoided patronizing the feelings of the victim: "An evil all-knowing spirit, I could see behind the scenes, while she was struggling, far, far away, in human loneliness. Her desperate eagerness to get well, her patience, her courage—it was all deceived. She would not be paid for any of her sufferings at all."[36] At this moment it is evident how the narrative voice controls our responses to the ordeal of dying, how clearly the quest for truth is nothing more than a search for a tolerable point of view. Devout Maman is eulogized by the secular voice of her daughter; but the mournful epitaph implicit in her words raises the question of how such suffering could appear to be redeemed without penetrating the consciousness of the victim too.

As long as death is narrated by an outsider, however close to the victim, the dying voice must be excluded from our range of imaginative perception. Simone de Beauvoir's sister narrows but does not span the gap separating the two by observing: " 'The only comfort I have . . . is that it will happen to me too. Otherwise it would be too unfair,' " but this generalizing of the human dilemma gives us no better glimpse into the dying consciousness. If de Beauvoir is correct when she says that the misfortune is "that although everyone must come to this, each experiences the adventure in solitude,"[37] then like the inhabitants of Plato's cave, all we have available to us is experience once removed—unless we find a way of overhearing the dying voice itself.

Even Simone de Beauvoir's mind has been so saturated by reflected images of death that she finds it impossible to withstand the steady glare of the reality, and retreats into her own cave at crucial moments, depending on safe and familiar premises to sustain her wavering vision. As the nature and prognosis of the disease seep into her mother's consciousness, Simone de Beauvoir cannot admit that she herself finds it too much to bear or discuss, and unconvincingly shifts the motive to her mother: "The truth was crushing her and when she needed to escape from it by talking, we were condemning her to silence; we forced her to say nothing about her anxieties and to suppress her doubts. . . . But we had no choice: hope was her most urgent need." Possibly this decision is correct, though the reasons for it are impure; de Beauvoir never gives her mother a chance to test Camus's contention that some crushing truths perish from being acknowledged. All we have is the daughter's insistence that her mother "had been taught never to think, act or feel except in a ready-made framework,"[38] and lacking any verifiable evidence for this claim, the reader is left with an inevitable lacuna in his response to the mother's death.

So even an observer as acute as Simone de Beauvoir has limited access to the experience of dying when her imagination is restrained by adherence to the literal facts. But she has few illusions about her power to venture further: "It is useless to try to integrate life and death and to behave rationally in the presence of something that is not rational: each must manage as well as he can in the tumult of his feelings." Rarely do love and friendship overcome the loneliness of death; more often, as in her own case, the survivor becomes an accomplice to the fate that is closing in on the victim, by supporting the illusion of hope. Simone de Beauvoir's ultimate insight, the justification for her narrative, appears in her discovery that one is *never* of an age to die, that even the old do not die from age but from *something,* and that whenever death arrives, it is violent and unforeseen: there is no way to *prepare* for a very easy death, because no death is easy. The challenge she flings at the imagination is born of twentieth-century man's experience:

There is no such thing as a natural death: nothing that happens to a man is ever natural, since his presence calls the world into question. All men must die: but for every man his death is an accident and, even if he knows it and consents to it, an unjustifiable violation.[39]

Unlike John Gunther, Simone de Beauvoir repudiates all formulas for immortality: her mother's death is an end in time, not a beginning in eternity, a lesson on the nature of *our* existence, now that hers is over. Unlike Lael Wertenbaker, Simone de Beauvoir is faced with a victim who lacks heroic dimensions, a strong will, a determination to choose her death: her mother suffers the physical and spiritual anguish of the unconfronting victim. If Death is the protagonist in each of these human dramas, the costumes he wears, the lines he speaks, his make-up, tone, and gestures are all determined by his collaboration with a director; and all this means is that any presentation of the theme will be more or less authoritative or persuasive, but never closer to an absolute truth. History, custom, language, and culture contribute to the portrait, but it is only a portrait, not a photograph, and one must be prepared for unexpected distortions in the features of the subject. My own investigation convinces me that the twentieth-century mind, goaded by the insights of Freud and his successors and harassed by the experience of atrocity, has been less dependent on common assumptions about death than its ancestors, and has struck out in fresh directions to open up vistas that we have yet to absorb. This does not mean that we are faced with the sudden demise of old attitudes; as we shall see in the next chapter, they survive even in the midst of atrocity. But the new ones need to be examined as closely as the more conventional (if occasionally more "modern") ones that we have just briefly surveyed. The implications of atrocity, of death as a generally inappropriate end despite its eventual necessity, are making slow inroads on our intelligence and emotions, but we will have to undergo a long period of synthesis before we can grasp their meanings. The hope for a single meaning is futile.

The hope for a new version of immortality, enabling man to conquer death with weapons honed by the whetstone of atrocity, is even more futile. The artists we will turn to in later chapters, though haunted by the contradictions in man's natural existence, have little interest in prophecy or utopia. They seek first to disclose the naked visage of death in its most modern guise, and then to create what human balance they can against its ravages in time, without illusions about man's power to live long in what Kierkegaard might have called the transcendental dimension. If a secular vision prevails among them, this simply reflects the logic of experience as they see it, though each wears his secularism with a different ease. They make no grandiose statements about the significance of human life, though some of them include characters who do, permitting the reader to weigh the value of traditional optimism against the more mournful vision of inappropriate death. Without banishing a sense of human dignity or man's opportunity to achieve it, they acknowledge the view of Melville's Ishmael that men must shift their conceit of attainable felicity if they are to endure life. And they accept as axiomatic Freud's corollary that to endure life one must be prepared for death, though they add some variations to his judgment. But they move beyond the conventional question of "how," to the more threatening one of "whether"—and their responses help to define the challenge to survival in an age of atrocity.

Rien n'arrive ni comme on l'espère,
ni comme on le craint—Marcel
Proust

2

DYING VOICES

Most dogmas about death are contradicted by experience. "Whether you think of it as heavenly or earthly," Simone de Beauvoir was convinced, "if you love life immortality is no consolation for death."[1] In our age of diminished faith, this may be true for those in whose ear hope still whispers its message of future possibility; but for those in whom hope has been crushed with a finality beyond any chance of revival, the future is dead and nothing beckons but the silence or transcendence of the grave. If we could hear the voices of men and women who knew in advance the time of their death, what would we learn? The existential torment that unconsciously governs the condition of human creatures who are "condemned" to die at an uncertain date and under ambiguous circumstances is part of the modern dilemma. But if the uncertainty and ambiguity could be eliminated, how would that affect the human condition?

Speculations are useless, since these too are so often contradicted by experience. The only valid testimony would have to come from the voices of the condemned themselves, and fortunately written evidence exists which provides a glimpse into the souls of men who have heard their death sentence, had their last appeal denied, and have been offered (or have seized) a final opportunity to communicate with the world of the living. *Letzte Briefe zum Tode Verurteilter: 1939-1945 (Last Letters of Persons Condemned to Death)* is a collection of letters written by members of resistance movements in fifteen countries of western and eastern Europe during World War II, who had been arrested by the Gestapo and sentenced to death. With a few exceptions, the authors knew that their executions would be carried out shortly. Invariably, the letters are directed to close relatives. Since many of the letters were transmitted by secret means or were accidentally discovered in their hiding places after the war, there is no reason to believe that their contents were "supervised," though here and there a phrase appears to have been censored. But last words represent a precious opportunity, particularly when they reflect such an unambiguous confrontation with inappropriate death, since neither natural illness nor accident nor will plays a role in the ultimate fate of the victims.

The authors, bound by their common opposition to the Nazis (though the tactics they chose varied), differ in almost every other way—sex, age, national origin, political affiliation, professional status. But they are united by a further detail, which has a major influence on their response to their grim destiny. They have the psychological support one gains from the knowledge that a pattern of cause and effect has been instrumental in shaping their fate. Although heroism may not have been a motive for those resistance members who drifted into the movement through chance or in search of excitement, it furnished a retrospective justification for their activity, and—the theme emerges vividly in letter after letter—for their deaths. Although all the victims die prematurely and violently (many of them not yet twenty), a spirit of protest or rebellion scarcely surfaces in their letters, as if they feared to disturb the equanimity they knew they would need at the final moment. They seem to fear death less than the absence of a myth to make their deaths as "liveable" as their lives.

By myth I do not necessarily mean a lie, though the rift between human dignity and self-delusion is very narrow. If the cultural institutions they draw on to pacify the terrors of creation and replace panic with acquiescence no longer address us with a vital voice, they offered adequate sustenance to the imaginations of the condemned only thirty years ago. Into the vacuum left by the collapse of these institutions pours renewed apprehension about inappropriate death, so that the testimony of those voices sounds like an echo from another era. The Communist victims die for the Party, for their comrades, in the war between capitalism and the people. The religious victims die for the triumph of good over evil, accepting death as the end of a journey whose course they do not control; the patriots die for glory, so their countrymen may live in honor and the dignity of their nation may prevail. They are familiar consolations, effective if the language of the condemned is to be believed; but one wonders, in an age when politics and war have been discredited as bulwarks for the spirit, whether such institutions will ever again afford shelter from the bleakness of our fate. With the loss of "sacrifice" and "martyrdom" as usable concepts, what new myths will appear to lighten the burden of the human condition?

The solace which prevails among most of the victims in this volume is that they are dying a memorable death—or so they have convinced themselves. One is astonished by the resourcefulness of the imagination when death grants it an opportunity to be allied with an idea beyond the self. A nineteen-year-old Belgian describes the beatings he endured to make him confess the names of his confederates, then heroically announces: "But never, truly never once did I name anyone. I could have saved myself, but I preferred to do and say nothing that might betray my country." To reinforce his heroism in his own mind and to his auditors, he continues: "Several people should be grateful to me, that I didn't mention their names. And now I'm proud of myself, because I've resisted everything and saved several lives." He reminds his parents to make sure they notify his friends and the members of his organization of the details he has just recorded, and signs himself, after his name: "Always a Belgian! Died for his country." Then in an additional note, apparently written at the same time but discovered in his clothing after his death, a repetition: "A final word to you to tell you that for my part I never betrayed or accused anyone, in spite of the numerous beatings I received with a blackjack, in order to make me talk. I might have saved myself in several ways, but I preferred execution to betrayal, so I die with dignity and proud of myself."[2]

The young Belgian's words betray a version of what Ernest Becker has called "transference heroics," though he practices it here in an extreme rather than a "safe" situation, and the process is partly conscious and partly unconscious. Transference heroics is a self-created mythology, "the establishment of a locus from which our lives can draw the powers they need and want." Such heroics seeks to validate the significance of our lives by transferring to another the authority to behold our conduct and declare it good. Becker might have taken his theory a step further, for in the situation we have just examined, this kind of transference represents an attempt to validate the significance of a *death*. The Belgian's anxiety, lurking behind the repetition-compulsion explicit in his language, can tolerate his inappropriate death only if his comrades affirm the last days of his life, which "cause" his execution. "People create the reality they need in order to discover themselves,"[3] says Becker, and he might have added, when death is in question, to have others discover them too. The Belgian's letter is a self-imposed therapy of a kind that individuals require if they are to survive creatively, but even more urgently if they are to die with a supporting vision beyond the loneliness of the human condition.

Unfortunately, the human condition does not naturally provide situations to sustain what we might call death-tolerance myths as easily as it nurtures transference heroics among the living. The crises which reality has thrust upon us—the threat of nuclear holocaust, assassination, political corruption, local wars dubiously attributed to the spirit of national liberation—all defame and diminish the image of man, making it increasingly difficult to establish a connection between one's inner self and the outer world of natural and spiritual reality. As a result, the "dying voice" has greater difficulty securing an audience receptive to its appeal for a memorable death, the equivalence of the young Belgian's surviving comrades. Their presence in his mind, together with his belief in the larger abstraction of patriotism, gives him the courage to "die with dignity, and proud of myself." It is what Becker might call his "vital lie."

A twenty-three-year-old Dane, a few hours before his execution, began his last letter, even before the salutation, with an armor of abstractions: "Faith, Hope, Love. Freedom, Truth. Duty, Honor, Loyalty." We are incredulous to learn that two of his resistance comrades, disguised as stonemasons, manage to enter the prison, where he is awaiting trial, to rescue him—but he refuses to leave! He has given his word to his captors not to escape, since they, like him, are bound by a principle of duty, and life without the sanctity of such principles would not be worth living. The only prop missing in this drama of ancient honor on the very stage of atrocity is a cup of hemlock! But it demonstrates that inappropriate death invades the imagination with horror only when that imagination lacks weapons to resist the assault. "Death and life give meaning and content to each other," writes this victim. "Both are introductory chapters to a new life." He weaves an elaborate account, rich with imagery, of death as a journey into a tunnel whose exit we cannot see but only imagine because it already lives within us. But most important of all, he is able to identify the act which will cost him his life with the political future of Denmark, and to ally both with his spiritual destiny, in a vision of a future, peaceful nation "lying in the shadow of God's wings."[4] The fusion of individual fate with political and spiritual continuity resolves the melancholy contradiction between human ideals and the mortal limitations of reality.

The heroic stance is thus a mutually reinforced collaboration between the ego and the outside world, with language, in these instances, as the vital—indeed, the essential—intermediary. Of course, without these recorded testaments to the dying voice, we would have no evidence that such heroism was possible; nor do we know whether the condemned men were able to sustain it when they stood alone before the final silence of extinction. Most of us are denied the grace of a last audience with humanity; if we could discover a way of making one available to more victims of mortality, we might ease the terror and isolation of the ultimate ordeal. But a few exceptional letters in this volume complicate the issue sufficiently to make one wary of simple solutions to the difficult contemporary problem of inappropriate death. For if the majority of these letters show that midway through our century there was still adequate support for the heroic posture in the face of death (given the special circumstances of the arrest and execution of the condemned), three or four of them are so openly rebellious against the terrible injustice of *such* a death that we are left humbled and dazed by the anguish and anger of the forlorn spirit when neither inner vision nor outer reality can furnish it with assurance of a memorable death.

Should we be surprised to learn that all of these rebellious letters are written by Jews—as it happens, Polish Jews? Not all of them, to be fair, were members of tightly organized resistance movements, though like the others, their words resound with the authentic tone of dying voices. But the tone is more muted, the final vision shrouded in gloom, and we discover to our dismay that in these instances the grace of the last audience is not enough. For many reasons, the Jewish experience of atrocity in our time is closer to contemporary man's anxiety about inappropriate death than the views we have just examined. The latter may reflect the last noble gasp of a collapsed continuity between life and death, while the ones we are about to confront illuminate the prospect of a life without appeal, of the grim challenge, in Becker's haunting words, of "the lived truth of the terror of creation, of the grotesque, of the rumble of panic underneath everything."[5]

But language traditionally gives order to our experience, while the rumble of panic opens into a universe of chaos that sanctions neither style nor myth for the condemned. "If heaven were paper," begins the last note from a fourteen-year-old Jewish boy to his parents, "and all the seas in the world were ink, I couldn't describe to you my suffering or what I see about me."[6] There is no need to rehearse his catalogue of horrors, which simply banishes the possibility of a memorable death—yet in our time this kind of death has been immeasurably more common than those described earlier. The sudden, violent, irrational extinction of vast numbers of people is part of the personal and historical consciousness of the twentieth century. Any confrontation with this fact should begin with a study of some of its earliest victims' failure to find an inner imagery to give meaning to their fate.

Unfortunately, the mind must first comprehend that fate, put it in a usable context, before it can try to translate the sense of personal loss into a meaningful image for the living. But by now we have gathered so much evidence from recent decades that a new kind of reality exists which of its very nature prevents the discovery of meaning in chaos, that it may be time to examine the chaos in greater detail before we dig further channels between it and meaning. Or if this proves too harsh a task, at least let us be genuine about what we are protecting ourselves from. In an action repeated dozens of times in towns and cities in eastern Europe, the Nazis massacred most of the Jewish inhabitants, locked the remainder in the synagogue, led some out in small groups to be shot, then set the building on fire leaving the rest to be burned alive. Amidst the rubble, after the war, last messages were found written on the walls, some in blood. One example will suffice:

The doors are opening. There are our murderers. Dressed in black. On their dirty hands they wear white gloves. They drive us out of the synagogue in pairs. Dear sisters and brothers, how difficult it is to take leave of such a beautiful life. You who are still alive, never forget our innocent little Jewish street. Sisters and brothers, avenge us on our murderers.

And after her name she adds, not "died for her country," but "murdered on September 15, 1942."[7]

The recognition of death's dirty hands beneath clean gloves is not the kind of image to make the contradiction between human aspiration and human fate more palatable, nor is the call for vengeance the sort of pious sentiment which centuries of tradition have taught us to rely on when facing death. Unlike the young Dane, who felt that he would be violating a principle if he escaped from his executioners, this victim sees her death for what it is—murder—and calls for the killing of her killers as a simple act of logic, an instinctive defensive response (though some might choose to interpret it as an expression of elementary justice). She has no illusions: death is ugly and brutal, and its ministers deserve to be destroyed. From this opposition between the Dane's heroic posture, his longing for a purposeful death, and the Jewish woman's helpless anger and despair, rose an attitude which Camus would describe as the "absurd." As we shall see, *The Myth of Sisyphus* in part responds to situations of this sort, in an attempt to mediate between meaning and chaos, to redefine the features of death and to give the imagination a myth for confronting it without succumbing to despair.

The Jewish victims in these letters share with Camus another conviction—their innocence. The spirit of rebellion in their letters differs from the mood of the other condemned, who seem psychologically more in the grip of institutional thinking. Although most of them believe their sentences are extreme— many are unprepared for it—few protest their innocence, as if the "law" making resistance to Nazi tyranny a crime somehow gained legal status in their minds and persuaded them they were in violation of it. Having risked their lives—whether they were conscious of the danger initially or not, they now realize it—they acknowledge the power of institutional "justice" (though of course they do not welcome it). But these Jewish victims, bereft of institutions to identify with, their religious community a shambles, torn by inner dissensions and fear, are forced to see death without intervening masks for what it is—a murderer of life. And until new masks are invented—or perhaps one should say "unless" they are—the white gloves on the dirty hands of death will fool fewer and fewer men—and the psychological consequences will be grave.

The problem is vividly illustrated by one last letter from an anonymous Jewish woman, who tells of the execution of five thousand men, including her husband:

Six weeks later, after searching for five days through the pile of corpses [left unburied in the cemetery] . . . I finally found his. Since that day life has stopped for me. Once, in my young girl's dreams, I couldn't have wished for a better and more faithful companion. I was permitted to be happy for only two years and two months. And now? Weary from searching through so many corpses, am I supposed to be "happy" to have found his? Can one clothe such agonies in words?

One is inclined to respond that *unless* we can clothe such agonies in words, our feelings will have no way of reacting to such experience—and this is part of the dilemma we suffer from today, as we are asked to absorb with increasing frequency the painful truth of apparently meaningless death. A surfeit of such deaths brings the danger (which we will turn to shortly in this chapter when we consider Robert Jay Lifton's work with Hiroshima survivors) of a psychic numbing that deprives us of our capacity to feel anything in the face of the death threat. The Jewish woman who found her husband beneath a pile of corpses presents a graphic description of this psychological condition:

In time you get used to anything. You're stupefied. If you lose someone very close to you, you scarcely react any more. You don't weep, you're not human, but made of stone, without any feelings. No news makes any impression. You even go to your death very quietly. The people in the square were indifferent and quiet.

Meaningless death mesmerizes the faculties of the victims; such hypnosis of the will and emotions makes them less than human. Recognizing the melancholy implications of this mournful spectacle, the anonymous Jewish author, virtually in her last words, introduces a countervoice, as if she would leave as her heritage a final protest against death's insult to the human spirit:

Why can't we cry out, why can't we arm ourselves? How can one see so much innocent blood flow and say or do nothing, but wait oneself for the same death? So miserable and bereft of mercy must we die. Do you think we want to end so, to die this way? No, no! We don't want to! In spite of all these experiences. The urge for self-preservation is often greater now, the will to live stronger, the nearer death is. It's incomprehensible.[8]

Less a split personality than a victim trapped by the paradox of her mortality at a moment in history when experience ruthlessly intensifies the paradox, this woman with her two dying voices embodies the twin but increasingly isolated impulses of the modern spirit, torn between a numb acceptance of meaningless death and the instinct to affirm the importance of the individual personality. This is the terror, says Ernest Becker, commenting on Kierkegaard's vision though his words fall on receptive modern ears: "to have emerged from nothing, to have a name, consciousness of self, deep inner feelings, an excruciating inner yearning for life and self-expression—and with all this yet to die. It seems like a hoax. . . ."[9]

Moreover, it is a cruel and inexplicable hoax, which artists like Samuel Beckett will transform into a macabre vaudeville. The condemned whose dying voices we have just examined did not survive to exhibit their scars, so we gain no evidence from them how a journey to the frontiers of death has altered their vision of existence. But the extraordinarily brutal nature of war and tyranny in our century has left us numerous witnesses who have made and outlived this journey, and their reports represent dying voices of another kind, analytical as well as emotional—voices that have suffered a death immersion and then returned, like Odysseus, Aeneas, and Dante's Pilgrim, from the land of the dead to tell their tale. If their narratives are less imaginative than the epic poets', they still cast significant light on our present concern—contemporary man's response to inappropriate death.

Jean Améry's *Jenseits von Schuld und Sühne (Beyond Guilt and Atonement)* is a primer for understanding the new image of death as atrocity that is slowly infiltrating the modern imagination. An Austrian Jew who survived Auschwitz and other concentration camps as well as the notorious SS prison between Antwerp and Brussels called *Festung Breendonk,* Améry has been one of the few to evaluate in detail the influence of his ordeal on traditional concepts like "human dignity," and to recognize that his confrontation with death released into history a unique version of the ancient struggle between the reasoning mind and unreasonable horror. Unable to accommodate itself to the kind of abnormal death that threatened in the world of the concentration camps, the mind capitulated to the terrible new reality and slowly began to see its fate as *reasonable.* "The last duty of the prisoner," says Améry, casting some eerie light on the motives of the Dane who refused to escape, "was death." Living as it were in the same room with death, seeing other inmates hanged for trivialities, one grew accustomed to the omnipresence of death: "I recall times when I negligently climbed over piles of corpses, and we were all too weak and indifferent to drag the dead out of the barracks into the open."[10]

But this apathy toward the fact of death did not obliterate all fear: it shifted the emphasis from "being dead," which now appeared as the logical and inevitable fate of all the prisoners, to the manner of dying. Fear of death became fear of dying an inappropriate death under conditions of atrocity. As a result of the camp experience, Améry argues, he and his fellow prisoners lost the power of distinguishing between the idea of death and the experience of dying, a privilege still available to free men outside the camp. Thus from his point of view the condemned men of the *Last Letters* could "bear" their death because they could put it in a social context, thinking of the family and work they left behind, and a mental context, because at the frontiers of intellectual possibility there was still a tiny space left for them to develop a heroic attitude toward their fate. They had little difficulty equating the manner of their execution with a tolerable idea of human dignity. Camp reality, on the other hand, caused a total collapse of any metaphysical framework for shoring up man's faltering spiritual courage; it became the microcosm of a world where self-knowledge no longer made life worth living and psychic numbing failed to conceal the terrors of the unliveable life. Améry's universe turns even Freud's clear-sighted exhortation—"if you would endure life, be prepared for death"—into a dubious abstraction.

The fear of dying under conditions of atrocity represented a failure of language, which in turn reflected a mind unequal—or not yet equal—to the task of conceiving or imagining what reality demanded of it. The old terminology was extinct. An intellect honed and hardened by the camp experience found metaphysical abstractions like "being" and "existence" superfluous and meaningless. "One could *be* hungry, *be* tired, *be* ill. But to say that one simply *was* made no sense. Indeed, Being was transformed permanently into a pointless and therefore empty concept." For a time, experience became a substitute for language, and the survivor was left with the difficult challenge of expressing mute responses. To reach out with words across the reality of existence, says Améry, "became before our eyes not only a worthless game, an unpermitted luxury, but also an insulting and evil one. . . . Nowhere else in the world did reality have so much effective power as in the camp, nowhere else was it so purely 'reality.' In no other place did the attempt to move beyond it prove so cheap and futile." The usual consolations of transcendence either intensified the victims' literal ordeal or sounded like hopeless babbling. "Where they meant anything, they seemed trivial, and where they weren't trivial, they didn't mean anything."[11]

In the extreme situation of the camp, logic and analysis, bastions of language, crumbled before the concrete images of atrocity: "One glance at the watchtowers, a sniff of the odor of burning flesh from the crematoria, sufficed" to remind the prisoner *who* reigned in this dominion of death. The immediate threat to existence was the utter vulnerability of the body, which suddenly disarmed all the devices the human imagination had invented—from the incarnation to the heroic defiance of martyrdom—to disguise the irreducible fact of physical extinction. "We came out of the camp," says Améry, "denuded, pillaged, depleted, disoriented—and it took a long time to relearn the everyday language of freedom. We speak it today, moreover, uneasily and without proper trust in its validity."[12] For the "language of freedom" was raised on the cornerstone of human dignity, and Améry had learned that you don't live among dehumanized men and witness their misdeeds and humiliation without doubting all notions of an inborn human dignity. When men are forced by their circumstances to acknowledge the overpowering influence of the fear of dying on their emotional and intellectual lives, they discard most of the illusions that sustain them during "normal" times: beauty, for one, and understanding, for another, which proves to be, in Améry's phrase, merely a "conceptual game" when grimmer rules are set by the other player, death.[13]

But Améry discredits the power of understanding as a palliative to human pain only *at the moment of atrocity in an extreme situation:* his testimony in this book affirms his belief in the value of insight for those who have been spared the experience themselves. Other men's fragility mirrors our own, and it may be that our ability to recognize our potential future in their ordeal should be the first step in making that ordeal psychologically manageable. Améry's most significant chapter is called simply *"Die Tortur"* ("Torture"), where he creates out of the harrowing account of his physical agony at the hands of the Gestapo an extraordinary metaphor for our time, one of those "inner images" which may not insure the unity of response to life that Lifton calls for, but which plays a vital and still unexplored role in the historical consciousness of men. History in our generation has sanctioned new dimensions to our fear of dying: the experience of torture, and—far more subtle in our response to a death stripped of heroic associations—the desire and will to be a torturer. Améry's reflections on torture introduce several staggering possibilities for our understanding of man's fear of dying by suggesting some relationships between the tortured and the torturer, between dying and killing, that open up new areas for psychological insight.

Ironically, torture restores to human existence what men for centuries have sought to suppress: the centrality of the body, what Ernest Becker prefers to call man's "creatureliness." It is a cruel way of reminding man of his physical fallibility. One wonders with a kind of dazed and timorous awe whether our increasing use of torture as an expression of institutionalized aggression is not a perversely honest way of finally acknowledging the fragility of our mortality. I frankly hesitate to wander through these marshlands of human motive, so infested are they with quicksand to trap the innocent layman, but I might venture the suggestion that as other resources for heroic transcendence fail, torture becomes for the torturer a way of transcending his mortality by creating the illusion that the power to inflict pain on others somehow exonerates one from suffering the same fate. The psychological burden imposed on all of us by nations who resort to torture and then are ashamed to confess their action—often, to see it even as shameful—must be inestimable, though investigators will have to devise complex means for assessing the effects of this burden. And one shudders at the prospect of more and more nations, faltering in their progress toward historical immortality, employing torture against "enemies," men and groups who appear to thwart that progress and whose victimization bolsters the tottering self-image of the nation.

One of the most sinister and melancholy discoveries of our era is that men and nations can kill under certain circumstances without having to face effective censure from civilization. The desolate heritage of Auschwitz, Hiroshima, Stalinism, fascist Spain, Algeria, Vietnam—the length of the list grows frightening—is that torture and atrocity have failed to outrage the sensibilities of men as one might have expected. Who can say whether this is because men identify unconsciously with torture and atrocity as distorted—or perhaps not so distorted—expressions of the impulse toward immortality, of uniting the self with a power beyond the self? The life-depriver is a demonic alter ego of the heroic life-supporter, the martyr who dies convinced that he perishes so others may live. The torturer lives so that others may die, a bizarre but logical bequest to the impoverished human image in an age of atrocity.

Ernest Becker, with his intense devotion to the psychoanalytic approach, offers us guidance and possible confusion here. Traditionally, the death-haunted individual alleviates his fears through transference, entering into a "cosmology of two," turning in some instances to a love partner, in others to God. But the disappointment or failure of these relationships in the modern era causes some men to shift their goal: "If the partner becomes God he can just as easily become the Devil. . . . One can be utterly dependent whether one needs the object as a source of strength, in a masochistic way, or whether one needs it to feel one's own self-expansive strength, by manipulating it sadistically." Later, in a chapter on mental illness, he elaborates by arguing that both sadism and masochism come naturally to man, not as grotesque aberrations of human behavior, but as reflections of "normal" mental health. Sadomasochism "reflects the general human condition, the daily lives of most people. It reflects man living by the nature of the world and his own nature as it has been given to him."[14] But Becker does not explore the nature of the world that makes his shocking conclusion acceptable, nor does he move in his discussion beyond the psychological framework of perversion, which has long presented the need to give or receive pain as unnatural.

His casual definition of "normal" requires further refinement, and here Améry's confrontation with torture provides an invaluable link. For when the sadomasochistic impulse is enacted on the larger stage of history, it ceases to be a private drama of "natural" perversion or mental illness. Absorbed into the general culture through repetition or familiarity, torture becomes a "normal" expression of human conflict (like local wars, which in our generation have become a "normal" means of settling hostility between rival factions); and extreme suffering (which one hesitates to equate with masochism) becomes a "natural" consequence of the logic of torture. Mental illness is no longer an excuse, though most institutions, whether of psychology, law, or government, continue to rely on it because the dreadful alternative, implicit in Becker's remarks and explicit in Améry's, would necessitate a radical revision of our view of human nature and motive. Torture as a form of perversion is acceptable to the human imagination because it leaves open some hope for a cure, just as death is "acceptable" only so long as it allows hope for transcendence through some form of heroic illusion. The "healthy" torturer, on the other hand, is a contradiction to the modern intelligence, like "welcome" death; yet under the public glare of history, we are being forced to face the fact that human life is no longer so precious and that "sacred" is no longer a term we can use accurately in connection with the human image.

Améry's testimony also is valuable because he speaks with the dying voice of one who has peered involuntarily beneath the canopy of creation and returned with an austere personal vision of the human spectacle. He is not a patient whose words must be interpreted by an analyst and incorporated into a general theory of human behavior. He is the first to disclaim any universal validity for his experience, though he offers his insights with the tentative firmness of unfamiliar and newly won truths. "Torture is the most terrifying event that a human being can verify by himself,"[15] he affirms. Determined not to thrust the uniqueness of his ordeal upon us, however, but the common practice of torture since the time of Auschwitz, he quickly cites examples from Vietnam, Algeria, South Africa, Angola, and the Congo. By 1967, when he wrote his essay, man's conscience had grown accustomed to the practice of torture; and it was able to do this, he suggests, because of the precedents established by the ordeal he suffered under the Nazi system. The reality introduced into the world by the existence of SS and Gestapo undermined man's approach to the world through imagination and destroyed—for a time—all those ramparts which the imagination had erected over the centuries between itself and the fear of dying. The reality of torture, and by metaphorical extension, of death as a remorseless attack on the human body, became a central fact of daily experience.

Améry's reeducation begins when he realizes how many of our attitudes are determined by inherited abstractions about reality, derived from hearsay, books, films, and our conception of how things ought to be. His arrest by the Gestapo at first follows the pattern of adventure stories: men in leather coats, handcuffs, pistols, the swift auto ride to prison; as long as events coincide with expectation, the mind can manage them. But then he is struck by the startling discovery that his captors' faces don't look as they are supposed to: they are not sinister, pockmarked, scarred, but like everyone else's— average and commonplace. And suddenly the victim finds himself up a dead end, because his responses to life have always been determined by presuppositions about everyday reality, and that reality has always confirmed them, even when life was unpleasant. "The truth is, " Améry abruptly learns when the knowledge is too late to serve him, "that only in rare moments of our life do we stand eye to eye with experience and reality."[16] Solzhenitsyn has dramatized with frightening detail this progress from abstraction to truth in the episode depicting the arrest of Innokenty near the end of *The First Circle.* For Innokenty and Améry, the humiliation of the body, suddenly reminding both men of its utter vulnerability, is the first stage in their journey toward a new understanding of the human condition.

The most difficult—because the most ingrained—abstraction to abandon is the certainty that because of a written or unwritten social contract, the "other" must respect one's physical, and hence one's metaphysical existence. In spite of repeated historical evidence to the contrary, the human imagination clings to this vital lie as the crucial prop supporting its image of the dignified self. "The limits of my body," insists Améry, "are the limits of my self. The surface of my skin separates me from the unknown world," and in order to renew confidence in that world, one has only to feel on that surface what one *wants* to feel. But with the first blow, that idea and the system on which it is based collapses. The torturer violates the integrity of the victim's body, and the blow "ends a part of our life that can never be reawakened."[17] Confidence in that abstraction we call "the world," in a social contract binding men, is displaced by the concrete experience of pain: once again the vulnerability of the body becomes the central fact of existence.

Here language falters in its efforts to describe the essence of reality. There would be no sense, Améry says, to describe the pains he suffered:

Was it "like a red-hot iron in my shoulders" [he had been suspended by his wrists from behind until his shoulders had been wrenched from their sockets] and was this "like a blunt wooden stake driven into the back of my head?"—a simile would only stand for something else, and in the end we would be led around by the nose in a hopeless carousel of comparisons. Pain was what it was. There's nothing further to say about it. Qualities of feeling are as incomparable as they are indescribable. They make the limits of language's ability to communicate. Whoever wants to share his bodily pain would be forced to inflict it and thus become a torturer himself.

Améry coins the word *Verfleischlichung* for this intense sense of one's physical vulnerability or "creatureliness." It is a total experience, complete and without appeal—a ritual of death. Having no other outlet leading to transcendence, the victim regards his feelings of pain as a foreshadowing of dying, and in his mind reduces his ordeal to the equation body equals pain equals death. Améry concludes with the hypothesis that torture, which transforms a man from something else into pure body, "obliterates the contradictions in death and permits one to experience his own death."[18]

But though he reminds us that his speculations are based only on his personal ordeal, Améry is concerned with more than his own confrontation with physical torture. He reflects on what the existence of torture as an integral part of reality does to man's image of himself and his world. He comments on the imprint it engraves on the victim's imagination: "Whoever has been tortured remains tortured. Torture is burned indelibly into him, even if no clinically objective traces are discernible."[19] But he imposes on the reader an even more difficult responsibility of interpreting this fact, of engaging in his own speculations, since Améry's account has entered into history and the general consciousness of our time.

At this point the various theories about death suppression and heroic transcendence give us little help, since torture is not a pathological circumstance for the victim, and Lifton's idea of impaired symbolic immortality does not apply. Nor does Becker's conception of life as a problem of heroics, "which inevitably becomes a reflection of what life ought to be in its ideal dimensions."[20] "Life in its ideal dimensions" was a senseless and futile phrase to Améry as he faced his torturers, whose complete dominion over his body abruptly eliminated all illusions that might justify his worth as a human being. It was not a question of failed heroics, but of *unavailable* heroics. For some men, in certain situations, traditions and culture no longer support the possibility of heroic transcendence. Failed heroics reflects a failing image of man, of the self. Students of human nature like Becker and Lifton struggle with the problem of inventing ways to restore that disintegrating image.

Responding to the kind of reality which has nurtured Améry and his fellow victims, Becker introduces a pertinent view of mental illnesses and perversions: "They all refer to the terror of the human condition in people who can't bear up under it."[21] But Améry sheds light on the terror of the human condition for people who have *endured* it, not through neurotic defenses but through actual experience. The result is a sort of grim lucidity, a clarity beyond tragedy that Charlotte Delbo, another survivor, will call *"une connaissance inutile"*—a useless knowledge. Memory is not a mental illness which can be cured; and insight that discredits all illusions, including the illusion of hope, is not a perversion of human nature to be treated by therapists.

Do we pay for psychological generalizations about mental disease by sacrificing the individual sufferer, his personal portrait, his private response to the challenge of integrating his life in a hopelessly contradictory universe? Psychology is concerned with guilt, but the literal victims of inappropriate death, or those like Améry, who through the equation of body with pain with death experienced a form of their own annihilation, were innocent. When reality, backed by history, burdens innocent men with the responsibility of living life in unideal dimensions, perhaps it is more important—certainly it is equally important—to perceive the harsh contours of that reality before we exhaust our energies on theories about the insufficiency of human response to it. The wonder is that the imagination has survived at all, given the historical brutalities of our era.

Améry's provocative image of a hopeless carousel of comparisons to describe any effort to communicate pain under torture through language provides an uneasy context for a passage like the following, from Ernest Becker's *The Denial of Death:*

The body is definitely the hurdle for man, the decaying drag of the species on the inner freedom and purity of his self. The basic problem of life, in this sense, is whether the species (body) will predominate over one's individuality (inner self). This explains all hypochondria, the body being the major threat to one's existence as a self-perpetuating creature.

Améry and Becker here confront each other like men from alien lands speaking strange tongues. Améry would wince to be told that the body is the hurdle for man, and he would simply ridicule (or deplore) a phrase like "the inner freedom and purity of his self." Yet Becker is far from a simpleminded optimist, and his choice of words may merely betray the difficulty of shaking one's allegiance to a language worn smooth by time. In an earlier section he develops a line of thought that in its main emphasis is compatible with Améry's experience, though by using it to support a general theory of schizophrenia he once more shows how psychology intrudes on events that were far more "innocent":

Here I want only to mention the main characteristic of the syndrome—why it is that the schizophrenic is in such an extraordinary state of terror. It took a long time for us to understand this state because we were dealing with a phenomenon so strange it seems truly like science fiction. I mean the fact that human experience is split into two modes—the symbolic self and the physical body—and that these two modes of experience can be quite distinct. In some people they are so distinct as to be unintegrated, and these are the people we call schizophrenic.[22]

Améry and Becker would agree that history reinforces the split between the symbolic self and the physical body, and that it should not be regarded as abnormal. But they would differ sharply over what constitutes normality, and on this difference depends the idea of inappropriate death that I have been trying to examine.

If part of the problem of our time is to find an inner imagery to reunite the symbolic self with the physical body, then a profounder dilemma is not the question of relationship but of exclusion—those inexpressible instances when the symbolic self simply disappears, effaced by the numbing truth that nothing can help the body defend itself against its unchosen fate. Unlike accused witches and heretics, Améry's tortured lose even the self-righteous justification with which these martyrs once opposed their wills to the zeal of their persecutors. "For the tortured," says Améry, "the torturer is only the 'other.'" In this respect, death loses not only its sting, but its drama.

Past martyrdoms, Améry argues, have wedded persecutors and victims in a kind of religious complicity that finds no parallel in modern police torture, and thus makes of dying a much less heroic affair. The modern torturer, and the death whose instrument he is, inverts the familiar social world where men collaborate in the common effort to survive and relieve human suffering. The first sensation of pain immediately transforms this social world into an illusion, and "fellow creatures" become those figures who possess total power over the flesh, "indifferent bureaucrats of death," in Améry's precise contemporary formulation. Nothing remains but the pain and the terrifying suspicion, gleaned from the expressions of "murderous self-fulfillment" on the faces of the oppressors, that for some men the will to torture is a form of transcending mortality and that killing, in the absence of more humane candidates, has emerged as a new form of heroics. There were moments, Améry confesses, "when I responded to the sovereignty which my torturers wielded over me with a kind of humiliated reverence. For isn't someone who can transform a human being into a body, a moaning prey to death, a god or at least a demigod?"[23] Améry specifically denies any connection between this attitude and the idea of perversion or sexual pathology. He prefers to interpret it as an example of how the historical moment "approved" a natural human impulse to pacify one's own fear of fleshly decay by driving others up to and beyond the frontiers of death into nothingness. We have yet to contemplate the consequences of this new form of heroics should it become a universal principle of psychological survival.

Men have always known that life is fragile. But modern history has bequeathed to this fragility a new status, whereby men become victims depleted of inner and outer resources to nourish the symbolic self and death becomes a torturer, with nature and other men its agents, reducing victims to such a throbbing consciousness of the flesh's vulnerability that they sometimes feel numbed by death even when still alive. Earlier in this chapter, in reference to the young Belgian resistance member condemned to death, I said that one is astonished by the resourcefulness of the imagination when death grants it an opportunity to be allied with an idea beyond the self. Here I must add that one is even more dismayed by the impotence of the imagination when death denies it an opportunity to be allied with an idea beyond the self. The inability to dramatize the ordeal of our dying is one sign of its ultimate meaninglessness—and who is prepared to deprive life of a significant denouement?

To be meaningful, a death must be part of someone else's life, but in our time too many deaths have belonged to no one—not even to the dying. We saw in the last chapter how Lael Wertenbaker's husband dramatized his death and thus infused it with meaning by enacting it in the presence of and indeed with the assistance of his wife. The drama lies in the literal collaboration between living wife and dying husband, or more precisely, healthy wife and ailing husband, since both recognized that only chance has prevented the roles from being reversed. The victim is able to keep the decision to die "now" in his own hands, repudiates the platitude that life on any terms is preferable to death, acknowledges without self-deception the sheer physicality of his ordeal—but preserves the quality of his life by the intensely human context of his death. He is able to meet his fate with a gesture that enhances his image of self: courage and determination are part of the symbolic expression of personality that sustains the imagination—of the victim, the wife, and the readers—in its effort to accept and transcend the fact of physical deterioration.

Stories like Wertenbaker's deceive us into concluding that the imagination is always free to engage in this kind of redeeming drama. But their appeal withers before another kind of death tale, equally if not more representative of our era, a life without denouement even though actors are present and the imagination is still ostensibly free to range across its symbolic stage to diminish the anxiety of physical extinction. This brief narrative, written by a concentration camp survivor and called "Conversation with a Dead Man," illustrates the abyss between inherited defenses against death (Gunther, Wertenbaker, Simone de Beauvoir, the European resistance fighters) and the utter defenselessness thrust into reality by the image of a tortured universe. It rehearses a scene, repeated so often in the extermination camps, when fear became more an ingredient of daily routine than hope—selection for the gas chamber. Only our knowledge of its truth keeps us from protesting that surely this is an account of a nightmare, a surrealistic dream:

I look around me—faces are pale, appearances are feverish, no one can speak any more. Even the bravest and most garrulous have grown mute. We wait. Who can describe this atmosphere of expectation and report what's happening inside us? There they are, they're coming. We're all naked and arranged in rows. The barrack leader counts, counts again, and with the appearance of these bandits, who hold our lives in their hands, we're all merely "living dead men." We look at each other, and with this look say to ourselves: "Whose turn is it? Which of us will be sentenced to death?"

This is a different kind of torture from Améry's, since the uncertainty about the outcome is quickly over, "in the course of half a minute a man's fate is decided," and the routine appears to be so ordinary that Améry's bureaucrats of torture have indeed been transformed into indifferent bureaucrats of death. This macabre display of the body, with human survival at stake, strips from the consciousness any concern except for one's "creatureliness," since the appearance of the flesh—do you look healthy enough to go on living for a while—is the sole criterion for continuing existence. The narrator "passes," one of his best friends does not, and then both their imaginations must contend with this somber fact:

The selection is over. We join each other again, as if nothing had happened. We're summoned to eat our soup. We, the rescued, and those condemned to death, are close to each other; and astonishing as it sounds, there is no revolt, no protest. No scenes of despair. It's so inconceivable that I still don't understand it, despite all the arguments that I try to find. A deathly silence surrounds me; those sentenced to the gas chamber seek out their friends. I am overwhelmed and lie down on my bed.[24]

If the victims themselves found the experience incomprehensible, how is the contemporary reader, seeking to understand this ineradicable part of his heritage, to respond? What symbolic dimension of experience could possibly pacify the unexpressed and perhaps inexpressible terror and despair that such a fate would inspire in an individual? Unanswerable questions breed neither security nor insight, as thirty years later one still searches for some usable orientation, unwilling to admit that such a crucial encounter with death is inaccessible to the human imagination:

Whoever was not present at this action, whoever has not seen the confused eyes of the condemned, who await the results of a friend's intervention [with the "clerks," who sometimes risked their lives by writing down a false number], knows nothing of hopelessness and nothing of genuine despair.[25]

Then the narrator's friend, one of the condemned, sits down beside him, and an uneasy confrontation transpires. We have a double vision: both are victims, but under the circumstances, one is closer to death than the other. We have the dying man's response, and the narrator's reaction to and interpretation of that response. We measure the narrator's expectation against the actual event, and from the tension between the two grows his insight—and ours.

As the narrator sits silently by his doomed comrade, a parable of man's fate in the presence of atrocity unfolds. The first scene takes place in the mind of the narrator, who remembers his friend's earlier words: "Me they'll never get. They'll pay dearly for my skin; I'll know how to die." And he waits for him to reveal his plans. But the uncanny indifference of the "murderers" to the human dignity of the victim divorces the symbolic from the physical self, and this rupture dislocates the will to action and paralyzes—almost literally prohibits—any response. The victim's resolution to die heroically assumes a psychological atmosphere that supports inner rebellion, while the abrupt, casual process of selection disarms the will and affirms not only the harshness but the futility of the human condition. The victim here rediscovers Améry's truth: that the essence of torture, of the condition of atrocity, occurs when the "other" refuses to acknowledge one's existence as a human being. "You're surprised," says the condemned man to the narrator, "that I eat and say nothing."[26] But it is clear to us, if not to them, that eating confirms the centrality of the physical self, and in the absence of hope for heroic transcendence, the victim desperately turns to the nourishment of the body as a useless if necessary gesture to convince himself that he is still alive.

The second "scene" enlarges the gap between expectation and reality, as the victim recognizes how removed is his doom from the social conventions which normally support a condemned man: "I'm thinking about death," he says,

but not as you imagine. I know that even criminals and bandits who are legally condemned are asked for their last wish before they die. Usually alcohol or cigarettes. And for us nothing, nothing at all. I'd like to have one last pleasure too before I die. The only thing left to me is eating! Eating! To die full! I've suffered so from hunger!

The silence at this secular last supper intensifies, as the scene shifts back to the mind of the narrator, who is still struggling to find some shape for the fate of his friend (which of course at the time would appear to be his own eventual fate too):

Something dreadful was taking place inside me. I had another conception of death. I thought he would speak of his family, vengeance, send greetings through me. Nothing. . . . He is completely emptied. All the words that he had used earlier were only attempts to cheer himself up. At the decisive moment nothing remained, and suddenly I understand why so many before him in rows of five went unresisting to their death. They have completely lost their vital energy: their existence crushed them, and the daily drama of death has destroyed in them every reaction.[27]

Deceived by what Camus will call the nostalgia of hope, possessing nothing to put in its place, both narrator and victim are deflated at the last moment and departure from life proves anticlimactic. Stripped to its core in an age of atrocity, is death never part of someone else's life, but always a solitary, isolating, incommunicable event? "My comrade stays at my side for a long time," says the narrator. "We don't speak. Finally he presses my hand, looks in my eyes and says: 'Be good, old man; be brave.'" And the narrator's response, followed by his closing words, persuades us that we still have much to learn about the mystery of death when a dying voice merely disguises a much deeper dying silence:

I have nothing to say in reply. I feel inside me an urgent need to tell him: "Defend yourself, at least show something, we'll help you!" But as he stands before me, I feel that he's already far away from us, that he's already gone and is not thinking of anything.

Silence loomed between us. I embraced him, and he left.[28]

None of the obvious categories—terror, despair, anger, acceptance, even the more technical phrase used by Lifton, "psychic numbing"—adequately describes the experience of the condemned man who has been "selected" by other men for death.

On its simplest level the episode does not differ greatly from more familiar death scenes: the survivor feels uncomfortable, casts about for words of consolation while knowing that the living have little to say to the dying. What neither confronts is that when the "daily drama of death" through selection leads to extermination in the gas chamber, nothing—literally nothing—in either of their prior experiences could possibly prepare them psychologically for the event. Such a fate leads the imagination beyond Freud's potentially tragic charge that to endure life we must prepare for death, into a realm where enduring certain kinds of death proves intolerable even when we have prepared for it by the most intense dedication to life. The question Freud could not ask, and we have not yet answered, is whether the age of atrocity imposes on our consciousness death burdens which in our inexperience we are too weak—or too untrained—to bear.

That question will remain open for a long time. Meanwhile, "Conversation with a Dead Man" provides us with a potential epitaph whose importance reaches far beyond the barbed-wire borders of the concentration camp: "Their existence crushes them, and the daily drama of death has destroyed in them every reaction." When atrocity makes headlines, as it has constantly during the past forty or fifty years, the average man retreats from the private implications of this public menace; surely the surge in studies of death and dying in recent years is partly a response to the vacuum left by this withdrawal. Such titles answer a need, not a desire. But they cast only a fragmented light on the shadowy issue of death and atrocity, which requires a systematic and comprehensive illumination if we are to greet it with more than the puzzled and embarrassed silence of the narrator in the episode we have just examined.

One of the few such studies is Robert Jay Lifton's *Death in Life: Survivors of Hiroshima*, a volume which recognizes the crucial importance for individual existence in our era of extreme historical situations. Although the book is about the Hiroshima experience, Lifton weaves into his narrative sufficient allusions to the concentration camp ordeal to convince us that, despite the radical differences in the instruments and manner of death, Auschwitz and Hiroshima are twin expressions of a similar human and technological will to destruction, and that we are all survivors of atrocity. He understands that naming a threat takes priority over exhortations to eliminate it, especially when the imagination is crowded with images of death that have been superseded in history if not yet in personal life by the phenomenon of atrocity. His analysis and interpretation of the process of replacement in the lives of a number of Hiroshima survivors becomes by association an exploration of the contemporary consciousness as it confronts or avoids new meanings of death.

The Hiroshima bomb, perhaps even more than Auschwitz, changed the quality of war and hence the quality of life and of survival itself. One of the "dying voices," a Japanese physicist who survived the attack on Hiroshima and the subsequent feeling of death-immersion (his first reaction had been "I think the world is ending") explained the difference between the two examples of atrocity with professional insight: "Auschwitz shows us how cruel man can be to man, an example of extreme human cruelty—but Hiroshima shows us how cruel man can be through science, a new dimension of cruelty." The "dying voices" of Hiroshima substitute the impersonality of a manmade natural force for the impersonality of Améry's "other"; and the new dimension of cruelty is that men now find it almost impossible to identify the source of their anxiety and suffering with any human agent at all. The private image of death is replaced by an indefinable and uncontrollable image of general destruction and annihilation. One of the main objections to nuclear testing, atmospheric or underground, has been the fear of polluting or disturbing natural forces, generating earthquakes, tidal waves, or rainfall carrying lethal radiation. The human imagination has no way of contending with the anxiety of nuclear-induced extinction; or, as Lifton has said of the original A-bomb: *The most striking psychological feature of this immediate experience was the sense of a sudden and absolute shift from normal existence to an overwhelming encounter with death."*[29]

How does an "overwhelming encounter with death" differ from the mortality which men have been doomed to face since their appearance on earth? Another Hiroshima survivor, commenting on the essential nature of the bomb, illuminates this question for us: "Such a weapon has the power to make everything into nothing, and I think this should be symbolized."[30] Death in its most literal sense has never been anything else; but twentieth-century reality has by now offered us so many vivid images of "everything" transformed into "nothing" on a massive scale that the imagination struggles for some manageable means of meeting the encounter. The most striking example for Americans in recent history is the missing Vietnam soldier, who was abruptly changed from "everything" into "nothing" and left behind no trace of his existence. More painful even than the dying voice is the whisper of mortality reduced to an anonymous silence. The threat of such a fate is the contemporary mind's most agonizing heritage.

The testimony of the A-bomb survivors gives us some of our most reliable information about the nature of this heritage. Lifton sums up much of it when he speaks of *"a vast breakdown of faith in the larger human matrix supporting each individual life, and therefore a loss of faith (or trust) in the structure of human existence."*[31] With the disruption of a familiar moral universe, the individual must find "new" reasons for living and "new" ways of confronting the prospect of death introduced into reality by atrocity. Such disruption mars not only an ordered universe, but the identity of one's self, one's conception of where he fits and how (and why) he is to act as a human being in a dehumanized world. The Hiroshima survivors felt a qualitative difference in their lives, partly because they knew that nothing could ever restore their prebomb identity, and partly because so many of them were literally engraved with a token of their ordeal. Although keloids or scar tissue from burns disfigured only a minority of A-bomb victims, they came to symbolize the conviction that their bodies had been permanently altered by the experience. Once again we see how closely death by atrocity is allied with man's physical identity; and the persistence of the idea is concretely illustrated by the fact that more than a decade after the event, survivors were still manifesting symptoms of A-bomb disease, often fatal.

It is appropriate, then, that the works we will examine in subsequent chapters pay so much attention to the body as the main target of death's assault on human dignity. Tuberculosis in Mann's *Magic Mountain,* plague in Camus, cancer in Solzhenitsyn, and the agonies leading to gas chamber and crematorium in Charlotte Delbo's uniquely artistic memoirs of Auschwitz and Ravensbrück, all reach out beyond the literal plane of disease and torture to the universal dilemma of dealing with one's "creatureliness"—of living critically and self-consciously while so vulnerable to the physical cruelties of men, nature, and science. The atrocities we have been discussing impose on the imagination as never before the human paradox, in Ernest Becker's words, "that man is an animal who is conscious of his animal limitations."[32] And to perceive this paradox, as these authors do, is to reinterpret the role of the human in a world with shrinking possibilities for its affirmation.

Implicit in this paradox is the realization that in an age of atrocity there are no limits to what a man can do or suffer, for destructive as well as creative purposes. A century born of progress, optimism, and technological discovery has been fed the nourishment of creative possibility; it has taken us decades to learn to live on a scantier diet. And with the spirit in a permanent state of malnutrition, the task of mastering death to make life more endurable offers us a meager feast indeed. Lifton speaks of "wandering through the eerie psychic terrain of death in life"[33] when alluding to a concentration camp survivor, though his phrase might equally refer to all literal survivors and, by extension, to the human condition of all men who need to assert the genuineness of their lives by heeding the dying voices of the victims of atrocity. We seem to have reached a point in history when ignoring these voices from the past and present affects the authenticity of our own existence. But their words conjure up a vision of reality that sometimes makes the superficial seem preferable.

The existence of the A-bomb and the concentration camp— supreme expressions of atrocity in our time—can eventually be traced back to the decisions of men. And Lifton does not conceal the frightening effect this truth has on survivors, "because at some level of psychic life they have been made aware that the world is a place in which man cannot be counted upon to control these terrifying impulses." The limited possibilities of heroic transcendence make the ordeal unbearable for the survivor, but equally so for the reader who listens to their "dying voices," since unlike Gunther, Wertenbaker, Simone de Beauvoir, and the resistance martyrs, they are speaking of a world we all still live in, not one in which someone *else* is dying. And although all the survivors are struggling to reestablish a form of continuity between the A-bomb experience and "normal" life, there is a quality inherent in the experience itself that inhibits such formulation. Their remembrance of the event—"The kind of death . . . faced by atomic bomb victims was different from natural death— something unprecedented in history—a total annihilation of human beings," as one of them said—threatens *us*, because if they are unable to make their ordeal, as Lifton puts it, "part of their ongoing self-process,"[34] how are we to absorb it?

There is a difference, if not a consolation—what was unprecedented for them is "precedented" for us, and we have the painful privilege of developing continuity with life based on *their* suffering rather than our own. Heard dissonances may not be sweet, but those unheard perpetuate annihilation—to say nothing of ignorance. Atrocity, with its emphasis on the grotesqueness of abrupt and violent death, intensifies man's latent apprehension that dying is an unmanageable event; it erodes culture's carefully nurtured postures for withstanding this threat, and leaves man with the options of terror or awareness—modest solace indeed. In addition, confronting death in a postatrocity world means abandoning the innocence (or self-deception) by which men lived in the past. For obvious reasons, survivors themselves are faced with the certainty of an unrecapturable past—personal suffering, injury, disfigurement, the loss of family and friends, not to speak of inner despair and humiliation, all conspire to shift the normal function of memory and their perception of the real. The survivor's mental economy, Lifton observes, "undergoes a permanent alteration, a *psychic mutation.*"[35] One of the chief residual bequests of atrocity, as we have seen earlier and as the Hiroshima ordeal confirms, is a perpetual obsession with premature or inappropriate death, and this becomes part of the inner dilemma for the survivor as he tries to justify his continued existence. Similarly, he struggles with the image of an unfulfilled or arrested life, of continuity frozen in time, so that the thaw of survival cannot undo the interruption in the original flow of experience.

Lifton underlines a vital difference between private dying and the public ordeal of atrocity when he concludes that "the shocking inappropriateness of death on a massive scale . . . causes a more fundamental disruption in the survivor's sense of the general continuity of human existence."[36] As in most dramatic tragedy, private dying usually represents a limited interference in this continuity; after a brief or prolonged period of mourning, social order reasserts itself and the individual finds consolation and support in the fact that society survives his personal ordeal unchanged, and welcomes him back into the normal rhythms of existence.

But mass atrocity in our time has altered the nature of society, of that "world" in which the individual once found refuge from his death-immersion. The taint of atrocity is universal as well as personal, and raises the specter of a return from inappropriate death to inappropriate life. Transformed inwardly by his unprecedented death-encounter, man then confronts a reality which itself shows the scars of the atrocity he has suffered—with one crucial difference. His response is self-conscious, and society seems largely unaware of its new visage—and often of his. The experience of atrocity purges the individual of his illusions about death far more swiftly than it purges society's institutions, which cling to their illusions in a desperate attempt to deny what man has learned. Lifton calls it "the temporary annihilation of the bonds of human identification through violently administered premature death on a mass scale."[37] On the reuniting of these bonds depends the psychic health of man and civilization. At stake is man's image of himself as a socially viable human being, a problem anticipated by Améry when he discovered that his torturers were not fellow human creatures *(Mitmenschen)* but anonymous "others" who denied his social and human reality. Like all survivors, he came back from a hermetic ordeal, an encounter sealed off from normal experience that created serious difficulties when he tried to return to that normality. The image of the hermetic ordeal has now become part of the twentieth century's literary heritage; as we shall see in later chapters, Hans Castorp's stay on the mountain in *The Magic Mountain*, the townspeople's quarantine in *The Plague*, Kostoglotov's hospitalization in *Cancer Ward*, and Charlotte Delbo's deportation to Auschwitz all represent modern death encounters in a hermetic atmosphere, and the problem of retaining or restoring human identity throughout and following their ordeals becomes a luminous imaginative commentary on Lifton's psychological research.

That research has its own limitations: Lifton's findings constantly challenge the intelligence, but only sporadically the imagination, as his mind reduces the original chaotic experience to the order of clinical categories—"psychic numbing," "death guilt," "counterfeit nurturance," and many others. It is in the nature of scientific investigation to make meaningful the apparently meaningless; the literary imagination, more ambitious in the complexity of its efforts, is more modest in its hope for clarification. The confrontation between meaning and chaos which it dramatizes thrives on ambiguity, as confusion persistently threatens insight with despair. Both Mann and Solzhenitsyn pay tribute to the importance of scientific research—after all, medical institutions are the setting for *The Magic Mountain* and *Cancer Ward*, and both Hans Castorp and Kostoglotov pursue the symptoms of their illness with intense fidelity to medical detail—but in the end the threat of death forces them to draw on resources which carry them beyond the frontiers of scientific investigation.

Questions about the role of literature in an age of atrocity return us to Freud's conviction of 1915 (at the onset of the first mass atrocity of our era) that we should seek in the world of fiction "compensation for the impoverishment of life."

Mann, Camus, Solzhenitsyn and Charlotte Delbo are less certain than Freud that in literature "we can enjoy the condition which makes it possible for us to reconcile ourselves with death—namely, that behind all the vicissitudes of life we preserve our existence intact,"[38] partly because Freud was thinking of literature *before* the age of atrocity, and partly because in 1915 he could have no conception of how in the next sixty years history would threaten the intactness of our existence. Words like "reconcile," "preserve," and "intact" belong to the vocabulary of social and psychological order, while the literature we are about to examine is united by the vision of death as a permanently disruptive force in our lives, and though the emphases of these four authors differ according to their absorption of the idea of death as a reflection of atrocity, they all regard it as an ordeal which negates old assumptions about heroic transcendence. Such a vision requires a redefinition of self, a reorientation of values, a new quest for an inner imagery to link mortality with survival, and especially a very cautious interpretation of Freud's appeal that we seek in literature "compensation for the impoverishment of life."

That impoverishment has been gradual, and neither Freud nor Mann (when he wrote *The Magic Mountain*) could have known how Auschwitz and Hiroshima would infect and weaken man's vital energy in his struggle to endure. At the time, World War I seemed an unsurpassable traumatic catastrophe; Camus's encounter with World War II reinforced his preoccupations with death in the prewar period; Solzhenitsyn's Gulag volumes confirm his belief, dramatized in the early novels, that the Soviet purges and death camps represent the central disaster of Russian personal and national existence in this century; and Charlotte Delbo's evocations of her concentration camp ordeal complete this cycle of literature relating death to the inhuman up to midcentury. When the imaginative literature on Vietnam begins to appear, we will have an additional grim chapter in the narrative. Meanwhile, such literature pursues the elusive goal of organizing insight into the question of how facing or avoiding the new perspectives on death unleashed by atrocity alters our image of ourselves.

How are we to decide whether such organized insight brings compensation or consolation for the impoverishment of life—whether, indeed, our lives are as impoverished as Freud preferred to believe? Literature reflects the human condition; moralists and others presume to improve it. Lifton himself admits that "the full recounting of a single death can evoke more direct and empathic response than descriptions of scenes of thousands of deaths,"[39] and the writing we will turn to shortly substantiates his claim. A volume of gruesome statistics speaks less eloquently than a simple painful narrative like "Conversation with a Dead Man." Much modern literature sees—has been compelled by recent history to see—man dying not as a continuum in the cycle of experience, not any longer as a tragic event, but as a dilemma which violates all previous patterns of human existence. If philosophy and religion and even literature have taught us in the past that human vision expands through discovery of the best, the history of atrocity has challenged us with an enlargement of consciousness through recognition of the worst. Who can say whether such insight will inspire men to transfigure the "worst" into a new "best"? Transfiguration may be another dead heritage. But where death is concerned, art is not yet ready to abandon the old myths merely to a new despair.

The problem is not: to be or not
to be. But rather: to be and not
to be. What it comes down to is
that man lives while dying, that
he represents death to the living,
and that's where tragedy begins.
—Elie Wiesel

3

THOMAS MANN AND DEATH ON THE MOUNTAIN

Thomas Mann speaks of *The Magic Mountain* as a swan song
to the kind of pre-World War I existence that made possible
and tolerated institutionalized dying, the main business of
the International Sanatorium Berghof, where the action of
the novel occurs. Institutionalized dying promotes an image
of health in the midst of decay and dangles the promise of
cure for a disease which Mann uses to represent man's fate,
the incurable affliction of his destiny—ultimate death. The
patients at the Berghof regard *time* as their enemy, not annihilation, and this misconception—or self-deception—is reinforced
by the directors of the Berghof, the healers of civilization,
who nourish the myth—compassionately, to be sure—that the
human dilemma is nothing more than a matter of patience,
resolution, and trust in the superior knowledge of experts.
By 1918 a civilization had perished behind the standards of
these withered truths.

Despite its prewar setting, *The Magic Mountain* is in many
ways Mann's World War I novel. Conceived and begun before
that conflict, it was to have been a brief companion piece to
Death in Venice, a humorous treatment of "the fascination
of the death idea." But then the war broke out, and by

Mann's own confession this "put an immediate stop to my work on the book, and incalculably enriched its content at the same time. I did not work on it again for years." The war experience transformed a humorous tale into the magisterial epic of one man's initiation into disease and death, an initiation inaugurated on a grand scale in our century by that first great war and continuing with more solemn intensity ever since. With startling clarity Mann perceived that a generation overwhelmed by the "death idea" might perish from immersion as its predecessor had from ignorance and illusion, so he sought new myths to blunt the conflict between what he called "bourgeois decorum and macabre adventure."[1] *The Magic Mountain* is a bridge between these two extremes: its protagonist, Hans Castorp, is an unsuspecting fictional agent of the modern challenge to recognize death as atrocity and still find a stance to preserve man's image of his human self. Mann found this task more amiable to the imagination than some of his literary successors.

Mann realized that the war reached out in two directions, cleaving bonds with the past but also creating consequences for the future that one could anticipate only dimly. He speaks somewhat ironically of the "historic mould" that covers his narrative, "due to its taking place before the epoch when a certain crisis shattered its way through life and consciousness and left a deep chasm behind." His tale is set "in the long ago, in the old days, the days of the world before the Great War, in the beginning of which so much began that has scarcely yet left off beginning."[2] If Mann's characters know nothing of the Great War until the narrative's closing pages, his readers bring their memory of its carnage to their experience of the novel; the dynamic interaction between what they "recall" and the "innocence" of his characters establishes much of the dramatic and psychological tension. Rather fancifully, it resembles opening a door to yesterday with the knowledge of tomorrow, a merging of history and imagined experience with the reader's mind as the catalyst. Much art draws on this tension, but the results are especially powerful here because the reader is already a "survivor" of the death encounter for which all of Hans's adventures prepare him. Hans's fictional confrontations highlight the real human waste and devastation that will follow, offering the reader, with provisional reassurance, a reverence for humanity that art affirms and history denies.

Both space and time make inroads on Hans's imagination, though at first they induce only a vague uneasiness, and Mann's narrator provides the language to prepare us for Hans's later ordeal: "Space, like time, engenders forgetfulness; but it does so by setting us bodily free from our surroundings and giving us back our primitive, unattached state" (p. 4). Poised between the familiar and the unknown, Hans finds himself in an incongruous situation precisely because what he has endured offers no explanation for what he is about to confront. The "primitive, unattached state" is menacing because it is morally neutral, unsanctioned by culture or society, invulnerable to illusion or defense, threatening to the very substructure of civilized reality, but mainly because it suggests that life is only a precarious balance between survival and dissolution, with the outcome continuously in doubt.

Time traps or liberates the individual, depending on whether he submits to its blandishments or penetrates its facade. Tradition protects man from the terrible; myth dissolves time and permits the self to wander freely, if temporarily, like Hans in the snow episode of the novel, in his "primitive, unattached state" across threatening terrain in quest of a balanced vision of existence which will acknowledge man's end as well as his beginning. Hans must unlearn the habit of relying on external expressions of time like family tradition and genealogy before he can address himself to the question of whether literal confrontation with death any longer leaves room for the pious vocabulary of time: persistence, recurrence, duration.

Hans's last memory of such piety is his grandfather's funeral, which dramatized for his youthful imagination the elaborate ritual men indulge in to avoid the desperate connotations of death. Thanatologically speaking, the history of culture has been a systematic effort to prove to the survivors that their dead are not really dead. On its deepest level, *The Magic Mountain* is a complex artistic commentary on Freud's simple statement of 1915 that "we cannot maintain our former attitude toward death and have not yet discovered a new one." The Castorp clan embody that former attitude, and the death of Hans's grandfather is a fictional swan song to its existence.

Mann offers a wry observation on art's complicity in the deception with his description of the life-sized portrait of Hans's grandfather, which silences the murmurs of mutability by bearing witness to "the perpetual continuity of things" (p. 25). An art that idealizes life disguises truth and deludes the imagination, which welcomes such delusion and joins the conspiracy willingly because it finds the truth unpleasant and is unequipped to face it. There is a lingering Platonic echo to the conviction that ordinary reality is only an imperfect version of a higher one, that "the old man's everyday appearance was not his real and authentic one," that the portrait was a "far finer and truer" representation of the man (p. 24); but the forms of death transcendence that Hans inherited and that history bequeathed to the generation entering World War I are nothing if not Platonic. The elder Castorp on his funeral bier, garbed in the ceremonial costume of his councillor's rank, betraying no hint of a decaying body, actually justifies the ordeal of mortality by providing the mourners with a reflected image of their own permanence; the splendor of the *idea* of man conceals the vulnerability of his flesh.

To his credit, Hans is not entirely immune to the other profile of death, though he and his contemporaries would only learn to know it in the mud and trenches of the Great War's battlefields:

In one aspect death was a holy, a pensive, a spiritual state, possessed of a certain mournful beauty. In another it was quite different. It was precisely the opposite, it was very physical, it was material, it could not possibly be called either holy, or pensive, or beautiful—not even mournful. The solemn, spiritual side expressed itself in the ceremonial lying-in-state of the corpse, in the fan-leaved palm and the wealth of flowers. . . . One and all of them . . . were there to palliate the other aspect of death, the side which was neither beautiful nor exactly sad, but somehow almost improper—its lowly, physical side—to slur it over and prevent one from being conscious of it [p. 27].

In the absence of concrete experience, Hans can only draw on epithets like "improper," "distasteful," and "unpleasant" to describe man's "creatureliness"; the fastidious inhibitions of bourgeois respectability forbade language more direct, nor was such verbal honesty considered desirable or necessary. Vision precedes expression, and when history provides us with the material for such vision, we still need to find witnesses with sufficient courage and talent to accept the challenge. An age of atrocity assures us of a new reality of death, not necessarily spokesmen in its behalf.

Continuity and permanence are part of the world that Hans has left behind him "down below," and as he approaches a more authentic vision of reality, he is to discover, and we with him, that the mind and imagination are sporadic faculties which in an unidealized world grope for occasional insights without any guarantee that they will grant sustained form to our experiences. The war had taught Mann that reality shifted too quickly for language or philosophy to hold it in check; and he was shrewd enough to realize that this required a new view of language and philosophy, and a redefinition of the nature of reality. The dilemma is concretely dramatized by the disquieting palpitations which suddenly afflict Hans Castorp. For traditionally, the heart is the organ which responds to external stimuli, so that its behavior can be explained in other than organic terms. No medical expert, Hans does not muse with scientific precision; but his distress at the lack of connection between bodily experience and some spiritual explanation or justification for it anticipates a major source of anguish in an age of atrocity:

For, you see, a person ordinarily has palpitation of the heart when he is frightened, or when he is looking forward to some great joy. But when the heart palpitates all by itself, without any reason, senselessly, of its own accord, so to speak, I feel that's uncanny, you understand, as if the body was going its own gait without any reference to the soul, like a dead body, only it is not really dead [p. 71].

A body "going its own gait" is like a headless torso to that part of Hans Castorp conditioned by the values of "down below." It may twitch with signs of life, like a dead body that's not really dead, but the imagination is too unaccustomed to the image to absorb it into a new vision of reality.

Fifty years later, Ernest Becker would identify with Hans's dilemma: "The body is definitely the hurdle for man, the decaying drag of the species on the inner freedom and purity of his self. The basic problem of life, in this sense, is whether the species (body) will predominate over one's individuality (inner self)."[3] Hans begins to bid farewell to the security that left his ancestors unintimidated by bodily decay when he confesses that "it is disturbing and unpleasant to have the body act as though it had no connexion with the soul" (p. 72), though his cousin Joachim, himself ill, finds the subject distasteful and asks that it be dropped. The question of reconciling the innate vulnerability of the flesh with the meaning of life is thus introduced, but soon suspended.

Hans's organic distress during the opening weeks of his sojourn on the mountain betrays a latent drift toward acknowledging his "creatureliness"; but before he can do this, before he can build an inner life based on its acceptance, he must understand and reexperience all those forms and rituals invented by the mind as momentary stays against the confusion of a palpitating heart and a body prone to decay. The first hurdle is the rhetoric of humanism, which had established a fixed vocabulary for defining human dignity in abstract terms. Settembrini, the Italian free-thinker, descendant of liberals (as Hans is heir to his ancestors' conservatism), is both spokesman for and victim of the humanist point of view: it gains control of his mind, he serves *it* instead of making it serve his own humanity. Each time he celebrates "freedom" and "liberty" his words are riddled by the mocking sound of machine gun fire echoing from the bloody battlefields of World War I. The war ridicules retrospectively Settembrini's optimistic dogma that "a sound principle can produce only sound results" (p. 99); history continually contradicts such verbal determinism, nations' false assurances against the threatening spectre of violent death. Although Mann's words are a version of experience, heightening our insight into the nature of reality, Settembrini's are not. Hans's education takes a great leap when he perceives that edification is only a secondary motive with Settembrini: "The important one, I feel sure, is the talk itself, the way he makes his words roll out. . . . He is very pleased when you notice the effect" (p. 101). A generation deceived by phrases like "making the world safe for democracy" easily sympathizes with Hans, while the reader witnesses a clever exposure of the distinction between language as artifact and language as art.

Paradoxically, out of context, Settembrini's aphorisms support the intellectual trend of *The Magic Mountain*. His insistence that "disease has nothing refined about it, nothing dignified" (p. 98) repudiates a romantic tradition that was a major obstacle to a more genuine confrontation with mortality. But instead of proposing it as a first step in gaining a more honest understanding of disease and death as tokens of man's vulnerability, Settembrini uses his idea—it is never anything more than that—to denounce disease as a degradation of mankind (as if men were responsible for its inroads): "The dilemma, my dear sir, the tragedy, begins where nature has been cruel enough to split the personality, to shatter its harmony by imprisoning a noble and ardent spirit within a body not fit for the stresses of life" (p. 99). Becker argues persuasively that this is the source of much of modern man's anxiety; but Settembrini blunts his "insight" by using it to celebrate the *idea* of the "noble and ardent spirit," to apologize for the limitations of the body: "A human being who is first of all an invalid is *all* body; therein lies his inhumanity and his debasement" (p. 100). There is truth here too, but Settembrini's aphorisms lead neither to compassion nor even despair, but only to the soulless dead end of rhetoric. Unable to cross the chasm between language and action, Settembrini is nevertheless a better individual than his words imply: "he has a kind of pride about him," says Joachim, "that makes an altogether different impression: as of a man who has great respect for himself, or for humanity in general; and I like that about him; it has something good, in my eyes" (p. 102). But the "something good" does not diminish the impoverishment of Settembrini's personal life, nor does it enhance the vitality of others.

Hans's mentors on the mountain—and beside Settembrini, there are many—cling to exhausted or eccentric institutionalized dogmas, each persuaded that his truth is sufficient to explain the mystery of being. But if institutions once helped man to "see" reality more clearly, they have lost that power in an age of atrocity; the mentor in our time is "politically suspect," and the journey toward insight is necessarily a solitary one. "Can he free others who himself is not free" inquires Mann's narrative voice, and continues:

The ailing physician remains a paradox to the average mind, a questionable phenomenon. May not his scientific knowledge tend to be clouded and confused by his own participation, rather than enriched and morally reinforced? He cannot face disease in a clear-eyed hostility to her; he is a prejudiced party, his position is equivocal. With all due reserve it must be asked whether a man who himself belongs among the ailing can give himself to the cure or care of others as can a man who is himself entirely sound [p. 133].

But since no one who suffers from mortality is entirely sound, the answer to these questions is evident. And if one were to promote the artist as the only remaining "sound" member of society, any reader of Mann's *Death in Venice* or *Doctor Faustus* would promptly dismiss that idea. The relationship between victim and physician—that last minister to man's physical fate, endowed with the power, we persuade ourselves, to halt the body's decay—looms prominently in major works of Camus and Solzhenitsyn as well as Mann. And the equivocal bond that develops between them confirms our intuition that atrocity has made concern for the body a central dilemma of the human condition in our time.

Hans Castorp too has an intuition of this fact, and thus turns slowly from Settembrini and his cult of the word to a private "cult of the body" that leads him eventually to a scientific investigation into the origins of organic matter. For Settembrini's republic of the world, his new age of enlightenment, is founded on the corpses of individual men: "Austria must be crushed, crushed and dismembered, first to take vengeance for the past, and second to lead in the new law of justice with truth on earth" (p. 157). His "logic" must be so familiar to dismayed readers fifty years later that one is dazed by the power of history to paralyze the imagination so effectively decade after decade. Mann thought he was sounding the death knell of rhetorical schemes to create the "universal brotherhood of man"; must we finally confess that all such schemes are rhetorical? We are forced back upon the paradox of language's insufficiency, whether as political declamation or literary form, to explore reality, and the equal inadequacy of any other tool available to the human imagination. History contradicts Settembrini's faith that "writing well was almost the same as thinking well, and thinking well was the next thing to acting well" (p. 159). Yet such simple formulations appeal to the mind because they divert attention from the more unapproachable problem of individual suffering—Settembrini's own failing health, and the impending chaos of the world catastrophe his ideas failed to prevent.

Settembrini, not surprisingly, is concerned with neither chaos nor catastrophe. The only sane, noble, and religious way to think of death, this last of the humanists announces, "is as part and parcel of life; to regard it, with the understanding and with the emotions, as the inviolable condition of life." Death is worthy of homage as the cradle of life, but to submit to its attraction as an independent power "is without any doubt at all the most ghastly aberration to which the spirit of man is prone" (p. 200). As an intellectual formulation, Settembrini's view sounds irreproachable; but like all his other views, when tested by subsequent experience, it reveals the poverty of his generation's effort to master reality by verbal disquisition. If death poetically is the cradle of life, then life in actuality is the helpless victim of death: Settembrini's aphorisms encourage man not to think of death at all.

Shortly after this conversation Hans has his first literal encounter with his own mortality when he visits Behrens's office for an x-ray. There is a mournful irony in Mann's choice of the most sophisticated instrument of radiation in his time as the device to reveal to Hans the essence of his physical vulnerability. Under its withering gaze the flesh is literally decorporealized, and Hans Castorp sees into his own organic interior. It is a wholly new experience in "seeing." Hans unwittingly furnishes an epigraph for the entire novel when he innocently declares that "we must wash our eyes with darkness to see what we want to see" (p. 216). First Hans peers at the image of his cousin on the screen, sees "something like a bag, a strange, animal shape," expanding and contracting regularly, "a little after the fashion of a swimming jelly-fish" (p. 217), and discovers that it is Joachim's heart! So much for this seat of love! Then he puts his own hand behind the screen, seeing "precisely what he must have expected, but what it is hardly permitted man to see, and what he had never thought it would be vouchsafed him to see: he looked into his own grave." Hanging loosely from his bony finger on the screen is the seal ring that he had inherited from his grandfather, emblem of continuity in change and the permanence of tradition; but now it is only "a hard, material object, with which man adorns the body that is fated to melt away beneath it." Are Settembrini's words then anything more than hard immaterial objects with which man adorns his mind? Hans gazes at his bones and "for the first time in his life," Mann tells us, "he understood that he would die" (pp. 218, 219).

But Mann is shrewd enough to realize that insights such as Hans's do not instantly transform the individual; they simply stir curiosity in some to pursue the equivocal nature of human existence. One is reminded of Ishmael's caution in *Moby Dick:* "Look not too long in the face of the fire, O man! . . . believe not the artificial fire, when its redness makes all things look ghastly. To-morrow, in the natural sun, the skies will be bright. . . ."[4] Shortly afterward, when Hans regards his hand in the light of day, he discovers no trace of the revelation in Behrens's office: "This was his living hand, that he was used to see, to use, to wash—not that uncanny scaffolding which he had beheld through the screen. The analytic grave then opened was closed again" (p. 225). Like Melville, Mann is ultimately equivocal about the demonic and the pure, artificial fire and natural sun, death and life, illusion and reality. And he shares with Melville too the conviction that survival requires an integrated vision, a balance of apparent opposites, the risk of venture if not a total immersion in fire or darkness. Hans is not yet prepared for such risk, though his future traffic with the uncanny will certainly carry him far beyond the perimeters of the analytic grave.

The body simultaneously glows with beauty and augurs decay, longs for freedom and is imprisoned by sensuality, clings to joy even as time and disease wear out its lineaments. Mann tempers Hans's solemn quest for truth, however—and this distinguishes him from his successors, for whom atrocity can never again be a laughing matter—with a deflating irony, even with a gently prodding humor, as if to caution him (and us) not to take too seriously the possibility of solitary man ever comprehending the profound mystery of the human being. Lest Hans become another Settembrini, Mann mocks some of his endeavors even as he applauds their serious intent. Much of Hans's early investigation into the secrets of organic life, as well as his long discussion with Behrens on the epidermis as the covering "form" of the body, is little more than a detour to understanding his own organic dilemma, not his disease but his uncontrollable physical desire for Clavdia Chauchat. If idealized love is merely disguised desire, then Hans will have to revise his inherited notion about the role of the body in life and admit into his imagination a dimension of experience hitherto excluded.

As we approach the closing decades of the twentieth century, Mann's insistence on the phallic basis of human relationships sounds a little old-fashioned, but his focus has reverberations far beyond the Freudian. Romantic love, "dying for love," the solace one gains from the knowledge that he will be remembered by a loved one—all these formed part of the "inner imagery" of Mann's contemporaries and furnished perhaps the most important link between the physical body and the symbolic self, making death a less harsh if not a welcome end to life. Wagner's *Liebestod,* fusing love and death with eternity, the orgasmic basis of Tristan and Isolde's union concealed in the music that celebrated that love, is parodied by Mann in the scene where Hans finally declares his love to Frau Chauchat. But behind the parody lies the serious suggestion that a romantic love hoping to transcend death by incorporating it into its vision of reality betrays an ignorance of both love and death. As we shall see in the snow episode, love still plays an important part in Mann's reverence for the human, but it is far more equivocal than Wagner's ennobling ideal, allied to death, but rooted in a recognition of the physical basis of reality.

Since pathology is not his vocation, Hans begins his investigation into the mysteries of life and death with a straightforward look at what the textbooks have to say about the biological foundations of existence. His shift in emphasis from the spiritual-philosophical to the physical is significant, but more so is his reversal of direction from ends to origins. Mann wipes clean the slate of human destiny for his initiate, as if Hans must duplicate in his intellectual inquiry the very path that matter itself followed in its evolution from the primordial to the "civilized." The "consequences" of life are known and shared by all without exception; but its antecedents remain shrouded in mystery (though scientific speculation has grown far more sophisticated since the appearance of Mann's novel). Still, Hans's conclusion that "death was only the logical negation of life; but between life and inanimate nature yawned a gulf which research strove in vain to bridge" (p. 275) will require further modification as his own experience with the dying and the living broadens. The immediacy of physical suffering—and the intensity of such suffering will increase incalculably from Mann through Camus and Solzhenitsyn to Charlotte Delbo—while not discrediting Hans's studies, casts an unremitting ironic shadow on all such inquiries which tempt the imagination away from confrontation with concrete examples of human experience to abstract speculations. Hans is finally "saved" by his sense of the equivocal; he uses science to raise questions he has never considered before, not to find simple answers.

Hans's scientific endeavors are less a quest for the truth than a search for an image of the human to maintain a precarious balance between the apparently irreconcilable opposites that have begun to trouble him—living and dying. Science provides him with a vocabulary for viewing the human in physical rather than spiritual terms, and for Mann in *The Magic Mountain* this is an indispensable preliminary step in building a more genuine reverence for the human. For Hans now, the human grows out of the nonhuman, the organic from the inorganic, matter from the immaterial, and this is the essential mystery of existence. Later generations, including Mann himself in the post-World War II *Doctor Faustus,* will bear witness to the more painful mystery of the human growing into the inhuman; Hans himself will get a glimpse of the relationship between the two in his snow vision, but it will remain tentative and undeveloped. As long as Hans uses "living" and "dying" as the main terms of opposition, his imagination can meet the challenge of finding a delicate balance to harmonize them; but when they are displaced by "survival" and "atrocity," as we shall see, the imagination must struggle to preserve any image of the human at all.

Hans's sense of the equivocal is firmly fixed in his new perception of man's "creatureliness." Life is

something brewed out of water, albumen, salt and fats, which was called flesh, and which became form, beauty, a lofty image, and yet all the time the essence of sensuality and desire. For this form and beauty were not spirit-borne; nor, like the form and beauty of sculpture, conveyed by a neutral and spirit-consumed substance, which could in all purity make beauty perceptible to the senses. Rather was it conveyed and shaped by the somehow awakened voluptuousness of matter, of the organic, dying-living substance itself, the reeking flesh [p. 276].

"Form" and "beauty" in man seem to be more a matter of attitude, of the view the beholder chooses to adopt, than an expression of qualities inherent in human nature. And if this is so we are at the frontiers of a disquieting revelation since, if man's "nobility" is merely an invention of the imagination, its persistence is as precarious as the traditions which once assured Hans Castorp continuity in the midst of change. The image of "reeking flesh," on the other hand, of flesh irradiated, incinerated, and napalmed, is a durable presence in an age of atrocity. Hans's quest does not take him as far as this unholy grail, though his alternating celebration of and disenchantment with the body prepares us for that time when its vulnerability will become a controlling image for the literary imagination.

Hans's penultimate concern in this difficult chapter called "Research" is finally with pathology, the theory of disease, the physical decay which, whether accelerated by time, nature, or man, always mimics the limits of human mortality. When we consider how many of Mann's contemporaries still paid lip service to the conviction that life's dignity consisted in the purification and refinement of the spirit, Hans's pessimistic speculations seem almost sinister. What if life *is* only an infection or sickening of matter, a "first step toward evil, toward desire and death," when "there took place that first increase in the density of the spiritual" that signified "the transition from the insubstantial to the substance"? This transition, thinks Hans, is a biological form of the Fall, and being born a second creation, but shorn of divine sanction and hence "only another fatal stage in the progress of the corporeal toward consciousness,"

just as disease in the organism was an intoxication, a heightening and unlicensed accentuation of its physical state; and life, life was nothing but the next step on the reckless path of the spirit dishonoured; nothing but the automatic blush of matter roused to sensation and become receptive for that which awaked it [p. 286].

Life as matter roused to sensation has one meaning in the context of Hans Castorp's experience; for Jean Améry, it would imply a more dreadful if no less accurate definition. The final image in this earnestly capricious venture into scientific research through books rather than experiments is a vision of Clavdia Chauchat in all her "flesh-borne loveliness," and we are suddenly plunged back into a realm where life rouses the body to sensations of pleasure. But Améry's later description of "that which awakened" in him the other sensation of pain makes one wonder whether history has added a new chapter to Hans's research, raising the corporeal to an even higher stage in its fatal progress toward consciousness, a consciousness of its vulnerability which cancels the consoling polarity between pleasure and pain, desire and decay, love and death, and leaves man wrestling with images of plague, cancer, and the crematorium in a desperate attempt to retain, however shrunken, some countervailing images of the human.

The last "test" in the first phase of Hans's development in *The Magic Mountain,* the ordeal of love, requires a direct confrontation with Clavdia Chauchat, which may culminate in the fulfillment of the desire that has been tormenting Hans physically since shortly after his arrival at the Berghof. Because this encounter occurs during Carnival, when by tradition the individual may disregard polite forms of address, he uses the second person singular when speaking to Clavdia. Ritual thus provides him with a chance to pierce the facade of form and express feelings that have been seething within him. He enacts his own version of a fractured *Liebestod,* discarding Wagner's holy alliance of love, death, and eternity, and substituting his own "unholy" one of love, death, and the body, thus replacing spirit by physical presence and creating a new seriocomic role for man as lover in the midst of decay.

Although Hans here sees his meeting with Clavdia as a culmination of his adventures on the mountain, Mann makes clear that her personality is only a catalyst, and the "love" she arouses in Hans only a transitory goal in man's quest for a durable image of the human. By placing the love episode midway through his novel—it ends volume one of the original two-volume German edition—Mann shifts our perspective away from romantic love as the highest expression of the human spirit. The novel concludes with war, not romantic love, perhaps history's ironic epitaph to a generation that depended on this "eternal" feeling to allay the hostility driving mankind toward armed aggression and mutual destruction. In his state of emotional inebriation, Hans links love with death, hinting that both represent a physical falling away from the idea of order, one in the natural and the other in the moral universe. He is beginning to realize that acknowledging this disorder as part of the human condition is a step in the direction of wisdom. To Clavdia he confesses that the idea of death no longer frightens him because it now seems a general and not a unique fate. His cousin's serious illness is not so different from his own unstrung plight: "He is dying, and I am in love" (p. 330).

Clavdia's attitude toward human experience, so much more "liberated" than Hans's (or Settembrini's), challenges Hans with a new plateau of understanding, a view of morality which is Faustian in its summons to a greater immersion in life's mysteries, Mephistophelian in its perilous appeal to discover good through evil:

One must search for morality not in virtue, that is in reason, discipline, sound morals, integrity, but rather in the opposite, I mean in sin, surrendering oneself to danger, to the harmful and destructive. . . . it is more moral to lose one's way and even submit to decay than to remain in a state of preservation. The great moralists weren't virtuous at all, but adventurers in evil, depraved, great sinners who teach us to bow down like Christians to misery [p. 340].[5]

Such "wisdom" may indeed have led "great moralists" like St. Augustine and St. Paul through sin to virtue and a Christian reverence for human misery; but to the secular ears of Hans Castorp, it gives license for his passion, which he babbles forth in a drunken panegyric to the human body, Clavdia's in particular. Behind the ludicrous confusion of his words, however, mingling lyrical celebration with anatomical detail, lies a serious new image of the human. It joins love and death with the body in a way that Hans will have to contend with on a deeper level in his more sober moments. Here Mann has dismissed the soul as the link between love and death, and as Hans struggles to substitute the body as the mainstay of this new trinity, we are present at the very modern drama of man seeking to uncover transcendence in materials consecrated on the altar of decay.

"The body, love, death," says Hans (*"Le corps, l'amour, la mort"*—the aural bond is much closer in the French), "these three make only one":

For the body is disease and desire, and that's what causes death, yes, they're both carnal [Fr.: *charnels*], love and death, and that's the source of their terror and their great magic! But death, you see, on the one hand is shameless and disreputable, making you blush with shame; and on the other, it is a very solemn and majestic power. . . . Similarly, the body too, and love of the body, is an immodest and awkward affair, and the body blushes and pales on its surface with fear and shame of itself. But it's also a noble, charming glory, a miraculous image of organic life, a holy wonder of form and beauty. . . [p. 342].

He continues in this tone of worship, but the vocabulary of the idealized spirit is incommensurate with his devotion to "living and corruptible matter," and he finds that he cannot exalt the mortal body as he might a portrait or a statue. His eulogy of the "marvelous symmetry of the human edifice" (p. 342) mocks even while it defines a love declaration which must resort to the bones and organs of the body in the absence of the transcendent language lovers usually employ. No less than Settembrini's rhetoric of humanism, the traditional rhetoric of lovers conceals a truth about the human condition, especially about the role of the vulnerable physical body in this most intimate of human relations. Mann combines insight with ridicule in Hans's closing description of Clavdia as a "human image of water and albumen, destined for the anatomy of the tomb" (p. 343).

Throughout *The Magic Mountain,* Mann manages to maintain an uneasy bond between love and death, as the body reaches toward one while the other casts its shadow over the body. In the authors we will turn to in later chapters, we will see this alliance slowly breaking apart as atrocity stains the image of love and corrupts its power to diminish the anguish or erase the memory of inappropriate death. The experience of dying under extreme conditions gradually transforms love in the imaginative visions of Camus, Solzhenitsyn, and Charlotte Delbo into a sad memento from a vanished civilization. One of the curses of an age of atrocity is that the urgency of survival can cripple the privilege of love, and the two sometimes become warring principles, with men forced to make a choice between them. The dilemma will become clearer when we turn to the works of these authors; but as we shall see, even Hans Castorp must arrive at a moment in his solitary journey toward insight and a more tolerable image of the human when he will have to reject renewed love—or will not feel the need for renewal—as he presses on to a higher integration of self.

This integration is accomplished by a pattern of recurring reflections on those abstractions, like love and death, which traditionally have established the boundaries for man's definition of the human. Time and space are similar abstractions and, following the Carnival episode, Hans Castorp launches some crucial speculations about their influence on human experience. Time and space, which on a metaphysical plane lead logically to the ideas of the eternal and infinite, assure man of continuity between his physical and symbolic self. Abandon these concepts, and what happens to our image of the human? Man's finitude is inconsistent with the timeless, as is change, the body's decay, fulfillment and loss in love, death itself— and as Hans Castorp ponders these possibilities, asking ultimate questions of a universe that replies only with an echo of his own voice, he faces the unsettling discovery that conventional notions of time and space may be only illusions, props to bolster the tottering imagination against the threat of mutability. No devout Christian, Hans has nevertheless subscribed unthinkingly to metaphorical versions of incarnation, of flesh embodying spirit—his grandfather's portrait was one; but as these metaphors collapse, he must find new ones, or learn whether he can live without them.

The recurrence of the seasons seems to mock the idea of eternity as a straight line from life through death to a realm of the spirit, and Hans cannot reconcile the two:

You feel you're being fooled, led about in a circle, with your eye fixed on something that turns out to be a moving point. A moving point in a circle. For the circle consists of nothing but such transitional points without any extent whatever; the curvature is incommensurable, there is no duration of motion, and eternity turns out to be not "straight ahead" but "merry-go-round!" [pp. 370-71].

Man is trapped by circular time, but if he can no longer believe in the "spiritual gravity" that once pulled him from the surface of this time-bound globe, his only hope is to discover new myths to exalt or mourn the limited scope of the human condition. Primitive man, says Hans, celebrated midsummer night because he saw it as that moment when the ascending year began to descend, when "the world went down into the dark" (p. 371), to rise again in the spring—a cause for tears and laughter. "Tragic joy, triumphant sadness [the German 'melancholische Übermut' and 'übermütige Melancholie' captures more exactly the reciprocity of the feelings]—that was what made our ancestors leap and exult around the leaping flames: they did so in an act of homage to the madness of the circle, to an eternity without duration, in which everything recurs—in sheer despair, if you like" (p. 371).

At this point ancient myth collides with modern history, as soldier Joachim objects to the "large concerns" that occupy his cousin's mind. To mollify him, Hans praises his diligence in studying Russian grammar: "That will be a great advantage to you if there should be a war—which God forbid." The clash between Hans's reality and his cousin's emerges from Joachim's rejoinder: "God forbid? You talk like a civilian. War is necessary. Without it, Moltke said, the world would soon go to pieces altogether—it would rot" (p. 371). Once more an authoritarian voice disputes Hans's deepening vision of the equivocal and, as his reply (that the Chaldeans, a Semitic people, almost Jews, themselves carried on wars) is interrupted by an encounter with Settembrini and a new arrival on the mountain, we have an uncanny sensation that much remains undisclosed in this aborted conversation between the cousins. Does a life without commitment to an equivocal vision of reality invite the war which Joachim so facilely interposes; or does the equivocal insure for society a rot that makes war inevitable? Can war, the most destructive principle in physical reality, ever be an expression of the spirit? How, indeed, can the idea of spirit be reconciled with the practice of war? Throughout *The Magic Mountain,* these issues threaten to demolish the integrated human image; hence it is dramatically appropriate that the latest arrival should be an eloquent spokesman for the power of the spirit in human affairs.

He is Leo Naphta, an Austrian Jew converted to the Catholic faith and become a learned Jesuit, resident on the mountain like the rest as a patient, though in lavish private quarters rather than at the Berghof. He introduces a fresh point of view, his religious dogmatism quickly establishing itself as the antagonist to Settembrini's free-thinking. Like the Italian, he has a fervor for words; Hans will have to suffer another baptism of language in his journey through uncritical assertion toward critical insight. By now Hans has confidence in his capacity for rebellion, as if maturity means nothing more than learning what to reject among the neat explanations of reality that surround him, and why. Settembrini had tried to ignore the contradictions between mind and body by disparaging the importance of the physical; Naphta approaches a more honest distinction by establishing a firm dualism, which he calls "the moving, the passionate, the dialectic principle of all Spirit. To see the world as cleft into two opposing poles— that is Spirit" (p. 374). Against Settembrini's image of *Homo humanus* Naphta hurls the counterimage of *Homo Dei,* whose hope lies in salvation rather than freedom, for whom redemption is transcendental rather than an achievement of reason. Hans listens with an attentive ear to the continuing disputes between these verbal duelists, but no longer as a potential disciple. He is now capable of mildly sarcastic rejoinders, while his inward comments are even more caustic. The process of discernment which we witness in him resembles the effort of a seeker in the dusty attic of the imagination cluttered with relics of a passing era, a seeker hoping to salvage a few items still usable in his daily life.

The danger of all such investigations of the meaning of existence is that they may deflect the imagination away from its proper goal—human suffering and the fate of individual men. Camus describes such inquiry as "spiritual affectation," recognizing that such an "apparent revolt of the mind is *the one that costs least*."[6] An attitude requiring no personal risk is a refuge from reality, an intellectual santuary, and after further exposure to Naphta's point of view—which like Settembrini's is not immune from unconscious self-contradiction—Hans develops a craving for risk, an adventure in the unknown. He flees from Naphta's conviction that a belief, "a given conception of the universe, an idea—in short, a will, is always in existence; which it is the task of the intellect to expound and demonstrate" (p. 397). With veiled irony he thanks Naphta for explaining that fleshly beauty is insipid, physical beauty an abstraction, while "only the inner beauty, the beauty of religious expression, has any actuality" (p. 393). Naphta's description of Innocent III's *De miseria humanae conditionis* as "an exceedingly witty piece of writing" astounds Hans (p. 394), while his defense of the grotesque wooden *pietà* in his room as a celebration of "submission to suffering and the weakness of the flesh" (p. 394) reduces to simple formulae all Hans's previous efforts to affirm a new vision of the human by reintegrating images of love, death, and the body.

Whereas Settembrini is well-intentioned if ineffectual in his abstract reverence for the human, capable of espousing a war against Austria for the sake of greater liberty for mankind, Naphta seems to betray a reverence for the inhuman: Mann unveils the demon of terror lurking behind his absolute. This unpleasant, authoritarian little man, wearing the mantle of Dostoevsky's Grand Inquisitor, addresses history with a doctrine we recognize when he argues ominously that "liberation and development of the individual are not the key to our age, they are not what our age demands. What it needs, what it wrestles after, what it will create—is Terror" (p. 400). Who can say, after half a century of wondering, whether man's deepest pleasure lies in freedom or, as Naphta insists together with his Dostoevskyan predecessor, in obedience? Time has vindicated much of Naphta's view, through violent imposition if not always through choice; though neither he nor Mann could have perceived the agonizing irony of his identifying the goals of communism with those of the "true" church: "To strike terror into the world for the healing of the world, that man may finally achieve salvation and deliverance, and win back at length to freedom from law and from distinction of classes, to his original status as child of God" (p. 404).

The "logic" of Naphta's appeal obscures the bloodshed behind his words, as he casually praises the early church for having "freed the world of undesirable citizens" (p. 396). Before our eyes a sinister drama unfolds, far more painful today than in Mann's time, for the price one pays for the secular version of Naphta's *Civitas Dei* is infinitely greater than the benefits Naphta ascribes to saving the soul from everlasting damnation. His declaration that "any system of pains and penalties which is not based upon belief in a hereafter is simply a bestial stupidity" (p. 396) is itself a shallow bestial stupidity to ears and bodies that have endured such pains and penalties in an age of atrocity. Dostoevsky pierced the facade of his Grand Inquisitor's solicitude for humanity by revealing that he did not really believe in God; Mann completes the portrait by suggesting that Naphta does not really believe in man, indeed feels utter indifference for the individual as a physical being. "The great danger," Camus quotes André Gide as saying, "is to let oneself be monopolized by a fixed idea."[7] The seeds of later atrocities germinate in Naphta's rhetorical contempt for the human body, the prison house of the soul. When the soul was discarded by the imagination of the agents of modern atrocity, nothing was left to cherish.

Naphta's rhetorical contempt for the body is balanced by the personal fate of Joachim who, though he serves an uncompassionate profession, remains a compassionate figure to the end. Unable to bear the strenuous demands of military maneuvers, Joachim pays for his rash devotion with his life. But after he returns to the Berghof, his larynx degenerating from the disease and his heart giving out under the strain, we witness the wasted death of a single human being, and suddenly all the colloquies on flesh and spirit, the nobility of suffering and the discipline of disease, wither before the sad and painful spectacle of an inappropriate death, a life extinguished early and without consolation. There is further ambiguity because, as a soldier, Joachim had never been troubled by the need for insight and his dependence on an organization to give form to his life exposes a major limitation of that life. Naphta, so often correct even when his reasons are uncongenial, unwittingly illuminates the "brotherhood" to which Joachim blindly belonged, and its effect on his attitudes: "It lifts the burden from the individual conscience, and consecrates in the name of the Absolute every means even to bloodshed, even to crime" (p. 509). Commitments to absolutes coalesce into undifferentiated and abstract versions of the human, finally disintegrating—surely this is a primary momentum of *The Magic Mountain* itself—into undisguised violence. Mann's novel is a dirge to the failure of human communion based on an idea of the absolute, and a caustically searching analysis of the reasons for this failure.

One reason is the imagination's inadequate image of the human. Finally exasperated by the jumble of speech which sought to define civilization with words and phrases, Hans Castorp resolves to seek his own answer to the question "Where lay the true position, the true state of man?" amidst the vast untrodden silences of the snow. The blurred surfaces of the snow beckon with a hypnotic appeal, enticing the gazing Hans to a dreamless sleep: "It was as free from the burden—even the unconscious burden—of organic life, as little aware of an effort to breathe this contentless, weightless, imperceptible air as is the breathless sleep of the dead" (p. 472). On his ski expedition he bursts forth momentarily from his hermetic bonds, heedlessly washing his eyes with a "whiteness" that dazzles and blinds his physical sight even as it unveils the profounder vision of myth. Man contends with nature on the field of the elemental, stripped of words, companions, orientation in space and time, face to face with the prospect of nihilism and annihilation, civilization now only a dim memory and perhaps the last illusory refuge of the lonely self.

The metaphor of man lost in the whiteness of nature is not new to the literary imagination. Hans has several unlikely antecedents, among them Huckleberry Finn who, lost in a solid white fog, "hadn't no more idea which way I was going than a dead man," reflecting with vernacular intuition: "If you think it ain't dismal and lonesome out in a fog that way, by yourself, in the night, you try it once—you'll see."[8] One is reminded too of Conrad's Marlow in *Heart of Darkness,* gliding up the Congo shrouded in milk-white fog while hostile blackness hovers along the banks. But the most elaborate use before Mann is Melville's chapter, "The Whiteness of the Whale," where Ishmael's meditations disclose hints of the uncanny in the universe which no imagination peering behind the facade of reality can afford to ignore. Like Mann, Melville is bemused and appalled by the riddling ambiguity of man hearkening to a primeval silence that simultaneously flatters and threatens his curiosity. Melville describes the "mild deadliness" of the white shark and the "irresponsible ferociousness" of the Polar bear "invested in the fleece of celestial innocence and love." Whiteness draws man to worship even as it evokes terror. Properly perceived, it is the "inner image" that joins spiritual transcendence in a dubious alliance to physical decay, combining the veil of the Deity with "the intensifying agent in things the most appalling to mankind." But it blends into a blurred vision, and in the end Melville's is more terrifying than Mann's, since it leads not to affirmation but doubt, and a boldness of speculation beyond what Mann chose to pursue. For Ishmael's question about cosmic whiteness—"Is it that by its indefiniteness it shadows forth the heartless voids and immensities of the universe, and thus stabs at us from behind with the thought of annihilation, when beholding the white depths of the milky way?"—might lead Hans Castorp down a path of numbing despair. And what would Hans make of Ishmael's even more paralyzing thought that the "dumb blankness, full of meaning, in a wide landscape of snows" merely betrays "a colorless, all-color of atheism, from which we shrink?"[9]

There is a closer parallel between Ishmael's ultimate speculation that "all deified Nature absolutely paints like the harlot, whose allurements cover nothing but the charnelhouse within," and the substance of Hans's vision at the end of the snow episode. But even here the comparison is inexact, since Ishmael includes the possibility of the seeker into life's mysteries, dismissing the rose-colored glasses of civilization, gazing himself blind "at the monumental white shroud that wraps all the prospect around him."[10] For Hans, such unimpeded sight will lead to vision, not blindness, one acknowledging the features of a palsied universe but using the human consciousness—as Ishmael himself will do later in *Moby Dick*—to reconcile the paradoxes of a nonhuman universe and preserve for himself an image of the human that insures survival if not untrammelled hope.

Alone in the snow, Hans encounters a heritage more ancient than his family tradition, and Mann links the two in a way that is lost in translation. As a boy, Hans had loved to hear his grandfather read from the family Bible the names of his great-grandfather (*Urgrossvater*), great-great-grandfather (*Ur-Urgrossvater*), and the long line of preceding ancestors. In the vastness of the mountains he meets a primeval silence (*Urschweigen*) and primeval hush (*Urstille*) that suggest a natural ancestry of another sort, emerging not from the security of tradition but "the menace of the elemental, a menace not even hostile, but impersonally deadly" (p. 476). As a child of civilization he had not the remotest idea of this possibility in his past; and even at the Berghof he could parry the rhetorical threats to his independence from the comparative safety of inward intellectual disapproval. Life in society, whatever its form, limits personal risk; only on his snow escapade will Hans experience the meaning of Camus's assertion that "thought alone, carried on in solitude, is a frightening adventure."[11] Mann shares with Camus the conviction that when the universe appears to be "impersonally deadly" to man, the individual is obliged to graze the perilous by choice in order to affirm his humanity. Hans succumbs to "the fascination of venturing just so far into the monstrous unknown . . . that it was just barely possible to put limits to it" (p. 477); and if this seems foolhardy, it merely confirms our suspicion that a genuine revolt of the mind is one that costs the most. Thus Hans must cherish a kinship with the menacing elements that he has been sheltered from up to now; if any mystery exists to death and life, it lies beyond the challenge of negation—the "haze" and the "nothing" at the summit of the peaks toward which Hans Castorp strives. He trembles on the brink of Camus's absurd world as the silence around him says nothing to his spirit and he deliberately loses himself in the "blind white void," matching his solitary "pulsating human heart" against "the icy void, alone with its question and its riddle" (p. 478).

Unlike the legendary heroes in quest of the Grail, Hans has no assurance that anything lies before him; not even the ambiguous voices from Kafka's castle summon him to a hearing. If love or faith was the source of courage for the Grail knights, nothing comparable drives Hans toward his uncertain goal: "His loneliness was profound enough to awake the fear which is the first stage of valour" (p. 478). It is a fear that comes partly from knowing how useless all the Grails of absolutism have proved for contemporary man, partly from the recognition that all quests for unity and form disregard the equivocal nature of reality. Once he had cavalierly dismissed form as "folderol"; now, as he examines the perfectly symmetrical snowflakes falling around him, freezing drops of water "of the same anorganic substance which was the source of protoplasm, of plant life, of the human body," he finally understands his impulse to reject pure form as a manifestation of the nonhuman: "They were too regular, as substance adapted to life never was to this degree—the living principle shuddered at this perfect precision, found it deathly, the very marrow of death" (p. 480).

Among other considerations, Hans regards his incautious ski adventure as an attempt to take stock of his rank and status as *Homo Dei,* the "higher" level of adaptation introduced to his consciousness by Naphta. We notice that the supernatural is not part of the elemental in which Hans loses himself, as if Mann would suggest that his excursion will require a redefinition of *Dei* as well as of *Homo*. Hans's unaided resources test the challenge to survival, when almost willfully he permits the "blind, nonsentient forces" (p. 482) of a snowstorm to burst upon him, and suddenly he is lost on the mountain, literally blinded by the soulless snowflakes, as regular as "the very marrow of death." It is Hans's way of submitting to the "worst," as he is about to discover that without it no vision of the "best" is complete. They partake of each other. He must literally taste the snowflakes, be baptized in their nihilism, if his survival is to have any meaning:

They flew into his mouth, and died away with a weak, watery taste; flew against his eyelids so that he winked, overflowed his eyes and made seeing as difficult as it was now almost impossible for other reasons: namely, the dazzling effect of all that whiteness, and the veiling of his field of vision, so that his sense of sight was almost put out of action. It was nothingness, white, whirling nothingness, into which he looked when he forced himself to do so. Only at intervals did ghostly-seeming forms from the world of reality loom up before him... [p. 483].

Mann is forbidden by the temporal bounds of his narrative from using a metaphor of atrocity drawn from history to initiate Hans into the desecration of the human, and particularly of the body. Camus and Solzhenitsyn will find it much easier to admit the Hitler and Stalin concentration camps into the background of their works, while for Charlotte Delbo the camps form the foreground of her art. A crucial difference between Mann and his successors emerges here, since for Hans the "world of reality" has not yet been transformed in his imagination by the heritage of atrocity; his rebellion against the assaults of the killing cold suggests that physical resistance can still be the measure of a successful *attitude* against death.

For Hans the struggle is thus not the "never-ending defeat" that Dr. Rieux will find it in *The Plague;* nor is understanding of the human condition as futile as it will be for Améry during the extremity of torture. Hans clings to a lucidity less pessimistic than Camus's when he declares that the powers threatening to overwhelm him "are two-faced . . . in the highest degree equivocal, everything depends upon the point of view" (pp. 484-85). In Mann, literary vision clarifies the possibilities of human endurance; drawing on her experience in Auschwitz, Charlotte Delbo will use the camp reality to design a narrower possibility for literary vision. The "point of view" that Hans develops in the snow episode is a tribute to the imagination's ability to maintain a precarious balance between the forces of unity and dissolution. But in placing it outside those other absolutes of time and space—Hans loses his sense of both, for in trying to reach the safety of the Berghof, he wanders in a circle, ending up where he began— Mann raises without answering the issue of how or whether this personal point of view can serve the society of man. If reverence for the human based on a perception of the "worst" is a solitary and not a communal vision, is it not as "hermetic" as the stifling experience Hans left behind him in the flatlands and the similarly insulated existence of the Berghof?[12]

Responses dissolve in the ambiguity of Mann's art, to say nothing of the brutal history that inspired it. As Hans lies dazed against the shelter of a closed mountain hut, exhausted by the raging storm, images of bliss and terror infiltrate his waning consciousness, and in a few minutes that seem like hours he "sees" with the mythical imagination a vision that finally permits him to reach a tentative accord with death. A pastoral landscape smites his heart with its natural loveliness. Human creatures move about with grave dignity, their acts conditioned by a "reasoned goodness" that recalls the enlightenment dream of a classical golden age. The graceful human form betrays an "ineffable spiritual influence" (p. 492), though the spiritual force seems to reside in men's instinctive reverence for each other rather than in some transcendent power. But the idyllic scene cannot extinguish the oppressive feeling that mounts in Hans's heart as he discerns in the background a temple concealing a sanctuary within a grove of columns. With "dread and anguish," those watchwords of existential man in our time, he enters the sanctuary, and confronts a hideous nightmare that shatters his vision and leaves him trembling in the snow:

Two grey old women, witchlike, with hanging breasts and dugs of finger-length, were busy there, between flaming braziers, most horribly. They were dismembering a child. In dreadful silence they tore it apart with their bare hands—Hans Castorp saw the bright hair blood-smeared—and cracked the tender bones between their jaws, their dreadful lips dripped blood. An icy coldness held him. He would have covered his eyes and fled, but could not. . . . It made him sick, sick as never before [p. 494].

The growth of Hans's own humanity proceeds in two stages, from recognition to interpretation: man uses the ambiguity of reality to establish a point of view for surviving within its paradoxes. And if this point of view does nothing to change or improve that reality, but only to illuminate it, we can blame neither man nor art. Insight, after all, provides limited refuge from the terror of being in an age of atrocity.

Surely Mann recognizes the irony of his own achievement, for Hans's interpretation of his experience is unshared—and unshareable—with his companions at the Berghof. We alone are privy to his final meditations on the mountain, his "dream poem of humanity" which reveals that behind man's courteous social state a blood-sacrifice is always consummated. If the human consciousness can acknowledge the claims of both and find an intermediate position between reason and recklessness, then man becomes, as Hans insists, the "lord of counter-positions" (*Herr der Gegensätze*) and the aristocracy of the human triumphs over the contradictions in nature that threaten to efface this image. His resolve to let death have no mastery over his thoughts, if a less strenuous affirmation than Dylan Thomas's, at least accepts death as the enemy of the human; Hans firmly enters the twentieth century when he explicitly repudiates the romantic tradition of Wagner's *Liebestod:* "Death and love—no, I cannot make a poem of them, they don't go together. Love stands opposed to death. It is love, not reason, that is stronger than death." Yet the blood-sacrifice in the temple, the literal desecration of the body, looms more ominously in the minds of Mann's readers, if not in the mind of his hero. For shall we read as eulogy or epitaph, as celebration of Hans's future or mournful commentary on his historical heirs, his determination to "keep faith with death in my heart, yet well remember that faith with death and the dead is evil, is hostile to humankind, so soon as we give it power over thought and action" (p. 496)?

Have the revelations of atrocity, the actual nightmares of Hiroshima and Auschwitz, wrecked Hans's equilibrium between reason and recklessness, love and death, making man the victim rather than the lord of counter-positions? For the blood-sacrifice, the power of death over thought and action, to say nothing of imagination—as Lifton, Améry, and others have demonstrated—does not await man's consent but invades his image of the human and cleaves his uneasy alliance between love and death, unity and dissolution. Mann endows Hans with a privilege of unifying vision that will wane and waver as we pursue its fate in the art of Camus, Solzhenitsyn, and Charlotte Delbo. But he is shrewd enough to recognize that vision exists in the realm of the imagination, that the "reality" of the Berghof cannot sustain the intensity of the "dream-poem" on the mountain, that Hans himself would absorb the experience but not be able to insulate it entirely from the forays of chronological time. An hour after his return, his vision "was already fading from his mind. What he had thought—even that selfsame evening it was no longer so clear as it has been at first" (p. 498).

The snow episode is a peak in Hans's ordeal of initiation, but not its summation. Hans has several crucial encounters with the mystery of the human being following it, and each adds to his insight into death's relation to life; one, indeed—his encounter with the art of music—carrying him even beyond his vision on the mountain. For man is never done knowing, in Mann's view; just as he rejoices in having reached a higher plateau of comprehension, experience intervenes to call everything into doubt and cause a readjustment of all prior convictions. Once Hans believed that his love of Clavdia Chauchat was the epitome of bliss, its fulfillment an ecstasy unequalled. He waits with rapturous anticipation for her return. Yet when she reappears as companion and mistress of a new patient at the Berghof, Mynheer Peeperkorn, Hans finds his romantic expectations displaced by a more comprehensive challenge to his inquiring spirit. Mynheer Peeperkorn is a personality and mentor unlike the others he has met and learned to regard with increasing scepticism. Although like them Peeperkorn is devoted to an absolutist view of reality, he radiates it with an Olympian incoherence that attracts all who meet him. If speech is civilization for Settembrini, gesture and fragmented phrases reign for Peeperkorn. If spirit prevails in Naphta's world, feeling rules for the Dutchman, which he affirms with a dogmatic ferocity that we now find familiar: "Man is godlike in that he feels. He is the feeling of God" (p. 603).

The fall of man is thus the defeat of the feelings, and this is a view Hans Castorp has not heard before, though his own feelings for Frau Chauchat have given him many uneasy moments. Peeperkorn forces us to confront man as essentially a sentient being, responding to reality entirely through his body, whose potency *becomes* the expression of the life force. But his formula is easily reversible, for if man is the feeling of God, feeling is the torment of man, the vulnerability of the body his curse or original sin in an age of atrocity. For Peeperkorn, pleasure is the summit of experience, impotence its base. No lord of counter-positions himself, he fails to pay tribute to the larger polar opposite to pleasure: pain. Hans is not immune to the darker implications of Peeperkorn's point of view, for he sees in Peeperkorn's horror of impotence—man's inability to "feel"—license for vice that by now seems a logical consequence of any absolutist position: "A vicious man appears not at all insensible of your horrors," he tells the exponent of feeling; "on the contrary he does them full justice, since it is the abdication of his feelings before the classical gifts of life that drives him to vice. Thus we need not see in vice any affront to life, it may just as well be regarded as homage to it" (p. 567). A sinister eventuality indeed, since a pagan reverence for feeling, for the emotions of the senses, as it were, makes of the body an instrument of self-indulgence; the centrality of the body in human experience, man's "creatureliness," when carried to an extreme, turns its abuse into a perverse homage to life. Reverence for the body verges closely on contempt for its limitations, while man as the feeling of God compels us to revise our image of the human, to say nothing of the divine. Hans shrewdly sums up the direction of Peeperkorn's point of view: "It indicates that civilization is not a thing of the reason, of being sober and articulate; it has far more to do with inspiration and frenzy. . ." (p. 568).

As a longtime resident of the Dutch East Indies, Peeperkorn has contracted malaria. His necessary interest in the chemistry of quinine has led him to study the properties of many other drugs and poisons. Hans discovers from Peeperkorn that the albumen which Behrens named as a major constituent of the human body is also a leading ingredient of snake venom; when introduced into the bloodstream, it has a swift and fatal effect. Peeperkorn's acute comment on the equivocal in nature casts an ominous gleam on the ambiguous quality of good and evil in man:

The truth was, in the world of matter, that all substances were the vehicle of both life and death, all of them were medicinal and all poisonous, in fact therapeutics and toxicology were one and the same, man could be cured by poison, and substances known to be the bearers of life could kill at a thrust, in a single second of time [p. 578].

Since man himself inhabits the world of matter—all Hans's previous investigations have confirmed this—he too must contain within himself all possibilities. Like the cinchona bark (from which quinine is made) obtained in the primeval forest (*Urwald*) of New Guinea, from which natives make love charms as well as poison, he must possess "dynamic virtue, for good or evil" (p. 579). Counter-position is thus modified by dynamics, an interplay of energies that admits no antagonism or opposition or polarity of the kind that sustains Naphta and Settembrini. The challenge to the human imagination is to recognize toxicology when it comes disguised as therapeutics; or more ambiguously, to find a point of view when one is faced with the problem that confronts Hans as he tries to distinguish between cleverness and stupidity: "It is so hard to draw a line—one goes over into the other" (p. 583).

Hans's dilemma results from his attempt to understand the mystery of Peeperkorn's personality, which now "seems positive and absolute, like life" (p. 583), now a riddling inability to accept the mortality of the feelings. Hans recognizes in Peeperkorn's zest for physical experience, his vitality that seems so inexhaustible but whose abuse sends him to bed for increasingly extended periods of recuperation, an intransigent affirmation of the human, an acceptance and even celebration of man's "creatureliness" which none of his other mentors approach. But he finds in Peeperkorn's assertion that the failure of feeling is a blasphemy against God, the same kind of one-sided "theology" that the other absolutists are guilty of. At least Peeperkorn lives the religion he preaches; but as the roar of a waterfall (an image of external nature) reduces him to silence on his last outing with his friends from the Berghof, so his excesses finally reduce to "silence" the potency of his physical being. Unwilling to accept permanent invalidism, the abdication of his feelings, he takes his life by injecting into his bloodstream one of those very poisons he had described so vividly to Hans Castorp. For this champion of feeling, therapeutics and toxicology are indeed the same, since the only narcotic to deaden his fear of not feeling is a fatal one. Personality on a grand scale cannot survive its own theory of the dynamic interplay between good and evil in man and nature because it has no image to embody it other than the limited vision of the physical self.

After Peeperkorn's death, Hans seeks refuge from boredom in the solitary card game of patience, his love-dream on the mountain apparently forgotten as he gazes imaginatively into the eye of "the demon, whose unbridled sway he foresaw would come to an end of horror" (p. 635). But before that end, a kind of musical interlude intervenes which restores to

Hans his "sense of what was formative in experience" and gives us a glimpse of his highest—and last—synthesis of the dynamic forces that constitute his shifting image of the human. To allay the lassitude of his patients, Behrens has invested in an expensively modern gramophone, which faithfully reproduces from its speaker—Mann twice refers to it as a "casket" and once as a "coffin of violin-wood"—selections from the great classics. If *The Magic Mountain* is Mann's personal testament to art's role in man's initiation into the mysteries of life and death, Hans's encounter with the art of music illuminates the reader's journey through the pages of the novel. Just as characters in fiction are disembodied reflections of the corporeal, creating the illusion of presence through the persuasive power of language, so the voices of those singing some of Hans's favorite operatic arias challenge the imagination to participate in the wedding of content with form through the persuasive power of sound. In all his previous encounters Hans had to adopt the role of adversary to a lesser or greater extent in order to preserve the integrity of his own self, as the speech of his "mentors" hardened into political rhetoric, church dogma, the jargon of analysis, or disappeared behind the domineering incoherence of gesture. But just as art refines language, music becomes a universal voice, the supreme example of form that includes the human and pays homage to the image of death. In ways impossible in actuality, these singers contribute to the heightening of Hans's vision: "He had their better part, their voices, and might rejoice in the refining and abstracting process which did away with the disadvantages of closer personal contact, yet left them enough appeal to the sense, to permit of some command over their individualities . . ." (p. 642).

Perhaps the ultimate paradox in this novel woven of ambiguities is that art, which pretends to illuminate the human condition, is itself the ultimate illusion, divorced from the reality it pretends to imitate. It is the final point of view, the supreme perspective for examining life and death, the image of the human and the blood-sacrifice which preys on it, making life endurable, as Freud thought it might, by preparing man imaginatively for death. The first of Hans's favorite selections is the last scene from *Aïda,* where Radames refused to "justify himself" to the high priests by renouncing his love for Aïda. War, death, honor, love, devotion to fatherland—themes which recur in altering contexts throughout *The Magic Mountain*—coalesce here as Radames is forced to choose death for love and acknowledge that "in reality" man cannot respond to all the claims of the ideal, though in art he can ennoble his image by choosing at least one. Mann combines the two—life and art—in a lucid juxtaposition, paying tribute to each, as Hans first admires "the triumphant idealism of the music, of art, of the human spirit; the high and irrefragable power they had of shrouding with a veil of beauty the vulgar horror of actual fact," and then the narrative voice disarmingly inquires:

What was it, considered with the eyes of reason, that was happening here? Two human beings, buried alive, their lungs full of pit gas, would here together—or, more horrible still, one after the other—succumb to the pangs of hunger, and thereafter the process of putrefaction would do its unspeakable work, until two skeletons remained, each totally indifferent and insensible to the other's presence or absence. This was the real, objective fact . . . [p. 645].

Mann's own art lies somewhere between the triumphant idealism of Verdi and the wrenching torment to the body that makes the art of Charlotte Delbo so unbearable. The terror that succumbs to ecstasy in the final aria of Radames and Aïda and that interacts more dynamically with love in *The Magic Mountain* resounds as the dominant theme in the art of atrocity, minimizing the "consoling power of this aesthetic palliation" that did Hans Castorp so much good. The contemporary reader finds little solace in accounts (like Delbo's) of inappropriate deaths that shatter the traditional frames of artistic form and present few occasions for idealizing the image of the human.

The other pieces that appeal to Hans Castorp alternate between their celebration of freedom or duty, love or restraint, though the mute threat of death hovers in the background of several of them. Hans delights in a symphonic prelude, unnamed but almost certainly Debussy's *Prelude to the Afternoon of a Faun,* whose timeless innocence opposes the "justify thyself" of *Aïda.* He revels in the dilemma of José in *Carmen,* torn between the call to duty and the call to desire, variations on a theme both Hans Castorp and his cousin Joachim have played in their lives. He is entranced by "Valentine's Prayer" from Gounod's *Faust,* partly because it again evokes the image of his departed cousin, partly because it plays an important role in one of the novel's last episodes, uniting Hans with his cousin in a bizarre encounter where art is used—or misused— to trespass on the realm of the dead. His last favorite is a *Volkslied* set to music by Schubert which would have a special meaning to the German imagination, *Der Lindenbaum,* "The Linden Tree."

The song is an epitome of the sentiments that Hans's "stocktaking" on the mountain have liberated in him. The problem for the reader is that Hans makes no effort to define them, and Mann dissolves in deliberate ambiguity his own attempt to do so. The song speaks to Hans's love for the "absolutely exquisite image" at its center, makes him "conscious of the 'meaningfulness' of his love and the object of it" (p. 651), tempting us with the expectation that we are about to receive a supreme revelation concerning the final fruit of his initiation. And we are, though one moves toward interpretation with a tentative step. For the world of the song that evokes a response in Hans's imagination is a world of forbidden love, and its object is—death. The art of the song provides an inner image which connects physical decay with spiritual transcendence and grants man *for the duration of the listening* a legitimate if vaguely illicit sympathy with death. The words of the song,[13] if one examines them, betray nature's message to man that he must die, and man's conscious resistance and unconscious acquiescence to this fact. The music echoes a mute appeal to that allegiance to death which, Mann would have us believe, lies deep within the heart of all men, and perhaps especially of his countrymen. A restrained response through the medium of art merely acknowledges a proper reverence for the mystery and power of death. But an un-restrained response—and this is the danger Mann foresees—may have sinister results. Mann's own language reaches its most equivocal pitch as he tries to analyze Hans's attraction to this popular German folksong:

This was a fruit, sound and splendid enough for the instant or so, yet extraordinarily prone to decay; the purest refreshment of the spirit, if enjoyed at the right moment, but the next, capable of spreading decay and corruption among men. It was the fruit of life, conceived of death, pregnant of dissolution; it was a miracle of the soul, perhaps the highest, in the eye and sealed with the blessing of conscienceless beauty; but on cogent grounds regarded with mistrust by the eye of shrewd geniality dutifully 'taking stock' in its love of the organic; it was a subject for self-conquest at the definite behest of conscience [pp. 652-53].

The paradox of art as conscienceless beauty inspiring insight into the image of the human and the way death distorts that image, calling on conscience to resist through self-conquest the temptation of moral dissolution which submission to death implies—this is a paradox that the language of criticism can restate but not resolve. Art illuminates the human condition, as "taking stock" (including reverence for art) illuminates for Hans his own life: but neither guarantees man's strength to embody or sustain the image of the human that the journey toward insight imprints on his imagination.

Unfortunately, the society of the Berghof never learns the syllables of "the new word of love" that might lead them to a more human future. In their craving for excitement—in Hans's own longing for insight into the relation of matter to spirit—they turn under Krokowski's leadership to the unsanctified revelations of spiritualism. Having encountered the nonhu-manity of nature, the humanity of man, and the inhumanity of blood-sacrifice in his snow vision, Hans now descends to the cellars of the Berghof to traffic with the subhuman dis-guised as the supernatural. The consoling power of aesthetic palliation exerts no permanent force over his personality, now that Krokowski's interest in the occult promises entry to a world of the dead which none of his other mentors could approach. For beyond dissolution lies the reappearance of the dead, the literal reembodiment of disembodied form, flesh reconstituted as returned spirit, as it were, bringing information straight from the mysterious realm of supposed nonbeing. Though finding such confrontation an "aesthetic revulsion" and "humanly valueless" (pp. 657, 658), Hans nevertheless assents to the plan to recall one of the Berghof's former residents from beyond the grave, partly out of sheer curiosity, but also because his intellectual awareness of the need for self-conquest cannot thwart the fascination of those uncharted regions of the self where a shadowy light illuminates, for those still alive, death's mysterious zone.

Krokowski asks the members of his curious circle whom they should recall, but they are terrified at the prospect of bearing the responsibility for even the naming of the dead, until Hans murmurs that he would like to speak with the spirit of his cousin Joachim. Mann calls the subsequent few hours the most important in his hero's young life, even though he also says that the episode resembled a revivalistic Salvation Army meeting and Hans himself is reminded of a half-tipsy visit to a brothel years earlier with fellow students. For others, it is one more optical diversion, the antithesis of insight; for Hans, it *seems* to be a new opportunity to tear away the last veil separating life from death and achieve ultimate revelation in a stunning display of secular incarnation. Hans expects nothing less than the spirit become flesh, an incontestable confirmation of transcendence, of a permanent bond between the physical and symbolic self. He cannot resist the temptation to seek explanations of man's fate beyond the view of counter-positions and dynamics that he has already achieved. But in his illicit quest he ignores the testimony of that fate hanging on the wall behind him, a copy of Rembrandt's "Anatomy Lesson." Reverence for the human must focus on man's "creatureliness": using a "medium," a newly arrived clairvoyant young patient at the Berghof, to summon back Joachim transgresses the limits of the human in the ultimate violation of the body for "humanly unthinkable" purposes—an abdication of reason and restraint, a submission to the very inspiration and frenzy that Hans earlier had equated with the vicious. The "organic mysticism" of the seance confuses the qualities distinguishing the organic from the mystical and the role each plays in man's efforts to identify what is human in his experience and what is not.

Historical time begins to crack the mold of hermetic life on the mountain as rumbles of imminent war resound from the flatlands, finding a responsive echo from the inhabitants of the Berghof. The ensuing personal animosities, as anti-Semitism and nationalistic pride turn men against each other, anticipate the effect of this world catastrophe on our image of the human. Men's frantic desire to reclaim from mutability some vestige of permanence by embracing an absolute collapses not only because the appeal to violence now seems deeper than the impulse toward unity, but because all absolutes—at least as Mann dramatizes them in his novel—themselves contain the seeds of violence, briefly insulated by a veneer of form. As the health of both Settembrini and Naphta deteriorates, Naphta proves unequal to the challenge of accepting his fate with equanimity, despite his devotion to the idea of spirit. He responds to his illness not with sorrow or aversion, "but with a sort of jeering levity, an unnatural lust of combat, a mania of intellectual doubt, denial, and distraction, that was a sore irritant to [Settembrini's] melancholy, and daily embittered more the intellectual quarrel between them" (p. 689). Naphta's celebration of spirit reaches an absurd (and by implication a sinister) dead end when he declares that "matter was so bad a material that the spirit could not be realized within it. . . . nothing could come of it but distortion and fatuity" (p. 690). His physical self-disgust ill conceals a more general misanthropy, while the ludicrous illogic that rejects matter while praising spirit ignores the obvious contradiction that, for man, spirit must be expressed *through* matter. Without reverence for the flesh the meaning of spirit disappears; this is the dismal secret behind Naphta's absolutism. Hence we are not surprised when he embraces history with the cry "War, war! For his part, he was for it" (p. 690).

Nor are we surprised when the interminable verbal disputes between Hans's two major mentors lead to literal combat, as the arsenal of words finally discharges more lethal weapons and Naphta challenges Settembrini to a duel. Neither is a lord of counter-positions, neither can reconcile in his imagination the blood sacrifice with a noble image of the human—neither cares to, since the premises of each forbid reconciliation and indeed thrive on controversy. As long as the discord remains intellectual, no one suffers; though Mann's canny point is that such discord never remains permanently intellectual, since intellectual dissension eventually crosses over into the personal, and "personal" disputes, especially between nations, are rarely settled with words. In trying to avert the duel between his friends, Hans reveals that he is still heir to a fundamental flaw in late nineteenth- and early twentieth-century perception of reality. Hans distinguishes between an abstract affront and personal insult: "The whole affair was in the intellectual sphere, and has nothing to do with the personal. . . . The intellectual can never be personal." Do we need to be reminded how theories about a world made safe for democracy, or about the class struggle, or about a master race, led to the extermination of millions? Here Settembrini is far shrewder than Hans Castorp as he argues that the abstract, the ideal, or the absolute "contains within it more possibilities of deep and radical hatred, of unconditional and irreconcilable hostility, than any relation of social life can" (p. 699). Yet Settembrini does not recognize the full implications of his position, since behind its "logic" is a license to terror scarcely less destructive than Naphta's: the duel between the two seems lamentably inevitable.

The duel is a microcosmic prelude to the conflict about to erupt across the landscape of Europe, abdicating to death the destruction that intellect could not prevent and indeed, as we have seen, unconsciously encouraged. One is dazed by Settembrini's fusion of insight with rhetorical self-deception as he regales Hans with a version of reality that equates humanism with the violence of war:

"The duel, my friend, is not an 'arrangement,' like another. It is the ultimate, the return to a state of nature, slightly mitigated by regulations which are chivalrous in character, but extremely superficial. The essential nature of the thing remains the primitive, the physical struggle; and however civilized a man is, it is his duty to be ready for such a contingency, which may any day arise. Whoever is unable to offer his person, his arm, his blood, in the service of the ideal, is unworthy of it; however intellectualized, it is the duty of a man to remain a man" [p. 699].

Mouthing Hobbes while using the language of Rousseau, this champion of the human image blithely signs its death warrant with a flourish of the philosophical tongue. Like Naphta, Settembrini has become a tool of the prevailing temper, the war that echoes from the flatlands; unable to shape history, the mind of man adjusts to its least flattering features and twists language to justify the event when the event exceeds what the mind originally desired. Hans deplores the duel, but discovers "in affright" that he is powerless to stop it. The insight of man may make him lord of counter-positions, but when his literal sight is confronted by the spectacle of conflict, imagination defers to history:

In [Hans] too the prevailing temper was strong, he was not the man to win free. There was an area of his brain where memory showed him Wiedemann and Sonnenschein [the anti-Semite and the Jew] grappled like animals; and with horror he understood that at the end of everything only the physical remained, only the teeth and the nails. Yes, they must fight ... [p. 700].

In the duel, the intellectual becomes personal through necessity rather than choice when Naphta, baffled and exasperated by Settembrini's firing in the air—to the end, the Italian's instincts prove more humane than the logic of his arguments—turns his gun on himself and commits suicide. Lacking the courage to kill without provocation, he is driven to express his contempt for the human by taking his own life. By refusing to fire at him, Settembrini has eliminated the "regulations which are chivalrous in character, but extremely superficial," those "regulations" which gave soldiers license to kill, and left Naphta no alternative but the violence of self-destruction. In Dostoevsky, the atheism of Kirillov or the total absence of active love in the heart of Smerdyakov naturally joins the impulse to murder with the impulse to suicide. Naphta is more simply a victim of his own absolutism, of the viciously inhuman principle that "matter was so bad a material that spirit could not be realized within it." He returns us to Ernest Becker's conviction that the human dilemma in our time is to accept our "creatureliness" without losing reverence for the image of the human. Naphta pays for his failure to do so with his life; now that history through atrocity has confirmed his irreverence for the "matter" that is man by abusing the body in ways that Naphta himself only played with philosophically, the imagination must face an equally grotesque but entirely secular version of the *pietà*—without the hope of salvation that this image promised to men of more serene faith than Naphta.

Unlike Naphta, Hans Castorp goes through "the deep experience of sickness and death to arrive at a higher sanity and health" (pp. 724-25). But the final unresolved problem of the novel (which ends with a question) is how to transfer the imaginative truth gained in the hermetic atmosphere of the mountain to the historical "actuality" of the flatlands, where we leave Hans Castorp slogging through the mud and splintering shells of World War I. Hans takes the risk of insight, "overcomes his inborn attraction to death and arrives at an understanding of a humanity that does not, indeed, rationalistically ignore death, nor scorn the dark, mysterious side of life, but takes account of it, without letting it get control over his mind" (p. 724). And no one can quarrel with Mann's summary of what his hero has endured or achieved. But Mann the artist is more complex than Mann the commentator, knowing as he does that history is no respecter of the imaginative vision. The human image in battle is reduced to "a body of troops calculated as sufficient, even after great losses, to attack and carry a position . . . there are so many of them, swarming on—they can survive a bloodletting and still come on in hosts" (p. 714).

One among that undifferentiated mass of potential victims is Hans Castorp, singing "half soundlessly" the words of Schubert's *Lindenbaum* that once had whispered to him with the consolation of aesthetic palliation its secret message of death. The shells shrieking over his head now echo a similar message, but with what consolation? The narrative voice introduces a dual viewpoint without attempting a synthesis— recalling the "human form divine" of Hans's timeless snow vision, and the war-doomed creature on the timebound battle-fields of history:

Ah, this young blood, with its knapsacks and bayonets, its mud-befouled boots and clothing! We look at it, our humanistic-aesthetic eye pictures it among scenes far other than these: We see these youths watering horses on a sunny arm of the sea; roving with the beloved along the strand, the lover's lips to the ear of the yielding bride; in happiest rivalry bending the bow. Alas, no, here they lie, their noses in fiery filth [p. 714].

No mention of the blood-sacrifice here, or the relativism of counter-positions, which the "humanistic-aesthetic eye" once synthesized into imaginative truth. History is the last absolute man must contend with; in its abstract name inappropriate death is elevated into a principle of existence—and destruction. Our penultimate image of Hans Castorp reminds us of his origin in matter and the fate to which his physical form will return: "He lies with his face in the cool mire, legs sprawled out, feet twisted, heels turned down" (p. 715). He eludes death this time, but as we last see him "limping on his earth-bound feet," we hear that his prospects for survival are poor. His epitaph as he "vanishes out of sight" are those ambiguous words from *Der Lindenbaum*, drifting through the battle: "Its waving branches whispered/A mess-age in my ear—" (p. 715). The word of that message is drowned in the whine of exploding shells, but also disappears beneath the ambiguous layers of Mann's art.

For once, in the sanctuary of the Berghof, Hans had convinced himself that "it was worth dying for, the enchanted *Lied!* But he who died for it, died indeed no longer for it; was a hero only because he died for the new, the new word of love and the future that whispered in his heart" (p. 653). Mann returns to this crucial moment in the closing lines of his novel, but with less certainty than Hans. Throughout *The Magic Mountain,* Mann has sought to dramatize a relationship between love and death, man's hope and man's fate, that would be more humanly valid than the spiritualized romanticism of Wagner and his predecessors in the tradition. A deficiency in imaginative vision had helped make possible the catastrophe of World War I, which could be justified only if "a new word of love and the future" emerged from its slaughter. Many atrocities later, we wonder whether that new word was "death" after all, the expectation of love only the last delusion to rescue man from the gloomy truth that one can take account of death "without letting it get control over his mind" in *art,* but not so easily in life. Indeed, *The Magic Mountain* is a prologue to the contemporary mind's failure to establish a balance between man in his physical embodiment as a victim of atrocity and man in his spiritual capacity as a vessel of love. The paradox is at the heart of the vision of reality revealed in the works of Camus, Solzhenitsyn, and Charlotte Delbo. They confront the question that ends Mann's novel with sober recognition of the fact that atrocity may have disfigured the human image beyond hope of an affirmative answer:

Out of this universal feast of death, out of this extremity of fever, kindling the rain-washed evening sky to a fiery glow, may it be that Love one day shall mount? [p. 716].

But they unite in their belief that the language of art can still wash the eyes of history with a darkness to illuminate what atrocity has done to that image of man.

There is but one freedom, to put
oneself right with death. After
that, everything is possible.
—Camus

4

ALBERT CAMUS AND THE LIMITS OF THE POSSIBLE

The history that swallowed up Hans Castorp and left his fate
a looming question mark obsessed Albert Camus in his life-
long search for a middle term between pure negation and
formal virtue. "Being in history" he asked, "while referring
to values that go beyond history—is it possible, legitimate?"
Against his longing for the human weighed the disfiguration
of man in an age of atrocity: how could the artist's imagination conjure up an image of dignity without betraying the
concrete events of the nineteen thirties and forties that reduced so many men to the helpless status of anonymous victim? Despair alternates with resolution in his journals as he
pays tribute to this melancholy fact: "Nothing is pure,
nothing is pure—this is the cry that has poisoned our century." While recognizing the need for a new hypothesis to
illuminate the human condition and make it bearable, he
confesses that any such hypothesis "has been *historically*
belied in a terrifying way, to such realities as misfortune,
murder, and exile for two or three generations."[1] Any affirmation of the human image in the twentieth century must
be honest enough to admit the horrors it is built upon.

The first half of Camus's literary career coincided with the darkest hours of modern European history. *The Myth of Sisyphus* and *The Stranger* appeared in 1942, when French liberty was strangling under the yoke of Nazi occupation.[2] *The Plague* (1947) was published when revelations about collaboration and concentration camps still challenged the credulity of "civilized" men. Camus's image of plague suggests a reality permeated by the infection of atrocity, afflicting both art and nature with its cheerless disclosures of what men did and suffered during the war years. The contagion is total:

> Plague. One cannot enjoy the cry of birds in the coolness of the evening— in the world as it is. For it is covered now with a so thick layer of history that its speech must get through to reach us. It is deformed thereby. Nothing of the world can be felt for its own sake, because a whole series of images of death and despair is bound to each of its moments. No more mornings without deaths, no more evenings without imprisonments, and no more noons without dreadful slaughter.[3]

This somber reflection appears more than a year before the Nazi defeat. Several years after the war, Camus jotted down a brief note for a novel concerning a survivor who is reluctant to answer questions about his experience in the concentration camp. The survivor offers a flat account, then never talks of it again. "He lives in the most ordinary way. Just one thing: he has no more relations with his wife. Until the crisis and the explanation: 'Everything human strikes me with horror.'"[4] Does his immersion in death, *such* death, clarify or distort the image of the human? History reflects one profile, the imagination yearns to create another, and from this confrontation Camus shapes a fragile portrait of a man trying to escape from the dilemma of his own imagined survivor, whose glimpse of horror embedded in the human has destroyed his reverence for love.

Camus perceives better than most writers of his generation the truth that history and atrocity have engraved on the consciousness of men: The death sentence cannot be avoided, and the traditions (or illusions) we have invented to deflect this truth no longer mitigate its finality. To live in spite of despair becomes the challenge to the human imagination, one Camus celebrated in the very title of his first novel, *A Happy Death (La Mort heureuse)*, unpublished during his lifetime, and later examined more soberly in *The Myth of Sisyphus*. The death sentence was not new, but its constant presence in the imagination, as Freud predicted, forced men to live psychologically beyond their means. Much of the art of Albert Camus is devoted to the difficulty of confronting this anxiety without abandoning faith in the image of the human. "Women's faces, delights of the sun and sea—that is what is being murdered," he writes on the brink of World War II, shortly after French mobilization. "And if one doesn't accept murder, then one has to hang on. We're living right in the middle of a contradiction, the whole of our century is stifling and living up to its neck in this contradiction, without a single tear to relieve its anguish."[5] The contradiction between sun and sea on the one hand, and murder (or death) on the other, becomes a central image in both *The Stranger* and *The Plague*. The war destroyed all previous judgments about reality because it was a new "fact" that required the reflective man to adapt his ideas to the alterations it imposed. "This is why," Camus concluded upon outbreak of war, "however vile this war may be, no one can stand aside from it."[6]

For Hans Castorp, as for the generation of writers nurtured by World War I, war could still be considered an initiation, the last stage in the loss of innocence that had fed the idealism of the late nineteenth and early twentieth century. What artist in 1914 confronted his destiny with the austere insight Camus exhibited in September 1939: "We die alone. They are all going to die alone. Let the man who is alone at least keep his scorn, and the ability to pick out from this terrible ordeal what serves his own greatness"? He mocks a journalist who professes amazement that the war of 1939 should not have begun in the same atmosphere as that of 1914, commenting on the naiveté of "simpletons who thought that horror always had the same face, who cannot escape from the physical images on which they have lived."[7] This had been Hans Castorp's dilemma when he arrived on the mountain, perplexed by the idea of frozen corpses brought down by bobsled because the physical image did not conform to any vision of death he had ever encountered. His final confrontation with the manifestation of his dead cousin's spirit supports Camus's implication that history continually revises the visage of this horror. In 1939 Camus himself had no explicit notion of the new countenance horror would display in less than half a decade. But his intuition counseled him that the collapse of values would be different: "Never before have these values and those we love been threatened all together and all at the same time. Never before have we been so completely handed over to destruction."[8]

This explains in part why Camus's art, while seeking life in the midst of despair, is so concerned with the physical images (and ideas) for which, one might say, men will die. Absurd life takes meaning from participation in absurd death. The same sun that warms the living bones bleaches the dead ones. In his first essays, *The Wrong Side and the Right Side* (1937), Camus balances the "smell of death and inhumanity" that he brought with him from a visit to Prague against the "Italian plain, peopled with trees, sunshine." This contrast leads to a "very clear awareness of what I did not like—renunciation and disinterest." But in the early essays this clear awareness of what he didn't like (as opposed to what he *did*) is less convincing than in the later works, because it seems fed by the mind without first being tested by the senses. His attitudes are simple and almost serene: "When we are stripped down to a certain point, nothing leads anywhere any more, hope and despair are equally groundless, and the whole of life can be summed up in an image." Nothing in the young Camus's Mediterranean sojourn equals the physical agony of the dying boy in *The Plague*. He would later call such observations both pompous and correct, founded on trustworthy intuitions but not on a genuine experience of despair.[9]

History thus did not contradict his earliest artistic impulses; it complemented them. Long before he objected to the inhuman implications of our century of murder, he could criticize society for blurring men's perception of death by inventing euphemisms like "He is going to pay his debt to society" instead of admitting "They're going to chop his head off." Did the habit of dodging one's destiny through evasive language invite some of the mass destructions that mark our generation? Camus will not venture an idea, but as he works through to a theory of "conscious death" which permits the imagination to anticipate the body's fate, he challenges each man to be his own artist, correcting creation and in a limited sense defeating death by the power of lucidity. "Lucidity" is probably Camus's favorite word, denoting a thoroughly human pride in living that justifies those men who urgently feel the loss of transcendence. "Creating conscious deaths," he argues in another early work, *Nuptials* (1938), "is to diminish the distance that separates us from the world and to accept a consummation without joy, alert to rapturous images of a world forever lost." Conscious death is an attitude that celebrates life while knowing its limitations—living without illusions about transcendence. It regards death shorn of pretense: "I want to keep my lucidity to the last, and gaze upon my death with all the fullness of my jealousy and horror." If the tone here betrays excessive exuberance for a melancholy subject, one must remember that Camus is still in his mid-twenties. "I have too much youth in me to be able to speak of death," he himself confesses. "But it seems to me that if I had to speak of it, I would find the right word here between horror and silence to express the conscious certainty of a death without hope."[10]

In his quest for a new image of the human, Camus stumbles on an old image of nature, a secular prelapsarian Eden where "the stone warmed by the sun or the cypress tree shooting up against the suddenly clear sky mark the limits of the only universe in which 'being right' is meaningful: nature without men. And this world annihilates me." For when man imposes his "creatureliness" on the prodigality of nature, celebrate the delight of the senses how he may, he transforms the enjoyment of that prodigality into a simultaneous mental "survey of a certain desert." The paradox of existence asserts itself as it did to Hans Castorp, who learned of the blood-sacrifice, the vulnerability of the flesh behind the beauty and grace of the body, *amidst* the splendors and terrors of nature. Human existence itself, as in the Genesis myth, eventually introduces discord into the harmonious rhythms of natural creation. If the world annihilates man through his mortality—the source of his tragedy—man defaces the world by annihilating the image of the human: perhaps this is what Camus meant when he later named "nothing is pure" as the cry that has poisoned our century. Although Camus's words here evoke the general tragedy of the human condition, against which the mind instinctively protests, they seem equally expressive of an age of atrocity that has taken us beyond the frontiers of conventional tragedy: "When we reach a certain stage of awareness we finally acknowledge something which each of us, according to our particular vocation, seeks not to understand."[11] Men long for love, but drift into disaster. When Camus comprehended the extent of that disaster, he realized the complexity of the challenge he had hurled at his contemporaries by asking them to absorb his principle of conscious death.

Missing from the sun-drenched sensuous landscapes of *The Wrong Side and the Right Side* and *Nuptials* is the concrete anguish of human suffering, which history had not yet imprinted on Camus's imagination. His philosophical jousting with death mutes without banishing his real concern, images of happiness to reflect "the simple harmony between a man and the life he leads."[12] This suffices only when man is free to choose the limits of that life; when life sets its own limits—the quarantine of the plague, for example—a new kind of hermetic existence appears, and nature assumes a more sinister role, as a murderer of men. The sun that conspires with Meursault's hand in *The Stranger* to trigger the fatal shot that shatters the equilibrium of his day—and his life—necessitates a reinterpretation of the idea of a "simple harmony between a man and the life he leads." The plague that descends on the citizens of Oran questions the value and the possibility of such "harmony" in a time of crisis, making it sound as nostalgic as the hope which Camus equates with resignation. And when history, through the revelations of World War II, leads to the concept of what Camus in *The Rebel* calls "logical crime," the idyllic Mediterranean world lapses into shadow and "through a curious transposition peculiar to our times— it is innocence that is called upon to justify itself."[13]

The romantic imagination, always half in love with easeful death, justified its longing for annihilation through some alliance with transcendence. Even in the absence of such consolation, as Camus recognizes, the appeal of nonbeing beckons with tempting vigor to the human heart that wearies of desire and suffering: "Every man has a deep instinct that is neither for destruction nor creation. Simply the longing to resemble nothing."[14] But to perceive this temptation is to reject it, since nothingness is only an inverted form of the ungraspable absolute that summons man to live beyond the limits of the possible and leads eventually to a denial of the human. Once the instinct for nothingness may have represented an adequate philosophical refuge in a civilization not deprived of transcendental consolations. But in a society so deprived—and this is one of Camus's stubbornly persistent assumptions—the contest between the mind and the world is so precarious that man's very survival depends on his determination to resist the temptation of nothingness.

One of the most challenging features of Camus's imaginative vision is its flexibility. It shifts with the urgency of the times, so that one may speak of stages in his artistic growth, plateaus of thought and design signifying deployments for further descents into the crevices and ascents up the peaks of contemporary history. In a 1940 essay he quoted a remark attributed to Napoleon: "There are only two powers in the world: the sword and the mind. In the end, the sword is always conquered by the mind." But Napoleon was perhaps the last hero of an age when the conqueror could speak with such "regal certainty." Images of force have changed, but nothing penetrates the imagination more slowly than the idea behind this truth, as dozens of defeated nations and millions of victims were to learn: "What a hundred years ago was true of the sword is no longer true today of the tank." The difference between sword and tank (and the more vicious instruments of destruction that would soon accompany it) is the distinction between war and atrocity. Frustrated by attempts to master it (vainly employing ancient weapons from the arsenal of intellect against a modern technological beast immune to both), the mind was reduced to cursing force. Like most Frenchmen, Camus must have found 1940 a crucially painful year, as his countrymen divided between resistance and armistice with a superior power. His initial response to the national disaster is curiously blurred, clear-sighted on the need for a fundamental revision of values but limited in its vision of what private virtues would be necessary to accomplish the revision. For one of the rare times in his writings, he speaks with a voice of hope that has temporarily discarded the image of death, and though one understands the reason for his encouraging words, his resolution here lacks the chiseled insistence of his finer art, that *includes* man's fate even as it opposes it: "We must mend what has been torn apart, make justice imaginable again in a world so obviously unjust, give happiness a meaning once more to peoples poisoned by the misery of the century."[15]

By 1946 Camus knew that he was facing not merely a threat to the strength and dignity of human character (conventional enough rhetoric, even though the spokesman could see behind the barricade of language), but "the unparalleled historical convulsion of our day." The war had opened an enormous gulf between the dazzling brightness of the Mediterranean celebration of life of his youthful years and the dark ordeal of atrocity that granted temporary triumph to death. In 1939 Camus had been planning a trip to Greece, following the voyage of Ulysses in quest of sunlight. But the war changed everything—history, man's sense of his fate, the artist's vision:

I did not get on that ship. I took my place in the queue shuffling toward the open mouth of hell. Little by little, we entered. At the first cry of murdered innocence, the door slammed shut behind us. We were in hell, and we have not left it since. For six long years we have been trying to come to terms with it. Now we glimpse the warm ghosts of fortunate islands only at the end of long, cold, sunless years that lie ahead.

The inspiration or consolation of nature retreats before the disproportionate image of disfigured man: "Man is everywhere, and everywhere we find his cries, his suffering, and his threats. . . . History is a sterile earth where heather does not grow."[16] The challenge thus becomes to master the kind of death that history has bequeathed to men as survivors while cherishing the memory of a beauty that may never be restored in one's lifetime but may receive fertile expression in the lives of later generations.

It is a vision considerably more humble than the exalted happiness of "the simple harmony between a man and the life he leads." Translating that vision into images, Camus asks whether his contemporaries, having betrayed Prometheus's gift of fire by choosing history over the Attic spirit of beauty, can ever make the heather grow again, enabling them to answer "yes" to the question of our century. Revitalizing the Promethean myth requires them to include the suffering they have endured and survived (since homage to the whole man can exclude nothing), and in one of his somberest moods (1946 was not a year of hope for those still reeling from men's "misuse" of fire in the holocaust just ended), Camus qualifies his belief that one can indeed still give an affirmative answer to the century's question: "I sometimes doubt whether men can be saved today. But it is still possible to save their children, both body and mind." The terms, however, are severe: if the myth teaches us that "any mutilation of man can only be temporary," history reminds us that today bread is more necessary than heather. Like Prometheus, men must learn to be more patient than their vulture, but at the cost of granting reality to the beak that has gnawed their vitals, the dark horrors that have corrupted the integrity of the human image. While most men sought to forget these horrors, Camus celebrated the Promethean stubbornness and determination "to separate and exclude nothing, which always has and always will reconcile mankind's suffering with the springtimes of the world."[17]

One of the most exasperating qualities of Camus's art is the frequent contradiction between the lyric tone of his language and the discordant facts of reality. One less sympathetic with his seriousness of purpose could accuse him of confusing style with truth and asking language to support a burden of insight beyond what words were ever designed to bear. Although the human dilemma has always been to "reconcile mankind's suffering with the springtime of the world," most readers need a more concrete definition of both "springtime" and "suffering" before they can identify with Camus's assurance of reconciliation. This is why it is essential to apply to a study of Camus the same principle he asks us to apply to a study of man: separate and exclude nothing. Style *becomes* truth when we recognize that the various expressions of his art nourish and illuminate each other through a complex network of interrelationships. If this is so for many authors, it seems more so for him: no single work stands alone as a consummate example of his artistic vision.

Thus "Helen's Exile" (1948), written two years after the essay on Prometheus, sheds important light on its ideas. Camus distinguishes between the solar tragedy of the Greeks, who knew despair through beauty, and the despair of his own world, whose intemperate European climate "has fed on ugliness and upheavals." Before the human image can be restored, including both suffering and renewal, beauty must be brought back from exile. This would necessitate an art *beyond* atrocity, and Camus writes as if this were possible— to believe otherwise would logically reduce him to silence— while acknowledging that behind the images of ugliness and beauty stand the historical mind and the artist, each seeking to remake the world. He has no illusions about the inequality of the contest at a moment when the artist has so much to hate in his times even as his heart surges with love for men. His conviction that art knows limits history ignores translates into his more familiar belief that the artist confronts the human condition (man's mortality) while history still seeks to transcend it. "In a way," he contends, "the meaning of tomorrow's history is not what people think. It is in the struggle between creation and the inquisition."[18] The process of art is an attempt to rescue men from the excesses of history and restore an image of human nature that has been mangled but not yet destroyed by an age of atrocity.

The problem for the artist intensifies when we try to understand how history has foreshortened modern man's perspective of time. Early civilizations passed from youth to age and eventual decline in centuries. Camus's generation had experienced this growth in less than a decade. The shock to artistic sensibilities was profound; one wonders why despair was not more universal. Returning in 1953 to Tipasa, an Algerian city he had written about in his early Mediterranean essays, Camus equates his awareness then with innocence, so profound was the darker knowledge of suffering that came with the war: "Where was innocence? Empires were crumbling, men and nations were tearing at one another's throats; our mouths were dirtied. Innocent at first without knowing it, now we were unintentionally guilty: the more we knew, the greater the mystery."[19] Unintentionally guilty of what? Of believing that innocence could forestall atrocity? Of living through the horrors that destroyed others, like Lifton's Hiroshima survivors? Of failing to distinguish between common mortality and the menace of inappropriate death?

Puzzled by the mystery, Camus retraces his steps in search of a solution to the question we have encountered before: how is man, shattered by the experience of atrocity, by unintentional guilt and the consciousness of inappropriate death, to rejoin his physical and symbolic self, the suffering which history imposes and the springtime which the imagination discovers in the innocence of its youth and loses in the labyrinths of time? The dilemma is crucial and more universal than we have been prepared to admit. Camus's formulation is as relevant to Solzhenitsyn and Charlotte Delbo as it is to himself and his contemporaries: "All of us, today, are dying of [the misery of not loving]. This is because blood and hatred lay bare the heart itself; the long demand for justice exhausts even the love that gave it birth. In the clamor we live in, love is impossible and justice is not enough."[20] Is love a luxury in an age of atrocity, a distraction from the immediate task of inventing a more human idea of justice to rescue men from the injustice of history and institutions? Although here Camus celebrates his memory of the ancient and innocent beauty of Tipasa during his prewar visit, preserving an "invincible summer" in his heart even as reality shivers from the frost of not being able to love, elsewhere (in *The Plague,* for example) he is more ambivalent about the relationship between love and justice. Atrocity enforces a conflict between the two that the heart is sometimes shocked into accepting, admitting a vulnerable winter which knows none of the consolations of Camus's invincible summer.

Camus is thus a spokesman for an art born of atrocity but unwilling to admit that its images can erase the memory of summer imprinted on his heart before that birth. This is what he means when he modestly asks: "What more can I hope for than the power to exclude nothing and to learn to weave from strands of black and white one rope tautened to the breaking point?" The tension of his art is an expression of his life and his age, creating the limits of his honesty: "I have not been able to deny the light into which I was born and yet I have not wished to reject the responsibilities of our time." The paradox of living two journeys simultaneously is the dilemma that afflicts the modern imagination, and threatens to reduce it to a permanent split: "There is, for man today, an inner path that I know well from having traveled both ways upon it, which leads from the summits of the mind to the capitals of crime." Hamlet had once traveled this path, from Wittemberg to Denmark, and could barely sustain the invincible summer in his own heart at the spectacle he discovered on his arrival. But personal tragedy still lent form to his world, even though for a time absurdity threatened his will to live. The memory of his father is a more durable ghost than the atrocities Camus must contend with. And in the end Hamlet can destroy the embodiment of corruption that threatens his ancient image of the world, restoring a semblance of justice to a society morally chaotic. The excesses of history afford Camus no such simple private gesture, thereby imposing on the mind a burden that Hamlet could finally discharge through action. Few times, declares Camus, "require to the extent ours does that one be as equal to the best as to the worst, to avoid nothing and keep a double memory alive. . . ."[21] What is this but the secret of Hans Castorp's snow vision, man as lord of counter-positions, the mind and heart consenting to the existence of the worst while cherishing an image of the best?

And what but language has the power to keep such a double memory alive, the language of art that sets limits to the excesses of history by inventing form where none existed and encouraging the individual to live with the informed restraint that, for Camus, justifies the work of art? He would have the same kind of imaginative effort govern life as governs art. Just as art imposes form on reality, the mind can set limits to the possible in experience. It does this first by acknowledging the ultimate limit that experience sets on life—mortality. Camus's idea of conscious death establishes the chance for a life that truly reflects the human condition, while permitting that condition to approach the desirable features of art. Defying history, conscious death transforms random events, through the experience of certain individuals, into the semblance of "lived works of art." And language is the catalyst.

In an essay on the French novel published during the war, while he was writing *The Plague,* Camus shows his preoccupation with this idea. Admiring a statement by a character in *La Princesse de Clèves,* he says: "It introduces art into life by giving man the power of language in his struggle against his destiny. And thus we see that if this literature is a school for life, it is *precisely* because it is a school of art. To be more accurate, the lesson of these lives and these works of art is no longer simply one of art, but one of style. We learn from them to give our behavior a certain form." This is what Camus means when he says that the artist, like the historical mind, seeks to "remake" life. It also prepares us for the distinction between man as rebel, whose acceptance of limits is born of respect for the individual, and man as revolutionary, whose commitment to unlimited historical possibility threatens to sacrifice the individual to an abstract ideal. Camus speaks of the novel as the political philosopher speaks of history. His words reflect a calculated choice to introduce a new voice of persuasion into the arena of society where the struggle for man's future is fought. The novel, he says, is "the perfect domain in which the forces of destiny collide with human decision. . . . None of our great novelists has turned his back on human suffering, but we can also say that none has surrendered to it and that they have all mastered it with an inspiring patience, through the discipline of art."[22] The intelligence of the artist, of art itself, can create a civilization and a way of life while paying homage to those "capitals of crime" where human suffering casts a shadow over the "summits of the mind." There is nothing theoretical to his claim. History has misused language so viciously in our time in the name of new orders, more harmonious futures, and more equitable democracies, that the very survival of the word may depend on some such effort by art to reestablish its native vigor.

An age of atrocity did not invent the habit of using ready-made expressions—"resettlement" for "deportation," "special handling" for "extermination," "final solution" for "racial genocide"—to "camouflage heart-breaking experiences," but it renewed the inquiry (as Camus suggests in a 1944 review of Brice Parain's *On a Philosophy of Expression*) into a fundamental question: whether "our most successful cries are not in fact empty of all meaning, whether language does not, in short, express man's final solitude in a silent universe." Like Joseph Grand in *The Plague*, "man has not managed to find his words," though his efforts to do so may represent one of the few options left to restore the shattered image of his dignity. Experiments with language following the disillusionment of World War I—Surrealism and Dadaism, for example—led to a license whose political counterpart finally cost men their liberty. Camus wants no replay of this futile drama. The tendency today, he announces, "is no longer to deny that language is reasonable or to give free rein to the disorders it contains. The trend is to recognize that language has the limited powers to return, through miracles or through absurdity, to its tradition." If Parain chose the first path and Camus the second, they nevertheless shared the belief (unlike writers after World War I) that "we no longer use the falsehood and apparent meaninglessness of the world to justify instinctual behavior, but to defend a prejudice in favor of intelligence."[23] Disillusionment seemed insufficient protection against a time when resistance to tyranny bred terror as well as defiance and saw some of Camus's friends shot by the Gestapo and others sent off to concentration camps. In his case, language lent strength to the superhuman effort to bear the weight of one's own daily life. Such a challenge leads not to the discovery of our capacity for heroism, but to the rediscovery of our banality; and this much-misunderstood term in turn leads directly to Camus's own initial efforts to use language and intelligence in behalf of an art that clarifies our image of the human.

Camus's prewar works are constructed on the principle that one may and must live so as to prevent death from taking one by surprise. It is an attitude born of crisis, but inconsonant with atrocity; hence it represents a point of departure for a study of Camus's art, but cannot stand alone as an illustration of his belief. Early publications like *The Wrong Side and the Right Side* and *Nuptials,* and the first novel that he never published, *A Happy Death,* are permeated by the spirit of André Gide's *Les Nourritures terrestres (The Fruits of the Earth),* a volume which for decades reminded French intellectuals that the body and the senses were unimpeachable features of the human image. Gide's early book was designed to liberate men from the banality of unawareness, of not being steadily conscious of the promises of physical existence. Camus took Gide's principle of a conscious happy life one step further by advocating the need for a conscious happy death, though in these works he shared with Gide a faith in the sufficiency of the imagination to achieve such ends. This faith could not last long, as Camus himself later testified in an essay on Gide: "I had to forget Gide's example, of necessity, and turn away very early from this world of innocent creation, leaving at the same time the land where I was born. History imposed itself on my generation. I had to take my place in the waiting line on the threshold of the black years."[24] History saturated the innocent landscape of creation in blood, making the idea of "happy death" an antiquated child of the imagination, an insufficient image of man's suffering in time. Perhaps this is one reason why Camus never permitted the novel of that title to be published.

But the experience of its protagonist, Mersault, an obvious sketch for Meursault of *The Stranger,* illuminates Camus's stubborn concern with the problem of finding for his own generation literary images of initiation commensurate with the nature of their reality. The experience which gave form to Hans Castorp's preparation for life through confrontation with death was no more appropriate than Gide's appeal to the intoxicated spirit in *The Fruits of the Earth.* Mersault (and Meursault) are difficult to understand because they have so few predecessors in the history of fiction. They must *encounter* the banality of their lives, not merely shed it, before they can begin a process of self-discovery. They must kill time before they can use it, then recognize what is happening in order to prevent time from killing them. Is the conjunction of metaphors accidental or deliberate that requires both men to kill literally before they can begin their journey to insight? The murders committed by Mersault and Meursault represent imaginative, stylized efforts of the artist to bring men in closer contact with the reality of their selves through the experience of death. And since both reject suicide—Mersault considers it more seriously than Meursault—the liberating impulse can come only through murder. The episodes have an antecedent—though not an exact parallel—in Raskolnikov's behavior in *Crime and Punishment,* where murder jolts the soul out of spiritual lassitude into an urgent if unacknowledged need to suffer (if not a convincing admission of human guilt). But unlike Raskolnikov, whose crime expresses a wish to dominate and exposes potential inner sources of redemption and fulfillment, Mersault in *A Happy Death* pursues a "patient self-abandonment" through surrender to the power of the world. The will to happiness, and ultimately, to a happy death, is born not of resentment and frustration but a desire for "a warm and an intelligent instinct for a relationship with the world—without anger, without hatred, without regret."[25]

It is a new form of self-discovery through estrangement, so one is not surprised that the process has led to confusion among some of Camus's readers. The formula that to find himself a man must first lose himself is a familiar one, on which Gide too played variations. But in an absurd world, that blurs and often obliterates the hierarchy of spiritual values which normally guides men through the labyrinth of experience, the individual must return to a point of moral zero, as it were, before beginning the laborious reascent to a world of values.   And that return means immersion in a miasma of beauty and suffering that guarantees no purification after this risky, unorthodox baptism. As Mersault gazes through a train window on a journey across the muddy plains of central Europe, he has a vision of how he must enter into collaboration with the universe to achieve the state of conscious death:

He wanted to crush himself into that mud, to re-enter the earth by immersing himself in that clay, to stand on that limitless plain covered with dirt, stretching his arms to the sooty sponge of the sky, as though confronting the superb and despairing symbol of life itself, to affirm his solidarity with the world at its worst, to declare himself life's accomplice even in its thanklessness and its filth.[26]

Does this clarify the ambiguous figure of Hans Castorp, sprawled in the mud with the message of love in his heart, excluding nothing by embracing everything, hoping that the worst of history does not destroy the best in man? Soot and sky, superb and despairing, affirmation and clay, life and filth—the very words wrestle with each other until they are interlocked, transformed into tokens of the reality they reflect.

But *A Happy Death* is more statement than art, guilty of the aesthetic breach that Camus charged Sartre with in his review of *Nausea:* "A novel is never anything but a philosophy expressed in images. And in a good novel the philosophy has disappeared into the images."[27] In both first novels, the theories do damage to the vitality of the art. The inadequately motivated murder with which *A Happy Death* begins leads to important philosophical consequences but insufficient dramatic ones, insufficiently dramatized: "Because of a single act calculated in utter lucidity, his life had changed and happiness seemed possible. Doubtless he had given birth to this new being in suffering—but what was that suffering compared to the degrading farce he had performed till now?"[28] Murder shatters the banality of his existence, as dying in *The Plague* and the idea of killing in *The Rebel* were meant to shatter the banality of ours; but the almost casual reference to suffering, never realized in images, leaves a lacuna in our imagined response to his ordeal. Perhaps we are to conclude that conscious death, like the absurd, leads nowhere but is a necessary preliminary step in developing an attitude toward the world that excludes nothing. As the iniquities that had to be "embraced"—imaginatively consented to—multiplied and intensified in horror, Camus turned to a stage beyond negation of banality and affirmation of life—dying and killing.

In *A Happy Death* and *The Stranger,* and in an early play like *Caligula,* the two are linked metaphorically. Mersault in *A Happy Death* commits a "perfect crime," successfully disguising the murder as a suicide, so unlike Meursault he is freed from the oppression of conventional justice. His victim had also been his mentor, urging him to use time so that at the end he will not feel that his life has been consummated without him. That might indeed be a definition of the banal existence, which a man must be conscious of before he can make the gesture that liberates him from its bonds. How is the novelist to dramatize the idea that one embraces life only by first participating in the death ritual that dooms all? Initially, it must be a drama of consciousness, since human justice cannot permit the happiness of one man to be built on the death of another. For this reason Mersault and Meursault must be "condemned" to death (the same is true of Raskolnikov, with his sentence to penal servitude in Siberia). In Mersault's case, the solitary night swim he takes to give birth to the will to happiness within himself, alienated from his unconscious past life and submissive to his present fate, hastens the death that must be included in his happiness and his fate. In his weakened physical condition, he contracts a chill which develops into the illness that kills him. But his awareness during the experience constitutes his baptism in conscious death and its alliance with a happy life: "Suddenly he thought of the depths which lay beneath him and stopped moving. Everything that was below attracted him like an unknown world, the extension of this darkness which restored him to himself, the salty center of a life still unexplored. A temptation flashed through his mind, but he immediately rejected it in the great joy of his body—he swam harder, farther."[29] His rejection of suicide, the celebration of his "creatureliness" while assenting to the nothingness of death, resembles the kind of fusion which Lifton and Becker perceive as the crucial need of the modern imagination. But, as we have seen and shall see again, the intrusion of atrocity complicates the possibility of establishing a metaphorical connection between the two.

When Mersault concedes that fate "is not in man but around him,"[30] he is unconsciously espousing one of the principles that distinguishes the twentieth-century mind from the nineteenth. In an essay on the novels of Roger Martin du Gard, Camus refines the idea: "Men learn not from circumstances themselves, but from the contact of their own natures with circumstances."[31] The truism is less simple than it seems, since in our age men are faced with the dual difficulty of knowing their own natures and understanding circumstances. This is why, in describing the absurd, Camus insists that it springs from a comparison or confrontation. Self-discovery is meaningless without the world; and the world is meaningless without men. They may both be meaningless in each other's presence, but that takes us beyond absurdity to nihilism, a direction, according to Camus, not justified by the mind's desire or the logic of history.

For Mersault, the confrontation is so explicit that the philosophy behind the images interferes with the aesthetic impact of the fiction: "What he really wanted was the encounter between his life—a life filled with blood and health—and death." During his last feverish nights, the face of his victim mingles with the final lucidity of his life, illuminating the meaning of conscious death but also of the "banality" that one had to return to and work through before arriving at the more desirable goal:

He realized now that to be afraid of this death he was staring at with animal terror meant to be afraid of life. Fear of dying justified a limitless attachment to what is alive in man. And all those who had not made the gestures necessary to live their lives, all those who feared and exalted impotence—they were afraid of death because of the sanction it gave to a life in which they had not been involved. They had not lived enough, never having lived at all.

Socrates' ancient aphorism about the unexamined life gives substance to its modern version that the unexamined death is not worth dying. The unexamined death sanctions the unexamined life; only through confronting death, as for Mersault, may one encounter "the secret image of his own life."[32]

To die with his eyes open—which is Mersault's last conscious desire—is to verify the fact that one has lived with one's eyes open too. Mersault has just begun to do so, having spent most of his energy learning what to reject from his past life rather than how to establish a relationship with the community of human pain. That is why *A Happy Death,* like *The Stranger,* shows the absurd hero in a preliminary and literally inimitable stage of development. His determination to be conscious to the end, "without deception, without cowardice—alone, face to face—at grips with his body—eyes open upon death"[33] affirms the paradox that man lives in spite of his fate, even though he must die because of it. At the final moment Mersault recognizes that death, not love or landscape, is a man's business, and that in a life without appeal the solitary joy in a man's heart is his sole defense against the finality of extinction. His admiration for living with sentient and intellectual awareness is verbally overstated and artistically underdeveloped in this novel. But it prepares us for the points of view in the later works, which will touch more widely on the social implications of the issue that Mersault confines to his private vision: how to reconcile joy in the heart with the agony of dying, and—a question which Mersault never has to face—how to escape despair despite the anguish of surviving. Learning to live—and die—within the limits of the possible is less difficult for a man alone.

But it is also less purposeful. In rebelling against his fate, the banality of his life, the death that sanctions it, Mersault (in *A Happy Death*) approaches a necessary truth but ignores what binds him to mankind. A more ominous error is to negate that bond, in a futile attempt to escape the limits of a common fate. This is the strategy of Caligula in Camus's play of that name: unable to accept death as the ultimate possibility in human experience, he develops a passion for the impossible. *Caligula* represents a dramatic effort to explore the consequences of this attitude, which is a legitimate subject for what Camus himself called a "tragedy of the intelligence."[34] We recognize it as a familiar nineteenth-century theme, embodied by those desperate exemplars of the Napoleonic temperament, like Melville's Ahab, who would risk their souls to transcend their mortality. Caligula's status is doubly dubious, because it is both doomed and partly out of date.

Camus uses for Caligula the same epithet that he devotes to Dostoevsky's Kirilov in *The Myth of Sisyphus*—a "superior suicide"[35]—though they do not die for the same idea and Caligula only metaphorically takes his own life. But they share the hope that somehow men without God can escape the melancholy truth that defines their lives: "Men die; and they are not happy."[36] The death that takes Caligula's beloved sister suddenly ignites the latent lucidity of his mind. He grows conscious of life's illusions—love does not endure, nor does memory mitigate mortality, for example—and with admirable resolution repudiates these self-deceptions that had previously made him content with his existence. The absurd begins with a recognition of the contradiction between human hopes and the world's denial of them. It continues with a rejection of *such* a world, but then brings man to a crucial crossroad, where the path he chooses creates the conditions for his survival as a human being.

Caligula decides to defy the world's rejection by inventing his own image of the impossible, and making it the goal of his existence: "I want the moon, or happiness, or eternal life—something, in fact, that may sound crazy, but which isn't of this world." And to an aide's objection that his admirable theory cannot be carried out in practice, he replies: "You're wrong there. It's just because no one *dares* to follow up his ideas to the end that nothing is achieved. All that's needed, I should say, is to be logical right through, at all costs."[37] For a brief moment, Caligula's words may sound like a quaint echo of the aristocratic ambitions of certain nineteenth-century literary figures like Ahab and Raskolnikov; but between 1938, when *Caligula* was composed, and 1945, when it was first performed, men were privileged to witness the consequences of their own Caligulas' perverse devotion to "courage" in the name of future absolutes that also ignored the human cost. A lucidity blind to the limits of the possible serves the very power of death it seeks to defeat.

Making the impossible possible, which is Caligula's ambition, presupposes no frontiers to human freedom, no boundaries to the use (and hence the abuse) of power, no terminus to what men expect to achieve from their lives. A heritage bequeathed us by an earlier time, we have little difficulty recognizing its manifestations, private and political, in our own. "I shall make this age of ours," cries Caligula, "a kingly gift—the gift of equality. And when all is leveled out, when the impossible has come to earth and the moon is in my hands—then, perhaps, I shall be transfigured and the world renewed; then men will die no more and at last be happy." His zeal to "infuse ugliness with beauty, to wring a laugh from pain" betrays a heedlessness of both ugliness and pain, if also an honest anguish at the contradictions inherent in the human condition. There is a germ of legitimacy in his rebellion against things as they are, as in his query: "What use is the amazing power that's mine, if I can't have the sun set in the east, if I can't reduce the sum of suffering and make an end of death?"[38] But when his ideas are tested by results—otherwise, they have nothing but rhetorical value—we see that he reduces the sum of suffering by diminishing the number of sufferers, and takes up arms against death by usurping its power and whimsically executing his own subjects.

Men acknowledge the limits of the possible only by abandoning the borrowed vocabulary of a Caligula, the "transfiguration" and "renewal" that belong to the rhetoric of hope and that once granted men—in literature and life—a means of transcending death. They are the blinders still donned, Camus would have us believe, by those who fear the vision illuminated by lucidity. Caligula's misdirected courage brings him closer to this crowd than he realizes, since his longing for the impossible implies an unadmitted inability to confront his own destiny. The secret solace that helps him endure, as he confesses, is "scorn," but he fails to perceive that a scorn for the universe not based on consent to man's human fate, on "conscious death," quickly turns into scorn for man, and ultimately into contempt for the limitations of one's own life. In this sense, Caligula's existence follows the logic of suicide that Camus in *The Myth of Sisyphus* attributes to Kirilov. One consents to death by affirming the vivid desire for life in one's own heart. Unable to understand fate, one chooses the path of survival, and this in itself is a gesture of defiance against that fate. Caligula instead (much like Captain Ahab, who is "the fates' lieutenant") chooses to play the part of fate: "I wear the foolish, unintelligible face of a professional god."[39] But men worship him through fear, and he can retain their "respect" only through terror. The contemporary flavor of Camus's play is abundantly clear.

But Camus is not in the habit of inventing villains; the murderous universe is villain enough for him. The source of evil is not Caligula's nature, but his dilemma, his inability to reconcile the knowledge that nothing lasts with his unquenchable desire to expect everything from life. If one were to reduce Camus's vision to a central belief—an impossible task—it might be that a man who must die cannot live by expecting everything from life. Caligula mistakes this enlightenment—that nothing lasts—for something godlike and solitary. Actually, it defines his humanity, but this is more than his pride can bear because it makes him as vulnerable as all men. Is history the last refuge of those who cannot live without appeal? "There's nothing in this world," weeps Caligula as the patricians break in to assassinate him, "or in the other, made to my stature." He is correct about the other world, but wrong about this, as some of his final words unconsciously admit: "The air tonight is heavy as the sum of human sorrows." But at the end his lucidity is clouded by the indomitable will to transcendence and, like Ahab hurling his spear at Moby Dick, he shatters his human image in the mirror with a stool and screams his epitaph to the world: "To history, Caligula! Go down to history!" His last gasp, the closing line of the play, mocks his fate and declines to accept the tragedy of his mortality: "I'm still alive!"[40] He dies with scorn for men, for the human condition, not for death, knowing that he has chosen the wrong freedom but ignorant that no "right" freedom exists other than reverence for the human in a world where possibility is permanently circumscribed by death.

The opposite of Caligula's impassioned desire for the impossible is capitulation to nihilism, to a world totally without meaning and thus without a basis for significant action. While Europe moved relentlessly toward war, this was the temptation that Camus chose to resist as history continued to offer support for the logic of a nihilistic point of view. For all its somber tone, *The Myth of Sisyphus* is an optimistic book: defending the possibility of a moderate human happiness before an age of atrocity required Camus to rethink his premises and conclusions. Finished early in 1941 and published in 1942, France's darkest hour, it offers a modest hope to men victimized by the violent frenzy that grows from misdirected scorn. Behind the guise of its philosophical intentions lies a very pragmatic book, answering the question of whether life is worth living with a resolute if occasionally uncomfortable "yes," and espousing an *attitude* for survival that met the immediate needs of men at a critical moment in history. Yet its impulses are less inspired by contemporary events than by the invincible summer of the heart that Camus retained from his Algerian days. *The Myth of Sisyphus* possesses the odd distinction of being both timely and anachronistic; but it could not have been written five years later.

The question of whether the absurd dictates death or counsels suicide appears academic when mass killing becomes a political habit and dying ceases to be, even metaphorically, a question of conscious choice. The absurd is neither a philosophy of behavior nor a doctrine of belief, but a statement about limits, a lucid vision of what man can still hope to live for after he has absorbed the principle of conscious death. When Camus's statement about limits was confronted by the experience of unlimited dying, many of his readers recognized the inadequacy of his ringing aphorism in *The Myth of Sisyphus* that there "is no fate that cannot be surmounted by scorn."[41] Yet the force of verbal persuasion, which is one of the unique qualities of this book, an immediate strength and an ultimate weakness, reflects the potency and impotence of language to clarify the dilemma of death. In 1951 Camus said of *Sisyphus:* "I was trying to make a *'tabula rasa,'* on the basis of which it would then be possible to construct something."[42] Imprinting new words on a clean slate was an attempt to give voice to what was left after the negation of a transcendence which once made that dilemma of death manageable.

But Camus also conceded the ephemeral if indispensable nature of his early work. "Even as I was writing *The Myth of Sisyphus,*" he admitted in the same interview, "I was thinking about the essay on revolt that I would write later on. . . . And then there are new events that enrich or correct what has come to one through observation, the continual lessons life offers, which you have to reconcile with those of your earlier experiences."[43] The last statement sounds like a description of Hans Castorp's career on the mountain, and it is exact insofar as it comments on man's (and the artist's) need to accommodate his view to the shifting contexts of death in our time. Since Camus begins with the assumption that death is *always* "inappropriate," he must adapt his vision to his changing perception of its inappropriateness. As history mocked his efforts to plot a way of thinking that would enable men to rescind the divorce between themselves and their experience, the passion for life and death's repudiation of that passion, Camus kept his eye steadily on those values that strengthened human endurance and supported man's life in time despite his fate. The artist's condensed vision taught him that man outlived the forces that mocked his humanity, though each new atrocity left the individual a little more bereft of a practical mode of thought to justify survival. The *Myth of Sisyphus* is Camus's prewar contribution to such modes of thought.

There is little reason for rehearsing the various interpretations and denunciations of a volume that has generated so much admiration and criticism. For our purposes, Camus's emphasis on absurd creation is worth exploring in detail, since in the absence of a Creator—a premise in Camus—the artist plays a vital role of mediator between death and survival, annihilation and happiness. Art enables man to live psychologically within his means by translating into images and thus making accessible to the imagination what Camus implies when he speaks of existing within the limits of the possible. The artist as creator brings down to a human level the transcendent desire for immortality and offers the conscious mind, as Camus wrote in 1955 in a preface to *The Myth of Sisyphus,* "a lucid invitation to live and to create, in the very midst of the desert." Men meet this challenge without illusions: "Creating or not creating changes nothing." Inappropriate death still prevails. But creating clarifies much, by deflating romantic formulas about unlimited aspirations: "The absurd work illustrates thought's renouncing of its prestige and its resignation to being no more than the intelligence that works up appearances and covers with images what has no reason." Absurd creation teaches a new modesty to art and hence to man, but it also reflects a human condition where death and the intelligence wrestle for advantage. Camus's idea of art resists the temptation to improve reality by "adding to what is described a deeper meaning that it knows to be illegitimate." But by giving form to what is described, the artist helps to make endurable what cannot be explained—we return once more to the idea shared by Mann and Freud of art as consolation. Is this why Camus quoted Nietzsche's aphorism with approval: "We have art in order not to die of the truth"?[44]

The work of art thus becomes a last refuge for the absurd, not an escape from it. It makes manageable Camus's conviction that "at the heart of all beauty lies something inhuman," a paradox rediscovered by Hans Castorp and so thoroughly confirmed by the experience of atrocity that for a time atrocity threatened to cancel beauty. One might even divide Camus's career into a prewar effort to preserve the balance between beauty and the inhuman and a postwar struggle to restore it. Early in *The Myth of Sisyphus* he speaks of "the different but closely related worlds of intelligence, of the art of living, or of art itself," a trilogy establishing important links among qualities that support survival in an absurd universe. Art gives the intelligence an attitude for enduring life, as earlier in Camus nature gave the body means to rejoice in it. If one accepts the premise that "everything begins with consciousness and nothing is worth anything except through it," then creating plays a vital role in reminding men of the reality that is the only stage of the human drama. In this sense art replaces transcendence instead of expressing or challenging it or conducting the individual into its vestibule. It displaces all those disciplines which seek to provide man with the image of an existence other than his own. Art is not the only consequence of the absurdist position, but it is one of the most fruitful: "I want to know whether, accepting life *without appeal,* one can also agree to work and create *without appeal.* . . ."[45]

The connection between art and life is even more explicitly

outlined when Camus rejects the work of a creator as a series of isolated testimonies and likens it instead to a profound thought that "is in a constant state of becoming." As a description of a way of being rather than an ideal to be striven for, it is also a lucid observation on the condition of existence in an absurd world. Neither the ordered universe of the eighteenth century nor the organic vision of the nineteenth corresponds to Camus's image of a creation constantly corrected and contradicted. The amorphous shape of such a world admits no goal, no conclusion, no final harmony: instability appears to be one of its basic ingredients. The sole obstacle to art, the one irreparable wound to the life of man or artist—who can avoid the painful irony of Camus's unconscious prescience here?—is premature death: "If something brings creation to an end, it is not the victorious and illusory cry of the blinded artist: 'I have said everything,' but the death of the creator which closes his experience and the book of his genius." And neither men nor artists should be surprised or dismayed, since earlier Camus had offered as one definition of genius "intelligence that knows its frontiers."[46] Art illuminates the frontiers that intelligence knows.

The creative act, with its reliance on will and discipline, patience and lucidity, is the most effective model for meaningful existence in an absurd world circumscribed by meaningless and inappropriate death. Camus may qualify this position later, correct and even "contradict" it as he lives out his own "constant state of becoming," but he will never repudiate his commitment to creation as a way of life. More than any other form of expression, art remains "the staggering evidence of man's sole dignity: the dogged revolt against his condition." Its value is not absolute but relative, however, contributing to the kinetic energy that links man to his world; like the Absurd, it is born of the encounter between human need and the finality of death. It has less importance in itself, says Camus, "than in the ordeal it demands of a man and the opportunity it provides him of overcoming his phantoms and approaching a little closer to his naked reality." As the image of Sisyphus and his rock (with which Camus ends his volume) confirms,

Camus believed that man was equal to the ordeal. But as the contest between death and the intelligence grew tenser during the ensuing years, death crowding its opponent into a narrower and narrower space, one sensed a singular irrelevance to Camus's assertion near the end of *Sisyphus* that outside of the single fatality of death, a world remains "of which man is the sole master."[47] So little world remained that time temporarily eclipsed the impulse to "rule," leaving the much more modest longing to survive.

Camus himself would recognize later the limitation of his eloquent celebration of Sisyphus' defiance. Although he does not flinch at the image of a tragic destiny—"There is no sun without shadow, and it is essential to know the night"—he does not yet see beyond atrocity, when the imbalance between sun and shadow obscured the vestiges of day. His confidence that "crushing truths perish from being acknowledged" attributes to lucidity and intelligence powers that disintegrate when faced by the kind of ordeal Améry described in his chapter on torture. And his belief that there is "no fate that cannot be surmounted by scorn"[48] owes more to traditional postures of martyrdom than Camus would have liked to admit. Although he was fond of insisting that *The Myth of Sisyphus* (like all his other works) represented only one way station in the artist's journey, he was unprepared, like most of his contemporaries, for the inroads that the Nazi excesses would make on the imagination's ability to organize a coherent response to reality. By the time *Sisyphus* appeared, the "normal" oppressions it was intended to confront had been replaced by abnormalities which few Europeans had been able to anticipate.

Similarly *The Stranger* and *The Plague,* separated by much less than a decade, seem a generation apart, and again not only because they represent different stages in Camus's projected study of absurdity and revolt. Moreover, when compared with some of the experiments of successors like Robbe-Grillet, both novels seem oddly conventional. Camus belongs to a tradition, shared by Mann and Solzhenitsyn, that refuses to reject literary antecedents even though their material seems unprecedented. If history represents a rupture, their art will reflect attempts to close the breach. Discovering original forms to contain the formless theme of inappropriate death was one way of facing the challenge that younger authors like Jakov Lind and Jerzy Kosinski met in less familiar ways. Camus chose a path parallel to the one followed by these spokesmen for a literature of atrocity, one that paid homage to the vision of prior practitioners of his art.

Thus, a novel like *The Stranger,* in its content if not in its style, owes an important debt to Dostoevsky, especially to the ordeal of Dmitri in *The Brothers Karamazov*[49] —not only in the "club" atmosphere of the courtroom, where those present seem to know each other and feel socially at ease, but more explicitly in the allusion to the case following Meursault's, which has even drawn a correspondent from a Paris daily—a notorious parricide case. Before he is finished, the prosecutor suggests that Meursault in some sense has "legitimized" the graver crime, and hence should be indirectly judged guilty and condemned for that too. Although the mockery of the judicial process is a subsidiary theme in both Dostoevsky and Camus, they share the belief that the process of law inhibits the individual from gaining insight into his human identity. Any growth in Meursault (as in Dmitri) is not because of but despite the legal inquiry. The will to crime in one case, the actual crime in the other, leads to a kind of exile that neither has anticipated: in thoroughly different ways, each begins to examine life more seriously than he had ever done before.

Camus does not follow Dostoevsky much further, since Dmitri had lived with a thoughtless passion and frustrating anguish that is the exact reverse of Meursault's tranquil indifference to experience. If he is "guilty" of anything, it is of a failure to distinguish between alternatives, to understand that decisions have consequences even when a man lives as if they do not. Returning from his mother's funeral, he plans to resume work as usual, concluding that nothing had really changed: but as we see, his mother's death will shape his fate and lead to his death sentence. The irony of the judicial process does not discredit the fact that a man who lives as if nothing matters invites disaster. He makes himself a victim, collaborates with those forces in society and the universe that will eventually "judge" him and destroy him. Through most of the novel, Meursault lacks scorn for his fate, and this is chiefly because he is unconscious of the absurd universe that determines it. In refusing to attribute to marriage or a job or even to grief more power than it deserves, Meursault shows good instincts: he is a ripe candidate for the absurd sensibility. But in his unconscious state his simple pleasures do not represent that affirmation of happiness which men fling in protest against an indifferent universe. For this reason his indifference is a collaboration with that universe.

Meursault's lethargic behavior at his mother's funeral demonstrates that he has not yet understood the principle of conscious death, which is expressed perhaps too clearly in *A Happy Death*. His story recounts the steps by which he is shaken out of his lethargy, or at least begins to be so, for Meursault's transformation is by no means complete. We get a hint of his initiation from his own language, which (with one important exception) is not much given to figures of speech; on the morning of his fatal encounter with the Arab, he notes as he leaves his house that "the day, already full of sun, struck me (*m'a frappé*) like a slap in the face." The image recurs, in reverse, as it were, in the closing line of the first part of the novel, after Meursault has shot the Arab as a kind of counter-assertion to this initial slap: "It was like four brief blows that I struck (*je frappais*) on the door of calamity."[50] Calamity admits him, but the responsibility for recognizing the implications of his new destiny lies entirely with him. The sun which oppressed him at his mother's funeral prods him again when he faces the Arab with a gun in his hand: with the first shot he acknowledges his fate, surrenders to the inevitable; with his next four, he defies the mortality which he cannot defeat. Although his motives remain obscure, buried in the richly metaphorical language, his *act* is unambiguous in creating the consequences that lead to his conviction and death sentence. It compels him to contend with his mortality and enter consciously into his heritage as a man.

Society, especially in the behavior of the examining magistrate, prosecuting attorney, and prison chaplain, does its best to tarnish this heritage. Much as Dmitri is baffled and exasperated by the refusal of similar officials to understand the reasons for his erratic conduct, so Meursault is vexed by their efforts to penetrate the facade of his indifference. Dmitri clings to the shreds of his tattered honor; Meursault does not feel like a criminal. To the magistrate's question whether he regretted his action, he replies after a moment's reflection that, rather than genuine regret, he felt "a little bothered" (*un certain ennui*) by it. The magistrate, not surprisingly, does not understand. But it is a healthy response, since so little has "bothered" Meursault in the past. The only challenge of his meaningless freedom was how to kill time, and this he had managed with little difficulty; his "meaningless" incarceration begins to crystallize for him the potential meaning of that freedom which he had never appreciated before. His longing to swim or be with a woman is contradicted by his physical situation, creating the conditions for confrontation with the absurd: as time passes, his thought approaches the frontiers of that confrontation.

A new relationship with time is an essential feature of his growing enlightenment. Although he continues to think in terms of killing time (*tuer le temps*), he gradually grows more sensitive to how time kills man. Even before he reaches this point, "killing time" (in prison) begins to mean internalizing experience, enriching the dimensions of existence by drawing on memory to reanimate the half-forgotten or ill-observed details of his life. "Thus I understood," he confesses, "that a man who had only 'lived' for a single day could live without any difficulty for a hundred years in prison" (p. 123). But Meursault still has only a limited comprehension of this principle, since he exercises his own memory on recollecting the items in his room at home; his previous indifference has impoverished the resources of his imagination. Sleep remains his major escape, in prison as it was outside, from the routine of his unexamined life. Failure to perceive the value of time, or to realize how much precious living can be condensed into a brief time, is the major source of his indifference, the legacy which must be rejected if he is to gain any insight into the human condition.

As the narrator of his own tale, Meursault is incapable of the philosophical inquiries into the nature of time that Mann introduced into the rhythm of *The Magic Mountain*. But his vacillation diminishes as he begins to sense the insufficiency of his previous uncritical acceptance of time as mere chronological routine. Similarly, Hans Castorp's far profounder growth depended on his discovery of an inner time that governed the imagination's response to reality. Meursault has never understood that to live consciously requires one to use time differently, to acknowledge the urgency of foresight in a universe where death allies itself with time to cut off the future. Raymond testifies at the trial that Meursault's involvement in the episodes leading up to the shooting of the Arab had been mere chance (*un hasard*), and though to a certain extent this is true, coincidences accumulate in Meursault's life (as in Oedipus', one suddenly recalls) to create his fate. Since the death sentence is irrevocable, living as if chance plays the most important role in one's existence is to remain blind to one's fate. Hence one test of Meursault's humanity after the shooting is his success in revising his idea of time by facing the challenge of foreseeing.

Camus offers us access to his unreflective character in a number of ways. Perhaps most important is through variations on a key phrase that begins to recur during the trial—"for the first time" (*pour la première fois*). It represents a series of shocks to Meursault's habitual indifference that gradually awakens him to a more meaningful perception of his separate identity. Aware of the prosecutor's hostility to him, he admits that "for the first time in many years I had a silly desire to weep, because I felt how much all these people detested me" (p. 140). Further injurious testimony leads him to confess to himself that "for the first time, I understood that I was guilty" (p. 141). Celeste's sympathetic testimony, on the other hand, elicits the response that "for the first time in my life I had the desire to kiss a man" (p. 145). After his conviction and sentencing, he grows more acutely aware of what he is about to lose: "For the first time in a long time, I thought of Marie" (p. 177). But we realize at this moment, even if he does not, how his earlier indifference has impoverished his memory and the content of his imagination. On the one hand, he recognizes that life and happiness require physical presence, not nostalgia; on the other, he exposes the limitations of his view of human relationships by concluding that people apart are as good as dead for each other. This is normal, he declares, as normal as other people forgetting him when he is dead. He has no inkling of Dr. Rieux's more humane insight (in *The Plague*) that memory nourishes the vital spark of life during periods of exile, or that after the death sentence has been executed, knowledge and memories may be all that is left to sustain a fraternal feeling for those who have died.

A second way of better understanding the taciturn Meursault is through the slow shift in his attitude after he is convicted. For the first time in his life (though he does not say this), he begins to *anticipate,* to consider alternatives, to admit, in others words, that life has its inevitable features that diminish the importance of chance and coincidence. He regrets not having taken more interest in public executions, that is, in that image of man's fate which testifies to the awfulness of death, a finality that cannot be a matter of indifference to men. He seeks a loophole in that inexorable destiny, his language using some of the key terms that have begun to define his place in the human drama. He wonders whether chance (*hasard*) or luck (*chance*) had ever once (*une fois*) changed that fate. Just once! The irony of his question lies in his failure—or inability—to perceive that although men may do many things "for the first time," as courage joins with intelligence in a defiant recognition of their fate, the death sentence never changes, life without appeal describes the limits of the human condition. There are no exceptions: Meursault must finally understand that the problem is not to escape death but to find an attitude that will preserve the image of the human despite death's "impudent certainty" (*certitude insolente,* p. 169). He inherits the dilemma of the absurd man without yet knowing who he is.

With death so near, his instincts rather than his intelligence teach him how precious life is. The failure to anticipate, to connect act with consequence, which had characterized his earlier experience, haunts him in an abrupt reversal as anticipation becomes his chief activity, waiting for the dawn, since this is the time for executions. He plays with possibilities as he waits, and here we see the effects of his earlier indifference, since he has difficulty purging himself of the attitude it had bred. He finds his own platitudes unconsoling—that life wasn't worth the effort of living anyhow, that it made no difference whether one died at thirty or seventy, that when the end came it didn't matter how or when you died. Crisis refutes these platitudes. No logic can still the rush of blood that is unleashed when the prospect of survival dominates his feelings. Thus, when the chaplain finally enters to counsel consolation rather than confrontation, Meursault erupts with a breathless fury that betrays his frustration at his failure to discover any consolation for an inconsolable event. Everything the priest says diverts Meursault's attention from his dignity as a man, a dignity based on rejection of all those conventions, like religion, which disguise the human dilemma with illusions like the promise of a future life. In a world where death chooses all, distinctions disappear, and "nothing matters" in the sense that ultimately mortality limits the value of human aspirations.

For Camus, as for Meursault, the chaplain's view encourages a false hope as an escape from despair; Meursault's outburst is an instinctive rebellion against a position which humiliates him and transfers grandeur from the human to the divine. If that rebellion appears incomplete or negative, it is because Meursault cannot yet make the leap from absurd contradiction to fraternal solidarity, the kind of reassertion of the human in the face of the death sentence which infuses a compassionate spirit into *The Plague.* Meursault's sympathy at the end is restricted to this mother, of whom he thinks "for the first time in a long time," (p. 187) approving of her taking a "fiancé" shortly before she died. Thus he repudiates the sentence of his judges, who condemned him for failing to mourn: since death is always inappropriate, grief is less a token of respect than celebration of the impulse to renewal. At last he has learned how to respond to his mother's death.

Camus takes Meursault no further. In a final assertion of his own series of renewals, Meursault consents to the universe whose sun had earlier oppressed him with such harsh and brutal insistence: "I opened myself for the first time to the tender indifference of the world" (p. 188). Having purged himself of the world of his indifference by denouncing the chaplain, he can now embrace the indifference of the world and feel the kinship between them. He cannot reach the level of kinship with men, which for Camus represents a higher stage in man's conflict with the death sentence. Meursault's desire to be greeted with cries of hatred by the spectators at his execution may signify his need to make his death part of someone else's life, to impinge on another's memory as those in his past have not impinged on his. It is a negative expression of fraternal feeling (*pour que je me sente moins seul*), an unusual but understandable assertion of the principle that in death any acknowledgment from other human beings is better than none—though as *The Plague* will dramatize, some are better than others.

The Stranger brings one man closer to the "naked reality" of existence—the death sentence. *The Plague* raises the challenge to a community level. In one of his *Combat* editorials shortly after the war, Camus argued that the truth of his age could be found "only by living through the drama of it to the very end. If the epoch has suffered from nihilism, we cannot remain ignorant of nihilism and still achieve the moral code we need."[51] In the earlier novel, the spirit of nihilism threatened the will to happiness; in *The Plague*, it mutilates men, and this requires a more complex consciousness and more concrete kind of revolt. In an absurd world, men suffer torment of the mind; the war forced them to endure torture of the flesh, which added a new dimension to Camus's untiring efforts to rethink an image of the human for an age of atrocity. The evidence of unjustified murder, the execution of innocent men and boys (hostages to the Nazi scorn for the human image), tested his devotion to concepts like "friendship, mankind, happiness, our desire for justice,"[52] though in the end he could not loosen his hold on them without destroying the intellectual coherence of his personal universe. The pestilence that overwhelms the city of Oran in *The Plague* is a trial for all its citizens, but particularly for the characters in the novel who routinely defended those values before the "torture of the flesh" challenged the logic and sufficiency of their commitment.

Camus's choice of plague as the controlling metaphor of the novel brings him closer to Ernest Becker's belief, in *The Denial of Death,* that man's need to confront his "creatureliness" is the central dilemma of the age. The age itself has accented that dilemma. In Camus's terms, the disaster of the intelligence with which Nazi domination threatened the European mind was a failure to recognize that the annihilation of the body lay at the heart of the menace. Political propaganda, geographical occupation, racist ideology—all these disguised the hidden inspiration of German power, a contempt for the integrity of the flesh. Although the Nazi mind did not invent indifference to human suffering or scorn for the idea of human dignity, its cold ferocity resembled nothing that Camus had encountered before; one can imagine how it must have traumatized his contemporaries. He echoed Jean Améry's numb astonishment when he confessed: "I did not understand that men could torture others without ever ceasing to look at them."[53] The plague reflects the bureaucracy of death that atrocity introduced to the modern imagination, dividing its potential victims, like the German occupation itself, into two clearly defined camps: collaboration and resistance. But the heart of the novel is not a dramatization of how men respond to plague (important as this theme is), but what plague does to men. Only by imprinting the ravages of plague on their consciousness can men live through the drama of their time "to the very end."

How adequate is Camus's image of the plague? In identifying the principle of destruction with an impersonal force, Camus extends the absurdist attitude by equating inappropriate death with a universe devoid of human features. By eliminating the agency of man (though human attitudes encourage the plague by failing to understand it), he saves the image of man but sacrifices part of the idea he hoped to communicate: "that men could torture others without ever ceasing to look at them." Ignorance displaces villainy as the confederate of evil, and as a consequence our hostility is deflected toward the world we live in rather than the one we as men have helped to create. Perhaps we have to sacrifice more of the human image than Camus is prepared to surrender in order to achieve a total vision of the consequences of atrocity. And yet Camus feared that surrendering too much could poison the remaining portion. This may explain the psychological naïveté of the remarkable passage from the last of his "Letters to a German Friend," written while he was working on *The Plague:*

At the end of this combat, from the heart of this city [which was Paris but might have been the Oran of his novel] that has come to resemble hell, despite all the tortures inflicted on our people, despite our disfigured dead and our villages peopled with orphans, I can tell you that at the very moment when we are going to destroy you without pity, we still feel no hatred for you. And even if tomorrow, like so many others, we had to die, we should still be without hatred. . . . we want to destroy you in your power without mutilating you in your soul.[54]

It is a genteel notion of violence that verges on smug piety; but Camus would have been the first to admit that his version of revolt in *The Plague* (and in the "Letters to a German Friend") was neither definitive nor "true," merely consistent with his belief that in the struggle against death for survival, one never finally blames the human spirit, since there are more things to admire in men than to despise.

That spirit invites much initial blame in the opening pages of the novel, for the banality of the townspeople's lives encourages the encroachment of disaster. Habits insulate them from intimations about their fate, about mortality in general and the more immediate threat of inappropriate death. Dying (before the advent of the pestilence, hence in "normal" times) is a disagreeable event, bringing discomfort to the patient (and even more to the healthy populace?) because it interrupts the superficial serenity of their lives. They are as indifferent to their existence, as uncertain and puzzled on the question of how to respond to death, as is Meursault in the opening pages of *The Stranger.* Routine induces a kind of moral somnolence, so that when Dr. Rieux asks his house porter to remove the dead rat he has found on his landing, we are not surprised by the porter's categorical denial: " 'There weren't no rats here.' "[55] And the simple porter is not the only one to thrive on the spirit of denial. The human mind, by instinct, inclination, and training, is unequipped to imagine a future darkened by disaster. Even the wary Dr. Rieux's initial response to the magistrate, whose son will be a principal victim of the plague's ravages, is "The rats? . . . It's nothing. . . ." (p. 12). Tarrou casually calls them "the porter's headache" (p. 13); Father Paneloux, his unseeing eyes smiling behind his glasses, dismisses the inundation of rats with "I suppose it's an epidemic they've been having" (p. 17); Joseph Grand has "other things to think about" (p. 19); and the journalist Rambert, on assignment from another city, insists repeatedly that he doesn't belong in Oran.

The plague is Camus's way of dramatizing for his contemporaries atrocity's influence on the normal course of human fate. Time and custom permit men to postpone confrontation with death and live "as if" it is never an immediate threat. Plague disrupts time and lays waste to custom, so that those who are not willfully blind must accept the prospect of untimely death as part of their "normal" heritage. The shock to the human imagination is severe, as we have just seen from the various evasions of the major characters. The implications of atrocity thwart those qualities of mind and spirit that traditionally support the individual during periods of oppression: memory, love, ambition, faith, belief in the future. As the pestilence spreads and hope diminishes, the support offered by these values wanes too, and men begin to embrace an attitude that, for Camus, is the greatest danger of the age: the habit of despair. Even more than the disillusionment and nihilism of the twenties, the atrocities of the war (and its aftermath) furnish the intelligence with reasons for despair. For Camus, ideologies no longer suffice to justify the suffering that ensues when abnormal conditions of reality like the plague become routine. The art of Solzhenitsyn and Charlotte Delbo is also suffused with the noxious atmosphere of plague: the idea of inappropriate death dominates their vision too. And they share with Camus a theme that has become crucial for our age: what happens to the heart and intelligence when inappropriate death replaces "normal" dying as the measure of human experience?

The novel's narrator, Dr. Rieux, pondering the problem of bringing a sense of crisis to townspeople who disbelieve in pestilences, crystallizes the challenge faced by artists like the ones we are considering, since they write for readers who disbelieve in atrocity. "How should they have given a thought to anything like plague," he asks, "which rules out any future, cancels journeys, silences the exchange of views?" (p. 34). For Dr. Rieux and Camus, the issue is the same: how to press a vital nerve of the imagination so that a dead man can be given substance and one can avoid repeating the indifference which had greeted past pestilences, whose "hundred million corpses broadcast through history are no more than a puff of smoke" (p. 35). It seems that there are disasters in history that exceed the imagination's ability to conceive of them. Thus even Dr. Rieux at first concludes that the present outbreak will not be serious—always the initial defense against atrocity—then translates this intuition into concrete feelings when he unjustifiably decides that in a town where simple, good-natured eccentrics like Joseph Grand live, "the chances were all against the plague's making any headway amongst our fellow-citizens" (p. 42). He is mistaken, though the human decency that motivates Grand is, for Camus, one of the values that enables men to endure plague and survive it with a diminished but intact image of the self.

In short, the behavior of individual men "doing what needed to be done" (p. 37) creates a pattern for living psychologically within one's means when disaster of the dimensions of atrocity appears. It signifies, once again, living within the limits of the possible, a classical ideal of moderation adapted to a post-romantic age whose major bequest appears at times to be an unlimited power of execution.[56] The plague is Caligula writ large. And for a moment, Dr. Rieux has a terrifying vision of the world defenseless against its ravages: "he had a preternaturally vivid awareness of the town stretched out below, a victim world secluded and apart, and of the groans of agony stifled in its darkness" (p. 88). Against this apocalypse of woe Camus can offer only the limited aspiration of a Joseph Grand, with that single perplexing sentence which he polishes and repolishes like a semiprecious stone whose chief value is that it occupies his time and enables him to endure. Measured against the groans of human agony in Rieux's vision, Grand's pathetic hope for literary success seems minimal indeed. Yet his passion for the proper word, for the discipline of style, makes him an initiate if not a practitioner of art, one who wrestles with reality through language and acknowledges precise observation as one expression of "doing what needed to be done."

The conflict between limited aspiration and the plague seems settled when, near the end, Grand contracts the disease and in a fit of despair asks Rieux to burn his manuscript. But Grand astounds everyone by recovering and resolves to start all over again, eliminating all the adjectives. His difficulty in finding words had cost him the brief happiness of his marriage, but his quiet courage in fighting the plague, and his determination to proceed with his literary ambition after he survives it, confirm within the novel's framework the strength of human decency and deep feeling—if not for defeating the plague, since permanent conquest is out of the question, at least for giving value to survival. In this sense Grand is the true embodiment of the attitude that conquers despair. And Camus is shrewd enough to realize that such attitudes, a kind of ammunition for the imagination, are more essential than programs for action based on ideological formulas, since such programs tend to deaden one's sensitivity to human suffering.

Grand's response is a reaction to the loss of his wife's love. For this reason Camus is sympathetic with the dilemma of Rambert, whose sole desire is to escape from the quarantined city and return to the woman he loves. At first his love makes him immune to the general distress. His personal insistence on happiness through love is a strong weapon against the inroads of plague on the imagination. Yet the threat of common disaster taxes this private ideal, and introduces a paradox that Camus cannot easily resolve, one that reappears in the works of Solzhenitsyn and Charlotte Delbo. For there, in the labor and concentration camps, the need for fraternal feeling in extreme situations puts a strain on conventional love and makes it appear—this is the heart of the paradox—almost selfish. In Solzhenitsyn's *The First Circle*, Nerzhin's fondness for his *zek* companions displaces his feelings for his wife, who is only permitted an annual visit. The narrator of Charlotte Delbo's Auschwitz volumes develops a kinship with the women who share her barracks that interferes with the memory of her executed husband. And in *The Plague*, Dr. Rieux sends his ailing wife away to a sanatorium just before the pestilence breaks out. Her image fades too as he slowly develops a more comprehensive sense of human responsibility in the presence of atrocity. One of the muted themes of Camus's works, especially the later ones, is the question of whether romantic love is not one more absolute inherited from an earlier age which inspires man to embrace the futile hope of living beyond the limits of the possible.

In *The Plague*, Camus remains ambivalent. Love may be a luxury, indispensable in "normal" times but questionable as a supreme value under pressure of plague and what it stands for. But Rambert's position is not to be taken lightly. A veteran (from the losing side) of the Spanish Civil War, Rambert has come to believe that men capable of great deeds are incomplete unless they are also capable of great emotions. In a crucial discussion with Rieux and Tarrou, Rambert discredits heroism and dying for an idea: " 'I know it's easy and I've learnt it can be murderous. What interests me is living and dying for what one loves.' " To Rieux's quiet demurral that man is not an idea, Rambert replies passionately: " 'Man *is* an idea, and a precious small idea, once he turns his back on love. And that's my point; we—mankind—have lost the capacity for love' " (p. 136). The question left hanging in the novel is whether the dimensions of disaster in our time have affected our capacity to love in ways we do not yet suspect. Atrocity infects the future, and since love thrives on precisely that future, it may infect love in subtle ways yet to be explored. Both Rieux and Rambert will have something more to say on this subject as their experience of plague intensifies.

Watching men die who were meant to live narrows the scope of feeling available to the human heart. It is not the same as watching men die whose lives have reached a "natural" limit to existence: this releases an anticipated grief that diminishes the pain of outrage if not the anguish of the loss itself. The sense of innocence betrayed, of vitality wasted, of universal wrong evokes inconsolable horror and reduces earlier patterns of transcendence to sterile mockeries of the principle of life. Two crucial episodes dramatize this idea. The first awakens echoes of Mann's parody of the *Liebestod* theme in *The Magic Mountain.* One of the diversions of the people of Oran is to attend performances of Gluck's *Orpheus* by an opera company stranded in the town because of the quarantine. The opera itself explores love's fragility as death wrests Eurydice from Orpheus just when love seems destined to triumph over it. Art doubly confirms the new conditions of reality as, at the very moment when Eurydice is being torn from the arms of her lover by the ruler of the underworld, the singer performing Orpheus staggers and collapses, a victim of the plague himself. While watching Eurydice (who was meant to live) "die", the audience sees art and reality coalesce here in an image of feeling's failure to survive within the limits of the possible. The exile of feelings imposed by plague requires a reassessment of love's role in a universe where inappropriate death is a constant presence to the imagination.

Rambert approaches this insight when he decides to remain in Oran to work with the sanitary squads which Tarrou has established to fight the plague. For the moment Rambert confesses that leaving would make him feel ashamed of himself, "and that would embarrass his relations with the woman he loved." He does not yet understand Tarrou's warning that, by taking a share in other people's unhappiness, one may have no time left for happiness oneself. Rambert refuses to believe that the choice is so clearcut, yet he has no reply to Rieux's weary admission that for "nothing in the world is it worth turning one's back on what one loves. Yet that is what I'm doing—though *why* I do not know" (p. 170). Camus reluctantly but courageously confronts the consequences of the alternatives that an age of atrocity highlights: The personal happiness of love seems inconsistent with a world where the spectacle of inappropriate death makes man witness to episodes which violate the source of that love. A second crucial scene forces several of the major characters to face the logic of their existence and to reassert or reexamine the principles that give them the energy to endure.

The convulsive death of the magistrate's son crystallizes some of the central themes in Camus's novel. We are forced to witness an "execution," the death sentence being carried out on the body of an innocent child totally defenseless against the agony of pain that ruthlessly torments him until he dies. None of the observers, not even Father Paneloux, can discover a satisfactory "reason" for the suffering of this boy who was "meant to live." The clinical precision of Camus's description is designed to spare no feelings: the naked reality of premature death dominates the stage. The child's incessant wail echoes the ultimate futility of a forlorn humanity; Paneloux's hoarse prayer—" 'My God, spare this child. . . !' "— awakens no response from the spiritual universe, whose silence only intensifies the inarticulate sound that is unaccommodated man's last form of revolt against *such* a fate: "in the small face, rigid as a mask of greyish clay, slowly the lips parted and from them rose a long, incessant scream, hardly varying with his respiration, and filling the ward with a fierce, indignant protest, so little childish that it seemed like a collective voice issuing from all the sufferers there" (p. 176). This torture of the body offers no solace whatsoever to the mind tormented by the problem of discovering an attitude consonant with its existence. In its presence, the heart suffocates, the intelligence is left mute. In the boy's death, Camus has described the essence of atrocity for the victim. Rieux's response reflects its essence for the witness: "He felt like shouting imprecations—anything to loosen the stranglehold lashing his heart with steel" (p. 177).

The episode represents a crisis of faith for Father Paneloux —but also a crisis in logic for the learned Jesuit priest. After the child's death, he tries to refine his own attitude by working on an essay entitled *Is a Priest Justified in Consulting a Doctor?* Unable to reconcile the suffering he has witnessed with any principle of reason or theology, he abandons his work with the sanitary squads and preaches a sermon espousing the only attitude that enables him to preserve his faith— believing everything or denying everything. Not daring to deny everything, he chooses total belief. It is a point of view, but one that serves his own spiritual needs, not the medical needs of the community. Hence it marks a professional break between the man of God and the man of science. Paneloux rapidly contracts a disease which may or may not be plague, dies, and is marked a "doubtful case." He is scarcely mentioned again in the novel. Rieux, who is resolved to fight against creation as he finds it, realizes that Paneloux's position lacks *relevance* for an age of atrocity, since it requires the individual to accept the boy's death sentence as an expression of divine will. And this seems to be Camus's charitable judgment too.

Despite his learning, Paneloux misunderstands the nature of this pestilence, and some of the sophisticated distinctions with which it challenges the intelligence. "No longer were there any individual destinies," the narrator reports; "only a collective destiny, made of plague and the emotions shared by all" (p. 138). The mind, unwilling to withdraw into private solutions, faces the question of how to confront the image of mass disaster—the problem Freud had anticipated at the outset of World War I. For the plague brings with it a surfeit of corpses, and the literal dilemma of burying so many dead contends with man's desperate need to give meaning to his individual loss. Once more love and death encounter each other in a desperate struggle for superiority; but, as in Gluck's *Orpheus,* the odds are too great—separation triumphs over reunion. One of Camus's subtlest suggestions is that plague, the threat of inappropriate death, caused men to waste away "emotionally as well as physically" (p. 148). One of the most desolate bequests of the concentration camp universe, which the plague atmosphere increasingly resembles—and both Solzhenitsyn and Charlotte Delbo will confirm this—is the truth that under conditions of atrocity both memory and imagination lose the power to sustain love. Even shadows waste away, says Camus's narrator, and "by the end of their long sundering" the survivors "had also lost the power of imagining the intimacy that once was theirs, or understanding what it can be to live with someone whose life is wrapped up in yours" (p. 149). Atrocity assaults both love and friendship, since both ask something of the future, while the emotional stability that can project relationships into the future is poisoned by the vague uneasiness and fear which a surfeit of dying and killing introduces into our psychological reality.

This is not to say that Camus deplores either love or friendship—only the fact of their diminished possibilities. Responding to a moving image of Grand's lost happiness, Dr. Rieux reflects that "a loveless world is a dead world, and always there comes an hour when one is weary of prisons, of one's work, and of devotion to duty, and all one craves for is a loved face, the warmth and wonder of a loving heart" (pp. 213-14). And in a moment of pure fraternal lyricism reminiscent of the simpler mood of the Mediterranean essays, Rieux and Tarrou seek temporary respite from the hermetic prison of the plague by enjoying a swim together in the harbor outside the town gates. They swim silently side by side in a baptism of friendship that celebrates the physical vigor of the body.

It is an experience to cherish, but they as well as Camus realize that men enjoy such interludes of beauty—of relative beauty only—beneath the shadow of plague and death.

The swim is the culmination of a scene between Tarrou and the doctor in which Tarrou explains his reasons—one more point of view among many—for fighting the plague. And once again Camus is more interested in making consequences explicit than in justifying or censuring positions. Lucidity implies anticipation, knowing insofar as is humanly possible what may happen as a result of one's attitude or action. In this regard Tarrou pushes lucidity to its ultimate frontiers, beyond where even Rieux can follow him. In the past he has allied himself with a party that was forced to employ the "death sentence" to achieve more human ends. But he was soon to discover that inhuman means corrupt such ends, that his associates were part of a tendency characterizing contemporary history: "Today there's a sort of competition who will kill the most." His dilemma contains the seeds of Camus's own later volume, *The Rebel,* for Tarrou defines the conditions of existence in a modern revolutionary state that is, if anything, more accurate nearly thirty years later: "Even those who were better than the rest could not keep themselves nowadays from killing or letting others kill, because such is the logic by which they live; and . . . we can't stir a finger in this world without the risk of bringing death to somebody" (p. 206). Hence Tarrou refuses to be a "rational murderer" and chooses, on an earth where there are only pestilences or victims, to survive in this society as an "innocent murderer" on the side of the victims. In a secular parallel to Paneloux's question whether a priest should call a doctor, Tarrou asks whether one can be a saint without God. Rieux finds it hard enough to fight the plague as a man; for him, reality contradicts Tarrou's ideal, which resists the truth that "innocence" and "murder" are incompatible. To exist in a world where killing and letting others kill become part of one's daily reality is to admit (what Tarrou finds intolerable) that one shares the responsibility for such conditions. His dying from plague just when the epidemic appears to have broken may be an ironic commentary on his excessive expectations from life.

Yet his belief that one must do what one can to cease being plague-stricken is one condition for survival that lies at the heart of the novel's vision. A more selfless concern for the welfare of others—one that has less time for the problems of the secular saint—is another, though this position too represents only a bleak affirmation of man's power to resist the ravages of plague. Rambert and Rieux survive, the one as lover, the other as healer, but both have been scarred by their ordeal and the purity of their devotion diluted by the inescapable recollection of horror that "victory" is unable to erase from their minds. Tarrou's death confirms the doctor's earlier admission that his fight against the plague meant a never-ending defeat; the atrocities he has endured give him the feeling "that no peace was possible to him henceforth" (p. 235). Inappropriate death reminds one of the insufficiency of love; though the townspeople may reunite with their loved ones—those who have survived—as if nothing had happened, the committed participants like Rieux and Rambert (Rieux in particular) acquire a heritage of loneliness as part of their future, as if exile, once experienced, permanently limits the challenges of life. Rieux's sense that "all a man could win in the conflict between plague and life was knowledge and memories" (p. 237) pays homage to the ineradicable imprint of extraordinary suffering that has been engraved on his imagination by what he has witnessed, but especially by the pressure of Tarrou's death, just when their friendship was beginning. The atrocity that abruptly transforms a living warmth into a picture of death is the paradox, multiplied a millionfold, with which his generation has had to contend. The somber tone of *The Plague* is a cosmos away from the spirit of joy that infused Camus's early Mediterranean essays, despite his concern there with death—though the works are separated by less than a decade in time. Once a life without illusions was a call to happiness; now happiness is a refuge from the threat of further pestilences.

Rambert's fate sheds light on the problem of love's relationship to death (in the context of atrocity), though it offers no solutions: ostensibly he has endured to rejoin the woman he calls his wife. As he awaits her arrival in Oran, he feels a nervous tremor "at the thought that soon he would have to confront a love and a devotion, that the plague months had slowly refined to a pale abstraction, with the flesh-and-blood woman who had given rise to them" (p. 240). Camus touches on the theme without elaborating; that would be another story, whose ramifications Solzhenitsyn and Charlotte Delbo will explore. What *does* daily contact with constant sorrow do to the human feelings, to the natural longing for happiness through love that inspires most men? With Rambert, Camus is evasive, though he recognizes the issue: "For the moment, he wished to behave like all those others round him who believed, or made-believe, that plague can come and go without changing anything in men's hearts" (p. 241). It may be that Rambert has a courage to love that Rieux lacks. But part of the "knowledge and memories" that Rieux inherits from the plague is that happiness through love in an age of atrocity must be built on denial, and though he will not ask men to forsake their happiness, he insists that *we* recognize the illusion it is built on.

As he walks among the ecstatic crowds after the gates have been opened and the hermetic nightmare ostensibly comes to an end, he measures his own pensive awareness against the momentary delirium of the townspeople, and the imagery of the passage is so precise that no one can miss the allusion to the grim history of our age:

Calmly they denied, in the teeth of the evidence, that we had ever known a crazy world in which men were killed off like flies, or that precise savagery, that calculated frenzy of the plague, which instilled an odious freedom as to all that was not the Here and Now; or those charnel-house stenches which stupefied whom they did not kill. In short, they denied that we had ever been that hag-ridden populace a part of which was daily fed into a furnace and went up in oily fumes, while the rest, in shackled impotence, waited their turn [pp. 242-43].

The ordeal of the "return," the appeal of happiness after

such return, is a theme that Solzhenitsyn will explore with equal sobriety in the closing episodes of *Cancer Ward,* and Charlotte Delbo in the last volume of her Auschwitz sequence as her survivors try to adjust to the "normalcy" of freedom. With his Tolstoyan compassion, Camus does not censure the calm denial of plague; men in general could probably not survive without it. But it precipitates the exile and loneliness of others like Rieux, who recognizes that present delight built on denial of past atrocity imperils future joys. His conclusion that he knew "what those jubilant crowds did not know but could have learned from books" (p. 252) may be less ironic than it first appears, or ironic in a different sense. What men fail to discern from history they may yet rediscover in art, which transfixes in images what eludes them in the swift flow of time. As the ordeal of atrocity slips from human memory, books like *The Plague* put it in a perspective that makes it accessible to the human imagination. There it may remain as dormant as the plague bacillus itself, or erupt briefly (like the infection in Hans Castorp's own body) and drive men to reconsider how its ravages affect love and hope in the modern world.

One thing is absolutely definite:
not everything that enters our
ears penetrates our consciousness.
—Solzhenitsyn

5

ALEKSANDR SOLZHENITSYN AND
THE JOURNEY THROUGH HUMILIATION

Aleksandr Solzhenitsyn seems resolved to prevent the ordeal
of atrocity from ever slipping out of human memory. His
substantial prose expeditions through the taigas and tundras
of Russian repression in the twentieth century indict a state
of mind and a condition of being that reduce the human
image to a Giacometti stick figure. "Our brothers are breathing under the same sky as we; justice is a living thing," sang
Camus on the closing page of *The Rebel*, in that stylized,
celebratory mood which occasionally substituted a poetics of
human nature for a clear-sighted view of the inhuman lurking
behind the human. "Our brothers are dying under the same
sky as we," Solzhenitsyn might have replied, "while guilt and
innocence have been repealed, and justice has perished."
Camus had no illusions about the blind, destructive power of
modern history, or the "men of Europe" who used ideology
to justify murder: "They no longer believe in the things that
exist in the world and in living man; the secret of Europe is
that it no longer loves life."[1] But he never lost his faith that
there was more to admire than despise in the hearts of individual men, whose capacity to love life could not be extinguished by a century of political violence.

Solzhenitsyn examines this premise from another point of view, from within the perimeters of those labor and death camps where so many have learned the meaning of atrocity in our time that the camps have become a metaphor as well as a locale of inappropriate death. On the fringes of civilization, hidden from a society that still believes it can satisfy its longing for the best without acknowledging its capacity for the worst, they represent a subterranean impulse in human nature that permits some men to destroy the lives of others without guilt or remorse. Camus would have us believe that ignorance is responsible for approving in one's heart that which causes the death of others. Solzhenitsyn suggests that indifference to suffering (and at times even acquired cruelty) would be a better explanation.

Solzhenitsyn's Gulag studies accumulate overwhelming evidence of the precariousness of what we call civilization. When the mutual respect for what men once regarded as a common human nature breaks down, the values supporting its dignity disappear. The individual is left wondering how to survive in such an atmosphere. This is the burden of much of Solzhenitsyn's art, certainly of those novels which dramatize the human dilemma in an existence permeated by death. Past experience and past literature, Solzhenitsyn argues, have infused the mind with a naive faith in the strength of moral weapons. Present history and some present literature have exposed the futility of such faith. The challenge, as with Camus, is to find an attitude for survival without lapsing into nihilism or despair. But under the conditions of atrocity in Solzhenitsyn's world, neither human solidarity nor the vision of the absurd suffices. All may be well with Sisyphus, but in the Gulag Archipelago, his rock crushes men.

Affinity with death cells, as with plague, confirms the necessity of learning to live within the limits of the possible. What do men live by when they finally realize that they are "sentenced to death"? Solzhenitsyn makes this a central issue in *Cancer Ward;* here he offers a naked statement whose complexity he will dramatize concretely in the novel: "Live with a steady superiority over life—don't be afraid of misfortune, and do not yearn after happiness; it is, after all, all the same: the bitter doesn't last forever, and the sweet never fills the cup to overflowing. It is enough if you don't freeze in the cold and if thirst and hunger don't claw at your insides." Such a mournful stoicism could hardly expect to convert a society devoted to the pursuit of hope and the future; nor can mere words cross the "unbridgeable chasm" that separated the prisoner Solzhenitsyn from his fellow countrymen outside the camps. Both Hans Castorp and Camus would endorse the principle of living with a steady superiority over life, as well as the desirability of confronting misfortune and acknowledging the fragility of happiness. But the rhetoric verges on platitude unless one keeps steadily in the imagination the somber image of death-cell doors being swung open in "the deep, deaf stillness of midnight."[2] That portion of reality haunts Solzhenitsyn, makes him a ghost himself amidst the solid indifferent masses of people whose imaginations are still unaffected by this image.

Solzhenitsyn is uncompromising in his demand that a medium be created to impress such images on minds hitherto immune to them. Otherwise, daily existence becomes a form of duplicity by which men ignore those insights into human nature which modern atrocity reveals. The camps, as nowhere else, disclose "in detail and on a large scale" one of the most harrowing trials of our time: "the special process of the narrowing of the intellectual and spiritual horizons of a human being, the reduction of the human being to an animal and the process of dying alive."[3] Charlotte Delbo will be even more explicit in her efforts to analyze the implications of "dying alive" as a contemporary phenomenon. Both she and Solzhenitsyn, like many other camp survivors who transformed their experience into literature, seek to generalize their personal ordeals to make them reflect a neglected feature of the human condition. But Solzhenitsyn pushes further into the controversial area of why the Gulag world should be recollected in such exasperating and unappealing detail: one of the dangers of atrocity is a desensitization to inappropriate death as a form of protection against its horrors.

After a painfully naturalistic description of how men die from various prison diseases as a result of malnutrition—scurvy, pellagra, alimentary dystrophy—he raises the obvious question of why it is necessary to record physical decay in such detail. "Why keep talking about all that? . . . Why remember all that?" And he quotes an "answer" from Tolstoy, who never heard of the Gulag Archipelago as Solzhenitsyn knew it:

What do you mean, why remember? If I have had a terrible illness, and I have succeeded in recovering from it and been cleansed of it, I will always remember gladly. The only time I will refuse to remember is when I am still ill and have got worse, and when I wish to deceive myself. If we remember the old and look it straight in the face, then our new and present violence will also disclose itself [*GA Two*, p. 211].

Although in some of his public statements Solzhenitsyn adopts the pose of a moral crusader, here he concentrates on recognition rather than reform, recognition that the life we lead does not prepare us for the one we may be forced to live. The victim of atrocity, of what Tolstoy in his day called "our new and present violence," loses the power to control his own destiny. And this is partly the result of an absence of an inner imagery equivalent to the worst possibilities of that destiny in his present life. The difficulty of making such a challenge a source of insight results from the unpleasantness of reproducing an initiation rite that degrades the human image instead of ennobling it. But if a human being, to say nothing of a new tragic figure, is to emerge from the ordeal of atrocity, it must come from that very degradation.

When is the "rock bottom" of a human being revealed? Solzhenitsyn offers a portrait of engineer Lev Nikolaiovitch Y. (noting the ironic coincidence of first name and patronymic with Tolstoy's). Y. is a "last-legger," a prisoner who has abandoned all pretensions to dignity other than the minimum effort required to keep himself alive. In his sluggish behavior and grotesque appearance he resembles one of those "muslims" from the Nazi concentration camps, hollow-eyed victims who had lost the will to live and wandered around in their own filth like zombies until they died. Y. differs from them because he has preserved an instinct for life, though this barely raises him to a level that we consider human. The body's basic needs disregard the "supplementary awareness" that elevates a man's self-image in civilized society. The portrait of Y., though neither exemplary nor fully representative, nevertheless provides an authentic image of man's "creatureliness" under conditions of atrocity, when survival replaces living with dignity as the challenge to the imagination:

Something with a resemblance to a human being sits in a declivity above a pit in which brown peaty water has collected. Set out around the pit are sardine heads, fish bones, pieces of gristle, crusts of bread, lumps of cooked cereal, wet washed potato peelings, and something in addition which it is difficult even to name.... The last-legger begins to dip out the dark slops from the mess tin with a wooden spoon and to wash down with them one after another the potato peelings, the gristle, then the sardine heads. . . . His nose can hardly be seen in the midst of the dark gray wool that covers his neck, his chin, his cheeks. His nose and his forehead are a waxy brown color and in places the skin is peeling. His eyes are teary and blink frequently [*GA Two,* pp. 211-12].

Since he is reporting someone else's account of this episode, Solzhenitsyn embellishes it with some artistic touches. The result has resonances beyond the photographic.

It seems as if the "rock bottom" of a human being must be the foundation for a revised image of man, based on an intimate familiarity with the worst that cancels most previous ideas of the best. When an outsider approaches Y., he gathers up the remains of his mess, presses them to his chest, "falls to the ground, and curls up in a ball like a hedgehog." (*GA Two,* p. 212). Man is forced to retreat to his animal nature in order to preserve the strength to remain alive. But it is a kind of humiliation that Solzhenitsyn endorses, since it permits Y. to exist without doing harm to others. However, the price he pays in traditional human resources is enormous, and one is forced to ask the question that Solzhenitsyn does not: of what value is an unsoiled conscience to this shrunken image of a man who resembles his animal ancestors more than his fortunate contemporaries beyond the frontiers of the Gulag Archipelago?

Solzhenitsyn calls engineer Y. a "last-legger theoretician," because he has calculated the pattern of his existence with the single goal of surviving. A chemist by profession, Y. has determined "that one can get everything nutritionally necessary from refuse; one merely has to overcome one's squeamishness and direct all one's efforts to extracting nourishment from this source" (*GA Two*, p. 212). The discovery has a more generalized value, since for Solzhenitsyn the ability to endure "with a steady superiority over life" requires a preliminary imaginative immersion in just this kind of "nourishment," suppressing the squeamishness which ordinarily directs one's eyes away from the experience of men like engineer Y. His outlandish costume is an equally graphic reminder that a rehabilitated image of man must acknowledge the failure of traditional costumes to depict the human image in an age of atrocity. In his patched and tattered padded garments, "he looked like a bat shaking its wings." But they provide insulation against an offending universe; beneath the heavy layers of rags his garbage-fed body "did not feel pain when he was struck. He could be kicked and beaten with sticks without getting bruised" (*GA Two*, pp. 212-13).

Y.'s behavior begins with a knowledge of his body (rather than his "self"), and ends with an insight into the motives of others—thus confirming the virtue of "knowing others" as a premise for survival in our melancholy age. Like Jean Améry, Y. discovers that "giving beatings" is a necessary condition of existence in the camps, not only for the authorities but for certain prisoners too. Their behavior confirms Améry's suspicion that some form of torture has become a widespread manner of justifying the self in a society which no longer supports other kinds of transcendence. Thus Y. has learned how to howl hideously even when he is not hurting, to gratify the needs of his tormentors. For in the camp some men are fond of beating up the weak "so as not to feel completely weak themselves." Torture itself is one means of surviving, a way of living with a superiority to life that was far from Solzhenitsyn's intention when he adopted the phrase from the stoic philosophers. In a world where "people simply could not believe in their own strength unless they subjected others to cruelty" (*GA Two*, p. 213), survival may mean living with the minimum hurt rather than the maximum joy. But when the definitions of pain and pleasure are themselves so blurred by the unprecedented dimensions of atrocity, the example of engineer Y. offers little consolation to those who still cling to ancient ideals of human dignity.

The graceful beauty of the human form which warmed the visionary heart of Hans Castorp while lost in a snowstorm has disappeared from view: we may have read its requiem there. For Solzhenitsyn, engineer Y. is a consequence of that "special process of the narrowing of the intellectual and spiritual horizons of a human being" which atrocity bequeathes to man. "Dying alive" supplants the body's potential glory, and if that too is built on a more terrible "blood sacrifice," even the counter-position is presented in a diminished image, an icy rather than a sanguinary fate. The opposition is not between vigorous health and violent death, but two stages of immobility. The motionless figure of engineer Y., curled up on the ground about the remnants of his scanty meal, can be measured against another kind of fixity, found in victims who succumbed to the building of the notorious White Sea Canal, as reported to Solzhenitsyn by a survivor:

At the end of the workday there were corpses left on the work site. The snow powdered their faces. One of them was hunched over beneath an overturned wheelbarrow, he had hidden his hands in his sleeves and frozen to death in that position. Someone had frozen with his head bent down between his knees. Two were frozen back to back leaning against each other. . . . At night the sledges went out and collected them. The drivers threw the corpses onto the sledges with a dull clonk.

And in the summer bones remained from corpses which had not been removed in time, and together with the shingle they got into the concrete mixer [*GA Two*, p. 99].

Myth metaphorically enables Hans Castorp to survive the threat of a frozen death. Unprotected by metaphor or any other source of strength, Solzhenitsyn's victims embody the harsher fate that now serves the imagination of the artist in search of a legitimate image of the human.

In a chapter he calls an "ethnographical essay" on the "zeks" or prisoners of the Gulag Archipelago, Solzhenitsyn outlines the inverted values that enable these unorthodox offspring of modern civilization to endure. By the time he has finished, one has the uneasy feeling that they have a clearer perception of how to live in the modern era than we do. "Those things that are precious to us, dear reader," says Solzhenitsyn behind the anthropologist's mask, "such as ideological values, self-sacrifice, dedication, and the desire to labor selflessly for the future, these are not only quite absent among the zeks but are even considered worthless" (*GA Two*, p. 514). His facetious and often mocking tone in this section should not deflect us from his earnest intent, because here we get his clearest statement of how the experience of atrocity affects traditional values like self-sacrifice, dedication, and hope, and forces the individual to adopt others that will preserve his humanity while insuring—or at least prolonging—his survival. A new culture emerges, apart from the cannibal "thieves" who merely prey on the weak.

To men and nations nurtured by the idea of dialogue as a means of establishing human community, the first principle of this new culture sounds discouraging: "The most important condition of success in the life struggle of the Gulag islanders is their *secretiveness*" (*GA Two*, p. 517). For the zeks—whose survival may depend on a piece of information, an extra ration, a heavier garment—to disclose is to lose the security of that life-preserving source or affiliation. In an atmosphere where there is neither psychological nor social support for self-sacrifice, where gestures of fellowship only mock one's own mortality without providing the solace of transcendence (to live on as a hero in the memory of others, for example), the individual slowly exhausts those resources which once contributed to his sense of personal dignity. "With the years," we are told, "the zek becomes so accustomed to hiding everything that he no longer has to exert any effort at all to this end; the natural human desire to share what he has experienced dies in him" (*GA Two,* p. 518). But Solzhenitsyn suggests an even more subtle reason for this reversal of the human desire to share. In an open and peaceful society, men can prepare psychologically for death, either honestly or evasively, but without fear of the sudden threat of extinction. But in the closed society of the Archipelago (and insofar as it reflects our era, in contemporary experience too), when death by atrocity is part of our consciousness (and hence unconsciously, of our expectations), concealment becomes a defense "against the *secret course of events* in general." Since the members of the camp administration "do all they can to conceal from [the zek] information concerning his own fate," his behavior mirrors the sense of his destiny imposed on him by his reality (*GA Two,* p. 518). Conscience, like other ethical ideas, has value only when one feels that it is supported by some portion of society, or a power beyond society. When this approval vanishes, Solzhenitsyn implies, most men lack strength or will or reason to sustain the force of conscience unaided.

When one's sense of the future is governed by annihilation rather than hope, we enter Camus's absurd world, but so reduced in aspiration that the longing for harmony shrivels and almost disappears. The zeks die, says Solzhenitsyn, like everyone else, "only more densely and more prematurely. And their funeral rite is gloomy, meager, harsh" (*GA Two,* p. 506). And anonymous, he might have added. The humiliation that this destiny imposes on the individual excludes the option of tragic defiance; and though it leaves the possibility of a point of view, the image of man which results can best be described—literally, as we shall see in *Cancer Ward*—as mutilated. If we recognize its features, it is not because it resembles ourselves, but because we have followed in the imagination the painful ordeal it has suffered. "Picture to yourself," Solzhenitsyn urges,

that the island environment differs so sharply from the normal human one and so cruelly confronts a man with the choice of immediate adaptation or immediate death that it grinds and masticates his character much more thoroughly than could a foreign national or a foreign social environment. And the only thing it can be compared with is a transmutation into the animal world [*GA Two*, p. 503].

When history forces a choice between adaptation to a humanly insupportable environment or immediate (and hence premature) death, the individual who would survive psychologically must surrender some of those values we traditionally identify with human dignity and acknowledge a heritage from the animal world that the veneer of civilization desperately seeks to disguise. First psychology, then history, confirms Darwin's biological insights. The era of modern atrocity continues an erosion of the human image that began over a century ago.

The ensuing fatalism, which exhausts the springs of compassion, is a natural consequence of the feeling that the future is obscure and beyond one's power to control. In the Gulag volumes, Solzhenitsyn's approach is documentary rather than evaluative; the implications of such fatalism reappear in dramatic form in his novels, where some individuals reach a cold-blooded moral calm and then try to rebuild human responses commensurate with it. The quest for happiness and fulfillment through love or some other form of personal achievement still inspires characters in *Cancer Ward,* but coexists with the knowledge that joy plays a diminished role in the lives of those who confront premature death daily with both mind and imagination. There are moments when Solzhenitsyn seems to suggest that love is the last self-deception or illusion invented by man to conceal his "creatureliness" from himself. The constant expectation of misfortune undermines love's captivating power.

The difficulty Solzhenitsyn encounters in reconciling the tensions of atrocity is implicit in his historical approach to the theme. Facts about human nature cannot clarify the ambiguity of character which the abrupt shift from "normalcy" to the world of the Archipelago released. The constant pressure on the imagination to find ways of accepting one's "creatureliness," to survive while deciding how much of a price one is prepared to pay for continued existence in a lethal atmosphere, to endure when the choices are so scanty—this pressure cannot be conveyed by the hundreds of fragmentary portraits Solzhenitsyn sketches in the Gulag volumes. A single day in the life of Ivan Denisovich is more valuable for one seeking insight into the world of atrocity than seven years in the lives of countless anonymous victims who grunt after having been called "pig" every day of their ordeal. Together with *Cancer Ward*, the story of Ivan Denisovich makes death a daily antagonist, so that any initiation into life must coalesce, as it did for Hans Castorp, with a frank acknowledgment of mortality as a fact that shapes every decision of one's existence.

The protagonist of Solzhenitsyn's first novel, Ivan Denisovich Shukhov, is one of those innocent victims of atrocity who resolves to develop an "outer" prowess to rebuild his fate on private terms. He begins his day at the "rock-bottom" of the human, with a vivid sense of his "creatureliness": "His whole body was one big ache."[4] It is his way of acknowledging that "dying alive" is his fate, though unlike engineer Y., he is not yet reduced to a primitive level of existence. But he does recognize that nourishment is the principal means of survival, so that his most important activities serve the needs of his body. All his human gestures are modified by these needs: cooperation alternates with competition in his relationship with others, and cooperation always has a selfish base, determined by whether it advances or retards his physical stability.

When survival depends on ministering to the body on such a rudimentary level, human alliances take unprecedented turns. Returning from their work site, Shukhov's group spots a labor detail moving toward the guardhouse from another direction. A race develops between the two columns, since the first to arrive will be searched first and will not have to wait so long for their bowl of hot, watery soup for supper. "So everything was turned upside down," thinks Shukhov. "Everything was all mixed up now—bitter was sweet and sweet was bitter. Even the guards were with them. They were all in it together. The people they hated now were the guys over in that other column" (p. 143). When an exhausted Moldavian falls asleep at the work site and fails to appear at roll call, the other prisoners are filled with murderous resentment because they have been made to stand in the cold while the search for him was going on. The spirit of camaraderie that prevails is never based on pure self-denial or loving one's neighbor as oneself.

Solzhenitsyn dramatizes the consequences of reversing this long-accepted theoretical basis for western civilization. Men do not become animals, but the intermediate realm they inhabit between the world of nature and the world of grace has been scantily portrayed in fiction before. Shukhov's behavior confirms the principle, long since proved by history though reluctantly accepted by the imagination, that evolution brings adaptation, but not necessarily progress. Shukhov lives by the philosophy that "it could be worse," and though this enables him to endure, it eliminates the future as a goal for contemplation and reduces the idea of "happiness" to the relief that another day has passed without catastrophe and that he has finagled an extra bit of food. It reminds us once more of Ishmael's conclusion in *Moby Dick* that if men would survive in a tempest-tossed world, they must shift their conceit of attainable felicity. For Ishmael, satisfaction with home and hearth and family already represented a shrinking of the frontiers of expectation. In the atmosphere of atrocity, these consolations dissolve into a futile hope and unattainable bliss. When men care more for their bowlful of thin soup "than freedom, or for their life in years gone by and years to come" (p. 151), then we must confront a version of human nature that the nineteenth century could not have recognized.

In his search for rituals to preserve a semblance of human dignity, Solzhenitsyn adopts a strategy similar to Hemingway's after the disillusioning experience of World War I. For Hemingway, the physical prowess and grace of the body or direct sensuous contact with nature still afforded pleasure in a universe shorn of intellectual and spiritual order. The famous fishing scene in *The Sun Also Rises* gives Jake and

Bill a respite from the complex ordeal of daily existence. For Shukhov, eating is not a respite; it *is* his daily existence, everything else moving up to and away from it like water flowing into and out of a crested wave. The sequence of motions or gestures in Hemingway which lend baiting a hook or prodding a bull a kind of moral dignity have a rough equivalent in Shukhov's manner of eating:

He began to eat. He started with the watery stuff on the top and drank it right down. The warmth went through his body and his insides were sort of quivering waiting for that gruel to come down. It was great! This was what a prisoner lived for, this one little moment. . . .

He drank the watery stuff on the top of the other bowl, poured what was left into the first bowl and scraped it clean with his spoon. It made things easier. He didn't have to worry about the second bowl or keep an eye on it and guard it with his hands [pp. 169-70].

The ritual is solitary, not shared, and its paradox is that its success depends on mistrust rather than mutual affection. Every extra ration for Shukhov deprives one of his fellow prisoners of a similar insurance for survival.

"Who is the prisoner's worst enemy?" asks the narrative voice in *One Day*. "The guy next to him. If they didn't fight each other, it'd be another story. . ." (p. 146). But in this novel atrocity strips the mind of that longing for communion and solidarity which nourished the meaning of transcendence before the hermetic camp-world sealed it out. For example, Shukhov needs a tray to carry the bowls of his work group. He spots another inmate about to give one up, and the following dialogue ensues:

"Gimme that tray when you're through, pal."
"But there's another guy over at the hatch waiting for it."
"Let the bastard wait. He should've been sharper" [pp. 165-66] .

The other guy, who was there "first," sees them and grabs one end of the tray. But he "was smaller than Shukhov. So Shukhov shoved it at him and sent him flying against one of the posts holding up the roof" (p. 166). The conventions which support justice disintegrate when survival of one's own body is the only impetus to order left to the individual.[5] Although Solzhenitsyn shares with his narrator the nostalgia for justice that would transform this competition into cooperation, as an artist he perceives that neither the simple-minded Shukhov, nor the world that gives him a number instead of a name and would be indifferent to his annihilation, supports such nostalgia.

Deprived of dreams, the ordinary man like Shukhov conquers death and protects his elementary dignity by fighting the system on its own terms. He accepts no absolutes which prescribe idealized attitudes for confronting present oppression. "I believe in God, all right," he tells an old Baptist prisoner who spends his nights reading the Bible and praying. "But what I don't believe in is Heaven and Hell." The idea of moral order is so contradicted by personal experience that the two worlds have drifted apart. The Baptist Alyoshka's conviction that a bridge still joins them is based on his withdrawal from daily reality, not an acknowledgment of it. He is an anomaly to be admired for the persistence of his faith, perhaps, but not to be followed by those like Shukhov who recognize that the injustice of history is incompatible with the vision of faith. "The thing is, you can pray as much as you like" says Shukhov, "but they won't take anything off your sentence and you'll just have to sit it out, every day of it, from reveille to lights out" (p. 198).

The same is true of the abstraction we call freedom. For Camus, the longing for freedom was in perpetual conflict with the indifference of the universe. But when the constant effort to defeat death stretches into years, as it did in the world of which Solzhenitsyn writes, then even the precious desire for freedom atrophies. Shukhov doubts everything:

He didn't know any longer himself whether he wanted freedom or not. At first he'd wanted it very much and every day he added up how long he still had to go. But then he got fed up with this. And as time went on he understood that they might let you out but they never let you home. And he didn't really know where he'd be better off. At home or in here [p. 199].

Just as Hans Castorp loses his enthusiasm for returning to the flatlands and Dr. Rieux recognizes that plague has permanently scarred the abstraction we call happiness, Shukhov vaguely perceives that "home" is no longer a meaningful aspiration. Charlotte Delbo will dramatize this insight as most of her returnees discover that the experience of Auschwitz has altered their attitude toward those values they cherished in a preatrocity world. Learning to be grateful for less, Shukhov slowly forgets those impulses which inspired him to long for more.

In such a circumscribed universe, one seeks gratification for its own sake. A deliberate gesture which achieves its end is sufficient to fortify one's image of one's humanity. Lacking control over temperature, one can only use ingenuity to secure better footcloths, warmer boots, thicker gloves. Keeping warm is a triumph over death. Shukhov is adept at this "outer prowess," which gives him a sense of superiority over life. Even more curious is his attitude toward his work. His gang is assigned to a bricklaying detail, which becomes for Shukhov a ritual of mastery over a chaotic world, similar to Nick Adams's fishing and camping experience in Hemingway's "Big Two-Hearted River" stories. The careful rhythm of movements is a kind of moral pantomime, keeping the wall firm and level and Shukhov's reality from collapsing in ruins about him:

He'd scoop up some steaming mortar with his trowel, throw it on, and remember how the groove of the brick ran so he'd get the next one on dead center. He always put on just enough mortar for each brick. Then he'd pick up a brick out of the pile, but with great care so he wouldn't get a hole in his mitten—they were pretty rough, these bricks. Then he'd level off the mortar with a trowel and drop the brick on top [p. 109].

It creates a precarious order which can be ruined by a blow from an angry guard or a few nights in the punishment cell. It seems a pitiful triumph, but only if we use a measure other than Shukhov's. Since the camps have eliminated universal terms for rebuilding his fate—his conversation with Alyoshka makes this clear—the only terms left are private ones. His decisions during the day have enhanced the well-being of his body; by nightfall, it no longer aches. Within the limits of his control, he has postponed the horror of physical annihilation for another twenty-four hours. But if Solzhenitsyn admires his persistence, he has few illusions about the larger irony of his efforts: "There were three thousand six hundred and fifty-three days like this in his sentence, from reveille to lights out" (p. 203). One day is precious, but multiplied by ten years, it seems less so. We are thus driven to question the value of "life at any cost."

Solzhenitsyn speaks here not of fictional time, but literally of the remaining period of Shukhov's sentence. That sentence floats in an atmosphere combining imagined and actual experience in a way that might have prompted a Polonius to describe Solzhenitsyn's art as a historical-autobiographical-fictional mode of writing. History fuses with imagination, forcing the informed reader to interpret the literal details of atrocity. For example, both Shukhov and Kostoglotov in *Cancer Ward* (as well as most of the zeks in *The First Circle*) are trapped by the notorious Article 58 of the Soviet penal code, which Solzhenitsyn analyzes extensively in *The Gulag Archipelago*. That work is a necessary gloss on Solzhenitsyn's fiction; no one unfamiliar with it, or the actuality on which it is based, can make full sense of his novels. History collaborates with imaginative vision to seal the fates of Solzhenitsyn's characters, and this judgment is even more relevant to an understanding of Charlotte Delbo's work. An important distinction thus appears between the imagined reality of these later authors and the artistic universe of Thomas Mann, for in *The Magic Mountain* Hans Castorp enters history *after* the closing pages of the novel.[6] Fiction then surrenders to history, whose guns, to be sure, have been booming ominously from the flatlands during the final chapters, but only on the fringes of the action. Hans's imagined experience leads up to but does not include the historical event it is designed to clarify.

Camus's shrewd perception of modern history's, and particularly modern atrocity's influence on present reality makes

The Rebel an important transitional work. Once, he argues in the introduction to that volume, the crimes of history were put on trial; today they determine law. Solzhenitsyn's *One Day* and *Cancer Ward,* and Charlotte Delbo's Auschwitz trilogy, confirm this point of view; they *include* the historical events the narratives are designed to illuminate, so that insight into human psychology and expectation is inseparable from the historical forces that shape them.[7] The metaphors of mountain and plague give way to the reality of slave labor camps, Stalinist and post-Stalinist politics, and extermination in Auschwitz. Through a cruel contemporary paradox that has made atrocity an *expression* rather than a violation of history, the individual who has survived the ordeal of atrocity has been compelled to redefine his or her humanity and to understand how that ordeal has tarnished the image of the self. Camus expresses the challenge precisely:

Slave camps under the flag of freedom, massacres justified by philanthropy or by a taste for the superhuman, in one sense cripple judgment. On the day when crime dons the apparel of innocence—through a curious transposition peculiar to our times—it is innocence that is called upon to justify itself.[8]

Solzhenitsyn's fictional figures suffer the consequences of that ambiguous challenge.

Cancer Ward is *The Magic Mountain* of the post-Stalinist era. Its imaginative vision blends the physical atrocity of cancer with the physical and moral atrocity of the labor camps, fusing the two into one giant metaphor of inappropriate death in our time. The disease has spread from the lungs, as it were, to all the organs of the body, metastasizing throughout the human image and permanently disfiguring the integrity of its form. "Dying life" now becomes a standard description of existence, for patients as well as physicians, including those who gain a temporary reprieve from the ravages of the malignancy. Survival has grown more precarious. Some patients are "released" simply to die, incurable. In *The Plague,* Dr. Rieux sided with the healers, and though his treatment was rarely successful, it never accelerated the death of his patients. Cancer treatment is much more ambiguous: diagnosis is uncertain because procedures designed to arrest one fatal growth are capable of inducing others equally fatal. Man's "creatureliness" is itself his chief vulnerability.

How can men survive intact in an atmosphere where every other human being reflects the condition of "dying alive" which one is trying to avoid oneself? A sense of community depends on shared life experiences; the mind is unequal to the task of basing community on shared death experiences. The patients in the ward discuss a book that two of them are reading, Tolstoy's *What Men Live By*. In turn they offer their answer to Tolstoy's question, and though Solzhenitsyn introduces it with total seriousness, his own novel raises an equally pertinent inquiry: what men die by. His story is the substance of that inquiry. But the initial response is that men live by formulas, and as each offers his own version—men live by their rations, their pay, their professional skill, "by their ideological principles and by the interests of their society"[9] — we quickly discover how insufficient these platitudes are until men also ask themselves what they are willing to die by.

Tolstoy's answer was not a platitude—men live by love, love of others. But the value of his reply in a cancer ward, to say nothing of the repressive age Solzhenitsyn is writing about, is equivocal. Tolstoy's twin principles of love of others and non-resistance to evil summed up an era and a civilization. Their validity for his generation is uncertain enough, but the facts of history since testify to their impotence to arrest an age of atrocity. Freud recognized that versions of heroic faith would not suffice to enable men to confront the scope and intensity of violent dying ushered in by World War I. The appearance of Tolstoy's philosophy early in *Cancer Ward* is not a nostalgic petition for a resurrection of its power over the imagination, but a reminder that old forms of transcendence, however appealing, are inadequate to combat the psychological menace of inappropriate death. On the other hand, through the figure of the KGB[10] patient Rusanov, Solzhenitsyn mercilessly satirizes the Party's corruption of the original purity of Tolstoy's thought. Rusanov first thinks they are speaking of the Soviet writer Alexei Tolstoy, and when he discovers it is really "tha-a-a-t Tolstoy," quotes Lenin's selective opinion of him as the "mirror of the Russian Revolution" (p. 105). Moreover, Rusanov's belief that men live by their ideological principles and the interests of society is rhetorically close enough to Tolstoy's intention to demonstrate how language detached from experience can distort the most salutary ideals.

Nevertheless, the themes of love and death are related early in the novel, where even more than in *The Magic Mountain,* the drama of romance unfolds beneath the shadow of mortality. Conscious of life, men long for love as the supreme fulfillment of their desires, the ultimate happiness; conscious of death—*truly* conscious—they no longer think of "ultimate" fulfillment, since the vulnerability of their bodies limits their life in time. They hope for love while simultaneously recognizing on a lower level that cancer mutilates this hope—in some instances, literally, in others, by suppressing or shifting the goal of one's desires. The novel is less a repudiation than a revision of Tolstoy's point of view that men live by love: it adjusts that attitude to a world where "man dying" is a more convincing portrait of the human image than "man living." Though for Solzhenitsyn, the designation is not as important as the behavior it inspires.

While another patient in the ward reads Tolstoy's *What Men Live By,* Kostoglotov turns to a textbook on what men *die* by—*Pathological Anatomy.* For him the enemy now is the force attacking his body, and the only way to overcome fear of that enemy—of death—is to understand its "strategy." Pain for Kostoglotov is what the camps meant for some of Solzhenitsyn's zeks: direct confrontation with death. And the result, similar to the state of some of Lifton's Hiroshima survivors, is a purgation of the emotions, a moral lassitude, so that any "recovery" excludes the possibility of returning to previous normalcy:

This autumn I learned from experience that a man can cross the threshold of death even when his body is still not dead. Your blood still circulates and your stomach digests, while you yourself have gone through the whole psychological preparation for death—and lived through death itself. Everything around you, you see as if from the grave [p. 31].

This is the clearest description of "dying alive" that we have in Solzhenitsyn, matched only by Charlotte Delbo's accounts of surviving in a post-Auschwitz world. And the result is not fear or frustration, not the psychic numbing which for Lifton meant the repression of the death experience, but an ultimate indifference to everyone and everything, as if this immersion by forced consent were the key to learning how to live psychologically within one's means. It is the spiritual equilibrium that Solzhenitsyn speaks of in his chronicle of the Archipelago.

"Why stop a man from thinking?" Kostoglotov cries in exasperation when someone protests against his expostulations on death. "After all, what does our philosophy of life boil down to? 'Oh, life is so good! . . . Life, I love you. Life is for happiness!' What profound sentiments. Any animal can say as much without our help, any hen, cat, or dog" (p. 137). His disillusionment, though more intense, reminds us of the shift in Camus's thought from the Mediterranean affirmation of physical joy to the somber reflections at the end of *The Plague* that pestilence is now a permanent condition of our existence. The happiness that Rambert insisted was his birthright somehow seemed frivolous in the presence of so much dying. He discovered that his joy was to be gained at the expense of another's pain, or at least through heedlessness of that pain. Kostoglotov has moved a step beyond Camus's rebel, since he protests not only against the injustice of the death sentence but also against how that sentence has poisoned the idea of personal happiness.

As his tumor responds to radiation treatment, Kostoglotov paradoxically begins to desire that very physical love whose consummation he regards intellectually as a superficial affirmation of life. Even more clearly than Camus, Solzhenitsyn sees that love in the conventional sense prospers only by excluding others. Once men may have believed, along with Tolstoy, that their common bond was love; now they must learn that their common enemy is death. Familiar forms of human unity and fellowship like physical and spiritual love are displaced by a new form of solidarity: "What can divide human beings on earth once they are all faced with death?" (p. 144). But the philosophical inquiry of the narrative voice penetrates the minds of the characters more slowly. Though Kostoglotov is a ripe convert for this philosophy, though he assents to it already in his mind, in the presence of Zoya the nurse and medical student, his natural feelings assert themselves even at the portals of the grave. Solzhenitsyn's description of the scene leading to their first embrace is a masterful dramatization of the tension between love and death in his world of atrocity.

Near Zoya, Kostoglotov suddenly forgets his earlier contempt for those who affirm life and its happiness as if death threatened others but not themselves. But we measure his moment of intense feeling against the shrunken image of the human lying not too far away in the hospital corridor: "That pitiful, yellow-looking patient with the pinched nose who was being eaten away with cancer of the lungs sat in bed, panting as he breathed through his balloon—you could hear the wheezing in his chest. Had he always been as small as that, or was it the disease that had shriveled him?" (p. 238). He is a spectral commentary on the romantic *Liebestod*, a reminder that love does not transcend death, but thrives by ignoring it. Made breathless by their kissing, Zoya and Kostoglotov forget the balloon they are filling with air for this patient until it nearly bursts; they shut off the cylinder just in time. Then they return to the patient, unconscious of how fragile that symbol is which separates them from (and joins them to) love as well as death: "They walked up the stairs, holding not hands but the balloon. . . . It was as if they were holding hands" (p. 242).

The complex affiliation of love to death is even more profoundly suggested when Zoya, prompted by the thought that Kostoglotov may one day be the father of her child, discloses the real nature of his injections—hormone therapy. Research has shown, she informs him, that injecting patients with hormones of the opposite sex sometimes stops the spread of secondary tumors. Thus the hope for "total" cure threatens to alter the very identity of the individual. Kostoglotov must now face the crucial question whether life is worthwhile *at any price*. The hormones, Zoya explains, first suppress potency, then libido; the result may be a man alive, but within the limits of a "possible" that he cannot accept. For a time, he submits to the hormone therapy, partly because he has not yet worked out a satisfactory attitude for the danger of living without it, partly because his feeling of well-being begins to deteriorate as the radiation treatment intensifies. It induces a state of constant physical nausea. He suffers from the dilemma of a man who knows that the threat of death diminishes "in perpetuity" the possibilities of the life force, but is not yet prepared to abandon that force, which men of previous generations have lived by: "If only he could somehow see the treatment through, escape the clutches of radiotherapy and hormone therapy, and avoid ending up as a cripple. If only he could somehow preserve his libido and all it meant. Without that. . ." (p. 272). It is the atmosphere of tragedy, but transformed by modern conditions that compel men to focus on their "creatureliness" rather than their moral destiny. The very terminology defines the new status of the individual in the age of Auschwitz, Hiroshima, and the Gulag Archipelago, all three of which we identify with assaults on the body and the terror of *physical* mutilation or extinction. Suddenly the survival of the imagination, the insight which ennobled Hamlet and Oedipus, seems less important.

In a lecture on the future of tragedy delivered in Athens in 1955, Albert Camus speculated on the possibility of a renaissance in tragic thought and literature in our own day, "when the most monstrous wars have inspired not a single tragic poet." The tragic figure thrives, he argues, when men cease to expect everything from life, but recognize that the adventurous spirit in quest of an absolute—love, power, immortality, world dominion, for example—unbalances the proportions that define the human image. Specifically, the twentieth-century mind has been committed to the absolute of history, a process whereby civilization unfolds endlessly into a "better" future. Our only reason for hope, Camus ventures, "is that individualism is visibly changing today and that beneath the pressures of history, little by little the individual is recognizing his limits." Reason and science, handmaidens of modern history, have promised a happy world, but have produced a monstrous one. "In a curious paradox," he declares, "humanity has refashioned a hostile destiny with the very weapons it used to reject fatality." That hostile destiny is inappropriate death, atrocity, versions of history which mutilate the human image, whatever else they may *promise* to do. They create the *climate* of tragedy, Camus suggests, though the actual tragic spirit awaits the formulation of a human point of view commensurate with it:

Today, man proclaims his revolt, knowing this revolt has limits, demands liberty though he is subject to necessity; this contradictory man, torn, conscious henceforth of human and historical ambiguity, is the tragic man. Perhaps he is striding toward the formulation of his own tragedy, which will be reached on the day when *All is well*.[11]

Although this sounds like a retreat from the affirmative ending of *The Myth of Sisyphus*, it is really an advance through the monstrousness of history and atrocity to a more tentative idea of human possibility. "Dignity" means accepting limitations without hope of transcending them. Unlike Hamlet, Kostoglotov has no Horatio to purify his wounded name; but even if he had, he would anticipate the futility of such an endeavor. Nor can he go forth like Oedipus to regain through suffering the favor of the gods. Ancient and Renaissance tragedy may have ended with a chastened but intact image of human pride; any renewal of the tragic spirit must begin with an image of man humiliated. Where it ends will depend on the consensus we reach about the visibly changing individualism of which Camus spoke—and all the authors we have been discussing wrestle with this—an individualism that finally abandons adages like "Know thyself" and "Trust thyself" and finds aphorisms compatible with an age of atrocity. Torn between the two worlds, Kostoglotov clings to an old vitality as he searches for a way of accepting the humiliation that threatens his manhood. The crippled body he fears is the price man pays for atrocity, a compromise between deception and annihilation. He has no illusions about the consequences of such a compromise: "First my own life was taken from me, and now I am being deprived even of the right ... to perpetuate myself. I'll be the worst sort of cripple! What use will I be to anyone?" (p. 333). He resembles Camus's individual formulating the terms of his own tragedy, proclaiming his revolt, knowing its limits, demanding liberty though subject to necessity: "This contradictory man, torn, conscious henceforth of human and historical ambiguity, is the tragic man."

Resemblance is not identity, however, since Kostoglotov wavers between the boundaries of revolt and acquiescence, depending on science even as he scorns the uncertainty of its decisions. He submits to a blood transfusion although he questions every step of the procedure, resenting the situation that defines his self through his body and eliminates informed choice as a condition for survival. The administering physician is the same Vera Gangart who earlier reflected on the dangers of radiation therapy. She is an agent of Kostoglotov's physical survival, though his feelings for her as a woman are even deeper than those that Zoya excites in him. Once again man and woman face each other in the dual roles of patient and healer and potential lovers, but the circumstances confound the two. Love requires mutual trust; dying cannot bind two individuals in the same way. During the transfusion, scientific and erotic images fuse but do not resolve the relationship: "Her fingers stroked the rubber tube that hung down from the instrument to the needle. It was as if they were helping to remove all obstructions in the tube" (p. 332). But medical process is confined by the anatomy of death, while human intimacy throbs with the anatomy of love. The blood transfusion betrays the inability of metaphor to unite the two.

An even clearer instance of love's limits in this universe of "dying alive" is the continuing relationship between sixteen-year-old Dyomka and seventeen-year-old Asya, whose illness has been diagnosed as a malignancy of the breast. Their intimacy represents what we might call an amputated eroticism,

a grotesque image which has literal references far more concrete than the metaphorical frustrations of a Captain Ahab.
Dyomka's leg, failing to respond to radiation treatment, has
already been cut off; and Asya has just been told that her
breast must suffer the same fate. The scene between them
when she imparts this information to Dyomka transforms
them into a Romeo and Juliet of the cancer ward; it is a
painfully moving encounter defining the limits of romance
in an atmosphere of atrocity. Shakespeare's lovers enjoy the
rapture of emotional expectation and the bliss of fulfillment
before chance, time, and the enmity of their parents combine
to insure the error of their untimely death. Their stars may
be crossed, but dying does not corrupt the purity of their
love while it endures, and the dignity of their images remains
intact beyond the grave. They enter into legend.

But when Asya visits Dyomka with her melancholy news,
she has already lost the exuberant sexuality which overwhelmed him at their first meeting: "She had sagged and
faded. Even her yellow hair, which couldn't change as quickly
as the rest of her, hung down pitifully now" (pp. 391-92).
Her grief as she sobs out the information about her impending
operation confirms one of the themes of Solzhenitsyn's
novel: the difficulty of creating a sense of community from
the shared experience of death or mutilation. Tolstoy had
answered the question of what men live by with the spiritual
certainty that they lived by love for each other. But in
Solzhenitsyn's imaginative world, death has numbed the
impact of that response. Even though Asya's shallow values
(as she complains that no boy will ever want a girl with one
breast) are a major source of her grief, Dyomka with his more
solid devotion to ideas can offer her no consolation. The absence of any prior shared notion of how death humiliates the
body excludes her anguish from the aura of common human
tragedy. Even if he could have argued that life was still
worthwhile, thinks Dyomka, "Asya's groan was enough to
tell him that neither he, nor anyone, nor anything at all would
be able to convince her. Her own experience led to only one
conclusion: there was nothing to live for now" (p. 393).

This may not be a final position, but it is a necessary preliminary one—death destroys the prospects for an unlimited future. Survival requires not only revolt, but a revolt that recognizes human limits. If the imagination is to move beyond atrocity to a renewed sense of tragedy, it must devise a dramatic gesture for the humiliation that the human image suffers as a result of atrocity. Asya intuitively discovers one form for this gesture when she loosens her dressing gown "to reveal her doomed right breast" and with passionate desperation urges Dyomka to be the last one to see and kiss it. The scene trembles on the edge of bathos, but assumes a ritual intensity as the breast becomes a talisman of the glory the human creature surrenders when acknowledging the disfiguration imposed by atrocity: "It shone as though the sun had stepped straight into the room. The whole ward seemed on fire. The nipple glowed. It was larger than he had ever imagined. It stood before him. His eye could not resist its sunny rosiness" (pp. 394-95). One is perhaps reminded of the closing episode of Steinbeck's *The Grapes of Wrath,* where a young girl suckles a starving old man in a gesture of human compassion that transcends her grief at the loss of her own child. No such transcendence is possible here. Dyomka bids farewell to a dying splendor, to the perfection of form, to a classical grace which once invested the human body with loveliness even in the midst of despair: "Nothing more beautiful than this gentle curve could ever be painted or sculptured. Its beauty flooded him" (p. 395). But his embrace is not an affirmation. It ushers in the mutilated universe that he and Asya will have to inhabit, where "dying alive" has supplanted "living immortal" as the necessary condition of existence. "Today it was a marvel," Solzhenitsyn drily concludes this prophetic chapter. "Tomorrow it would be in the trash bin" (p. 395).

Romantic love flourishes in celebration of the body. We do not know how Dyomka and Asya will fare, since we never see them together again in the novel, but this scene is enough to convince us that for Solzhenitsyn romantic love is no longer a sufficient hope for men to live by. We are on treacherous ground here, since ordinary reality continues to affirm what Solzhenitsyn appears to question imaginatively—but some such thread clearly twines itself through *Cancer Ward* and the other literature we have been examining. It is probably too soon to discern trends in contemporary literary vision. Nevertheless, the parody of courtship and reverence for the body with which Mann suffuses Hans Castorp's admiration for Clavdia Chauchat is replaced by a sterner commitment to human solidarity in Camus's plague-ridden society, where both Rambert and Dr. Rieux must surrender personal love to fight impersonal death. And imprisonment and exile in Solzhenitsyn have made suspicion and mistrust so "normal" that they poison the climate where love once flourished. On a literal level, the physiological prowess from which romance prospers has been diminished by a widespread malignancy. On the psychological level, society is so sown with discord by an ideology that threatens identity, manhood, family, and the values that support them, and so disheartened by a past that has injected fear into the national bloodstream, that men and women seem to lack energy for the sustained emotional intensity that romantic love requires. This heart-weariness also permeates the pages of Charlotte Delbo's post-Auschwitz world, where memories of wanton executions have tainted love and darkened the future of feeling with a paralyzing sadness. Such memories drive some individuals to seek refuge from the rapture that once tempted the heart with so much promise.

Solzhenitsyn confronts this theme more explicitly than Mann or Camus. On the night before his discharge from the hospital, Kostoglotov has a quiet conversation with a worn but efficient woman orderly, who reads French literature after her work is done. They instinctively recognize each other as exiles, victims of an ideology that interrupted the continuity of their lives and destroyed all opportunity for restoring the rhythm. The woman's daughter had died in exile, her husband had been rearrested after the war and has disappeared in one of the labor camps. She is left with a small son and no information whether his father is still alive. "How ought I to bring him up?" she asks. "Should I burden him with the whole truth? The truth's enough to sink a grown man, isn't it? It's enough to break your ribs. Or should I hide the truth and bring him to terms with life?" (p. 478). Although the childless Kostoglotov insists that she should burden him with the truth, she recognizes that belief in such valor may have more support from literature than from life. Heroic defiance, growing into tragic insight, needs a vision of moral order to nourish it, and this is precisely what the universe of atrocity, which has spawned both Kostoglotov and this woman, lacks.

"These literary tragedies are just laughable compared with the ones we live through," she protests. "Aïda was allowed to join her loved one in the tomb and to die with him. But we aren't even allowed to know what's happening to them" (p. 479). Art can no longer transfigure a love that life so brutally discards, leaving the imagination nothing with which to feed its hope. Her ragged and brittle existence has no context, nothing but eternal sadness, bitterness, and regret rather than expectation. Narratives of love's tragedy cannot illuminate the despair of victims of atrocity. "Children write essays in school," she complains, "about the unhappy, tragic, doomed, and I-don't-know-what-else life of Anna Karenina. But was Anna really unhappy? She chose passion and she paid for her passion—that's happiness! She was a free, proud human being" (p. 479). In fact, Anna was humiliated by her society and, in the end, by her irrational and uncontrollable jealousy, but she *is* the agent of her love and her death, which distinguishes her from the helpless, innocent speaker, who one day was ordered to leave her home with her family within twenty-four hours, "with only what your feeble hands can carry" (p. 479). Just as the spiritual conviction that informed Tolstoy's inquiry into what men live by lacked resonance in the debased atmosphere of the cancer ward, where extraordinary physical suffering silenced the longings of the soul, so his vision of tragedy appears irrelevant to a woman whose humiliation has no parallel in the history of literature. "So why should I read *Anna Karenina* again?" she asks. "Maybe it's enough—what I've experienced. Where can people read about us? *Us?* Only in a hundred years' time" (p. 479).

Confronting this woman without a future, Kostoglotov is vividly concious of how past humiliation has corrupted their image of themselves: "They were like insects pinned inside separate compartments, each in its own set place" (p. 481). The insect who would survive must take care not to be caught; once he is fixed as a specimen in someone else's "collection" his memories of the free life are as futile for renewing existence as the dim recollections of Beckett's Krapp or Kafka's caged hunger artist. The consequences of atrocity cannot be undone, nor can the "lessons" learned from it be transmitted as a ritual of rebirth to surviving generations. Its world lacks tragic energy because the contempt for the human which permeates it has combined with the pervasive fear of death to drown the protest of the individual will.

History perpetually requires of us redefinitions of the "worst" and the "best"; only those who accept this challenge, Solzhenitsyn suggests, stand a chance of living with a superiority to life. Kostoglotov has left behind him in his place of exile an old couple called the Kadmins, who like him have survived the wolfish existence of the camps and endure their perpetual exile, though innocent, with the understanding that only "the kinship of heart to heart and the way we look at the world" (p. 266) make for happiness. During the camp experience, as we have seen, such attitudes have limited value for individuals who are under constant threat of death. But Solzhenitsyn is equally concerned with what men live and die by *after* the crisis, when they have more power to control their point of view. Living in a mud-hut hovel, devoted to each other and to their dogs and cats, the old couple are like pioneers, though without any ambition to build a new life in a new world or create a "better" future for themselves and their descendants. They simply want to die together. They are optimists in Kostoglotov's redefined sense of the word, people who say "It's worse everywhere else. We're better off here than the rest of the world. We've been lucky" (p. 272). If their limited shared happiness is circumscribed by a larger shared loneliness, that loneliness is a heritage from the camp experience, a necessary consequence of a life where mutual mistrust corrupted some of the spirit that for Tolstoy and Dostoevsky once inspired mutual affection. The threads that linked Alyosha Karamazov to the entire universe have not been cut, but they have been drawn in so that they no longer reach out to all the stones of the earth and the distant stars. The love that would embrace the whole world had not discredited a legacy of hate; the Kadmins in exile simply practice a less ambitious charity.

In their tranquility they have passed beyond the yearning that still afflicts Kostoglotov's ailing body. Their peace is a stable center against which he can measure his own restlessness and uncertainty, so that a main momentum in the second half of *Cancer Ward* is his indecision whether to stay with Vera or rejoin them immediately in exile. Part Two of the novel begins with a letter from Kostoglotov to the Kadmins, in which he sums up his dilemma and examines the options open to him. "After all, I am not asking for a long life," he writes. "Why should I want to peer deep into the future? First I lived under guard, then I lived in pain, and now I want to live just a little while without guards and without pain, simultaneously without one or the other. This is the limit of my ambition" (pp. 294-95). At this point the distant steppes and the river Chu that runs through it crowd his imagination, though with an image of nature that bears no resemblance to the hope for renewal and creative expression that Pasternak celebrates in *Doctor Zhivago:* "Our Chu reaches no sea, no lake, no expanse of water at all. It is a river that ends life in the sands, a river flowing nowhere, shedding the best of its water and strength haphazardly along its path" (p. 295). It is an image of life without a goal, a life which exhausts its meaning as it flows to death but seems all the more precious because it enters no reservoir of transcendence.

For this reason, preserving the vitality of a body that exhausts its vigor in its struggle to survive is of supreme importance for Kostoglotov, as it was for Shukhov and all the real inhabitants of the Gulag Archipelago. But that struggle has its limits, and in the absence of spiritual consolations the individual is thrust back upon himself to decide how much he is willing to pay for the world beyond atrocity. As Kostoglotov writes the Kadmins, "The camps have helped many of us to establish that the betrayal or destruction of good and helpless people is too high a price, that our lives aren't worth it" (p. 295). Atrocity has permanently deflated the value of single lives, and Kostoglotov seeks no program for restoring that value—a vain enterprise at this point in time—but an attitude for living with the fact. Although with Vera's support he might grow accustomed to an existence which ignores the springs of his masculinity, when alone he is not satisfied with such a solution. He cannot easily accede to a treatment which resists death by destroying his capacity to love. "Can one accept a life of digestion, respiration, muscular and brain activity—and nothing more?" he asks. "Seven years in the army and seven years in the camp, twice seven years, twice that mythical or biblical term, and then to be deprived of the ability to tell what is a man and what is a woman—is not such a price extortionate?" (p. 296). In a sense, to pay would be to kneel before history, since both the army and the camps exacted just such a price of the individual, and if in freedom he perpetuates such servitude, he has not escaped their hermetic embrace. But to refuse outright would be to lose that medical certificate which keeps the authorities from sending him into more distant exile, away from his friends and too far from civilization, should he once more require emergency treatment.

With his dilemma unresolved, deploring the cunning and compromise he must resort to (he has persuaded Zoya to stop giving him hormone injections, but takes them from Vera), Kostoglotov agrees to accept three month's prescriptions for the hormone and take it himself if the hospital will temporarily discharge him. Vera, who lives alone, offers him a bed in her apartment until he decides to leave the town, and with this invitation to a "new life" before him, he enters the crucial day of his existence, when he must face the image he wishes to live by and determine the boundaries of the human still available to him. His sudden emergence from the atmosphere of death—in a chapter called "The First Day of Creation . . ."—tempts him with prospects of a rebirth, and in a traditional novel of education Kostoglotov would confront life strengthened by his long contact with death. But such growth in a fictional hero assumes continuity between the reality behind him and the reality he now encounters, and though Kostoglotov at first anticipates just such a continuity, he gradually discovers that the two worlds are separated and that there are no universal laws by which men in this society can live.

His first impulse is to search through the Old Town for a flowering apricot tree, whose delicate blossoms are to him harbingers of the joy he expects from his liberation. Leaving the hospital is like leaving prison, he thinks, and hopes to savor each experience of the day with an unhurried appreciation of its appeal to his senses. Beyond the cancer ward, he temporarily loses his affinity with death and succumbs to the illusion that he can leave its somber atmosphere behind him. The rhythm of his day gradually discloses the folly of this hope. He stops first in a tea house but, in his pursuit of the exotic, orders a green tea that turns out to be insipid and full of leaves. There are no women there, only men in skullcaps, which makes Kostoglotov wonder whether their gathering together meant to demonstrate "that the most important part of life does not concern women" (p. 488). It is a curious thought, but prepares him for his final decision later in the day to leave at once. Both Hans Castorp and Camus's protagonists linger on the brink of that melancholy view, without reaching such an explicit conclusion. In an age of unlimited possibility, the choice between love and "the most important part of life" did not seem urgent or even necessary. Kostoglotov's condition is symptomatic of a critical period when survival seems to support the cogency of such a choice.

But Kostoglotov moves obscurely toward this insight, which is always clearer to us than to him. One might imagine, we are told, that he "had sweated out the torment of his illness and had died in January, and that some new Kostoglotov, tottering on two uncertain legs, had emerged from the clinic" (pp. 488-89). And this is how he thinks of himself, as he finds a solitary apricot tree and admires its pink and white magnificence. He enjoys a skewer of shashlik, for which he pays more than he can afford, drinks a glass of wine, which like the tea has a disappointing taste, and both strengthen the delusion which is beginning to seize him: "Life seemed even better, even though it had been good to him ever since morning. . . . For he had already experienced and left behind all the bad things of life, as many as there are, and he was left with the better part" (p. 496). The heady delirium of being among "free" people, ostensibly untainted by death, diverts his attention from the humiliation of the body that he bears within him.

But not for long. He joins a crowd before a department store, lets himself be swept upstairs wondering what the turmoil is for—and finds himself in a line for women's cardigans and sweaters! The frivolity of his compatriots' eagerness, the frantic movement for nothing significant stirs his curiosity, but he is abruptly brought back to reality by the innocent request of ⌐ well-dressed, clean-shaven man for a shirt with collar size 16. Kostoglotov discovers that they inhabit different worlds·

What was this? There were men rotting in trenches, men being thrown into mass graves, into shallow pits in the perma frost, men being taken into camps for the first, second and third times, men being jolted from station to station in prison trucks, wearing themselves out with picks, slaving away to be able to buy a patched-up quilt jacket—and here was this neat little man who could remember the size not only of his shirt but of his collar too! [p. 498].

The outburst may sound a trifle melodramatic, but it defines the difference between points of view which absorb and ignore the vision of atrocity. All men pay a price for surviving, though the currency may vary: if the cost of his manhood is too high, the cost of returning to society on *its* terms is even higher. Why go back to this sort of life? Kostoglotov finally asks himself. "If you remember your collar size, doesn't it mean you're bound to forget something else, something more important?" (p. 499).

Finally he recognizes that his experience has transformed his image of the human while simultaneously transforming him. He gazes at himself in a huge mirror and an exhausted, stooped, and neglected figure stares back. His physical self dispels all the dreams of the morning, as he feels more and more alienated by the jostling swarms of people who appear indifferent to his past or future fate. He feels soiled by his contact with them, immune as they are to their mortality, and to his. "He wanted to lie down somewhere in the shade by a stream, just lie there and purify himself" (p. 502). One is reminded of his river Chu in the steppes, flowing nowhere, just into the sands, and it begins to seem inevitable that life will be possible for him only there. Survival here is too expensive, as he learns literally and metaphorically when he tries to fill one of his prescriptions at a pharmacist's, only to find that the cost is ridiculously beyond his means. He cannot pay the price others ask of him, even if he would. In desperation, depressed, searching for a way to restore his spiritual equilibrium, he heads for the zoo, where the alternatives open to him are ironically reflected by the images and behavior of the beasts.

The allegory that greets him at the entrance to the zoo is clear: a spiral-horned goat stands with motionless dignity on the edge of a towering rock, while nearby a squirrel on a wheel in a cage frantically rushes around, but always remains in the same spot. They represent, as we are perhaps too explicitly reminded, "two equally possible modes of existence" (p. 504), though we are left to interpret the difference between adding to one's humiliation in captivity by the furious quest of a dubious advantage, and the stolid courage which confronts reality with a firm stance at the edge of a precipice. The squirrel and the goat are two extremes of a continuum which joins all the animals in a single bond: "deprived of their home surroundings, they had lost the idea of rational freedom" (p. 505). Liberating them now would only make things harder, since once lost, such freedom could never be regained. The analogy with Kostoglotov, as with all those literal and psychological heirs of atrocity that we have encountered, is quickly established, though Solzhenitsyn disarmingly attributes it to his "twisted" mind: "Whatever he experienced from now on, there would always be this shadow, this gray specter, this subterranean rumbling from the past" (p. 505). The carnivorous beasts remind him of how history has preyed on his generation, eviscerating their humanity even as it consumed their bodies—and at this moment the final confrontation occurs between an inappropriate death that has corrupted the past and a love, however physically restrained, that promises some redemption for the future. Kostoglotov spots a graceful antelope whose trustful eyes resemble Vera's, and he resolves to accept her invitation to stay with her.

So "The First Day of Creation," the penultimate chapter of the novel, despite some disenchantment, ends with a promise of joy that belies the title of the final chapter: ". . . and the Last Day." With the fearful delight of a young lover on his way to meet his beloved, Kostoglotov goes straight to Vera's house, armed with two bunches of violets. But she is not at home. In his confusion at this unexpected disappointment, he is trapped between two images, both of which seem to mock the inadequacy of his masculine identity. Out of Vera's communal apartment comes "a great loutish, snout-faced young man with a flat, bashed-in nose" (p. 512), pushing a bright red motorcycle. During the entire scene, as Kostoglotov stands before the apartment wondering what to do, the harsh spluttering of the machine bursts on his thoughts, tearing him to shreds with its repeated efforts to ignite its latent energy into the smooth rhythm of motion. On an unconscious level it assaults his imagination in the same way that the other image discourages him through its more explicit references.

Hanging on a railing are some pillows, mattresses, and blankets that transform Vera's apartment into a bastion to be stormed, and they fill him with an overwhelming sense of his alienation from the life that draws him to Vera. "A prisoner sleeps on naked planks since he has no choice," he thinks, "and the woman prisoner, too, separated from him by force. But when a man and a woman have arranged to be together, the pillows' soft faces wait confidently for what is their due" (p. 514). His physical condition combines with his ordeal in the camps to make "normal love" an unassailable fortress. Wearied and disillusioned by the brittle energy of the motor-cycle and the erotic reminders of the bedding, he retreats in defeat, conscious of his sore feet and "how utterly physically exhausted he was, and that still unbeaten tumor rolling around inside him. All he wanted was to get away as quickly as possible" (p. 516). He has lost his conviction that mutual affection may be interpreted in uncommon ways too.

During his last hours in the town, during the closing pages of the novel, Kostoglotov's mood continues to waver, as Solzhenitsyn considers the consequences of his options rather than the single best path to follow. The foundations of his life shift so quickly that Kostoglotov can find no stable plat-form to stand upon. From Vera's he goes to the local security police, permanent arbiters of his fate, to validate his travel certificate. There he hears from a surprisingly polite officer that such registrations will soon no longer be necessary, and that political exiles will probably be released to live where they please. Once more Kostoglotov's point of view changes, as the prospect of living in freedom with Vera suddenly silences all the other objections he had just fled. He promptly takes the first trolley back to Vera's, affirming what he had earlier rejected: "Why shouldn't they try to rise above the common level? Why shouldn't they aim higher? Weren't they human beings after all? At least, [Vera] was" (p. 520).

The unintended irony of his last observation confirms the difficulty for the survivor of establishing a coherent image of the human beyond humiliation. Kostoglotov's immediate fate is settled (as was Doctor Zhivago's, curiously enough) by an episode on the trolley that reminds him what he has sacrificed to stay alive. Pressed against a young blond girl by the crowding passengers, he understands through his sensations that the hormone treatments have already begun to take effect, leaving him in the grip of a libido unaccompanied by any other power: "It was a happiness, and it was a sorrow. There was in the sensation a threshold he could not cross whatever his powers of self-suggestion" (p. 521). That threshold divides more than desire and consummation; it separates two worlds, the physical and symbolic self, solitary man from that transcendence which makes his death endurable. Such transcendence is a forsaken glory, Kostoglotov now realizes, and his dream of finding an ethereal equivalent to it is bound to lead to torture and deceit. His is simply a victim of his "creatureliness":

They had come to a high-minded agreement that spiritual communion was more valuable than anything else; yet, having built this tall bridge by hand together, he saw now that his own hands were weakening. He was on his way to her to persuade her boldly of one thing while thinking agonizingly of something else [p. 522].

In this instance, at any rate, man is doomed to live psychologically beyond his means. If he cannot eliminate the frustration of such a fate, he can at least ease it by refusing to live physically beyond his means too. He decides to return to his exile.

Kostoglotov's sole dignity is that he understands what his past has done to him, how atrocity has maimed his soul and mutilated his body. Conscious of human and historical ambiguity in a way that the heroic tragic figures of the past were not—few of them suffered similar humiliations, and most emerged with their moral stature intact—he resembles Camus's individual who has recognized his limits while striding toward the formulation of his own tragedy. Unlike him, however, he will never be able to proclaim that *all* is well, because part of what afflicts him is beyond his power to redeem. His happiness is that he has survived, that he has not died from cancer, that even his exile may be cracking like an egg shell. But his sorrow is that others did not survive, from "out there" and from the cancer ward: inappropriate death has effaced these victims, and there is no tribute appropriate to mourn their annihilation or to restore their memory with dignity to the human community. This knowledge forms a vacuum in his consciousness as he lies stretched out on the luggage rack in the crowded train that will bring him back (with a possibly doomed body) to where he came from. But it does not fill him with joy, or even tranquility: "in his heart, or his soul, somewhere in his chest, in the deepest seat of his emotion, he was seized with anguish" (p. 532). Its sources are complex, for he mourns not only the fate of his own body, but what it reflects: a part of him has been killed by the historical terror he has survived. With the atrocity of the Gulag Archipelago as his heritage, how can man ever again assert that "all is well"? The last image in *Cancer Ward* is of Kostoglotov's boots dangling "toes down over the corridor like a dead man's" (p. 532). The mystery of dying for nothing, of those who cause it and those who suffer it, remains the melancholy riddle of the modern era.

L'histoire
c'est fini
soyez heureux comme tout le monde.—Delbo

CHARLOTTE DELBO AND A HEART OF ASHES

Solzhenitsyn divides his creative energies between history and literature, reconstructing with painstaking detail the elaborate bureaucracy of atrocity in his time and using its reality, where appropriate, in his fiction. Charlotte Delbo makes atrocity the substance as well as the subject of her art. Auschwitz and the other camps provide her with a setting; their inmates are her characters; their experience and her own furnish the events of the narrative; and their common fate, its denouement, though survival in this case means for some an endless return to the images of fear and humiliation with which the narrative began. Recurrence vies with chronology to rule the temporal patterns of her story, forcing the reader, as Mann's narrator had done in *The Magic Mountain,* to recognize (though with a different emphasis) how past atrocity presses on the consciousness of the present and burdens its content. Since Delbo herself is a survivor of Auschwitz, she works with a reality reimagined rather than imagined, creating a disturbing and original alliance between memory and invention, history and art.

Her own contact with death was literal; her account of it offers one of the most lucid images we have of what it means to be a "survivor" in an age of atrocity. One way of measuring the distance we have traveled in fifty years is to recall Behrens's consolation to Hans Castorp as his cousin Joachim lay dying:

"But about death—no one who came back from it could tell you anything, because we don't realize it. We come out of the dark and go into the dark again, and in between lie the experiences of our life. But the beginning and the end, birth and death, we do not experience; they have no subjective character, they fall entirely in the category of objective events, and that's that."[1]

The "subjective character" of death is precisely what atrocity has intensified for the modern mind, and the authors we have been examining share the concern with a common question: what to do with its presence? During the war Camus jotted down in his notebook, in response to a novel he was reading, a characteristically paradoxical observation: "Only death is true knowledge. But at the same time it is what makes knowledge useless: its progress is sterile."[2] The title of the second volume in Delbo's Auschwitz trilogy, *Une Connaissance inutile (A Useless Knowledge)*, offers a gloss on Camus's remark, probably more melancholy than he intended. Charlotte Delbo explores the vexing problem of whether insight into the nature of atrocity ultimately *does* reach a point of sterility, beyond which the imagination can hope for no further renaissance of the human image. A line from her first volume, *None of Us Will Return*, defines the limits of this problem: "They expect the worst—they do not expect the unthinkable."[3]

The "they" include not only new arrivals at Auschwitz, but all those who seek meaning in the human condition despite the gloomy poignance of her narrative. She adopts a pseudo-Lockean strategy by virtually ignoring all prior conceptualizations of reality and leading the reader into a world of sense experience, where pain and physical deprivation accumulate until we begin to identify with the response of one of her characters: "I can't take it any more. Today I just can't take it any more" (p. 117). The later volumes gradually add layers of reflection to this portrait of life as painful physical sensation, but nothing ever displaces its quintessential distillation of the nature of atrocity. Such knowledge gained through the senses devours itself, remains hermetically sealed in a private universe of torture and suffering that cannot escape into the realm of ideas. Delbo exposes the insufficiency of Freud's aphorism that to endure life one must be prepared for death, by modifying it in a way that Freud could not have anticipated: having survived death, how is one to return to life?

Before one can speak of a renaissance of the human image, one must crystallize its disfigured form, and the horror which has defaced it. Unfortunately, the process of crystallization perpetually reminds both reader and artist of what man has been reduced to by atrocity, and complicates the attempt to rehabilitate an image of human dignity. Delbo's narrator acknowledges with bitter irony the futile but necessary compulsion that drives her to transform the "unthinkable" into the thinkable, when she realizes that her attempt to reproduce the horror of the experience is slipping into the form of "mere" narrative:

A skeleton of a woman. She is naked. One can see her ribs and hip bones. She pulls the blanket up on her shoulders and continues to dance. A mechanical dance. A dancing skeleton of a woman. Her feet are small, thin and bare in the snow. They are living, dancing skeletons.
And now I am sitting in a café writing this story—for this is turning into a story [p. 31].

The poetic style freezes the horror instead of transfiguring it, riveting the reader's gaze but offering no sanctuary for the awe and revulsion that such images evoke. As Delbo subtracts epithets in an effort to reach the physical essence of suffering, she interrupts the very momentum of art, by moving from expression to silence. Her language approaches the status of music with its lyric repetitions and incantations, though she seeks visual images equivalent to the rhythmic phrases of sound.

Certain distinctions are necessary to understand her vision, some of which we have encountered before. In the later volumes, she speaks of *"là-bas"* ("over there," the camp) and *"ici"* ("here," postcamp reality) much as Hans Castorp referred to "up here" and "down there" after he had grown accustomed to the Berghof. Delbo also distinguishes between those who know and those who "think they know," emphasizing the imaginative distance that the experience of atrocity cleaves between literal and indirect survivors. Entry into her universe requires nothing less than a redefinition of frontiers, and in some instances their dismissal, leaving the individual wandering uneasily in alien terrain. A portion from one of the lyrics interspersed through *None of Us Will Return* captures the essence of this challenge:

O you who know
did you know that one can see one's mother dead
   and not cry
O you who know
did you know that in the morning one wants to die
   that in the evening one is afraid
O you who know
did you know that one day is more than a year
   one minute more than a lifetime. . . .   [p. 14]

This kind of "knowledge" is comparable to Camus's unsettling discovery in World War II that one can torture even while looking at one's victim. In a bizarre way, Delbo's works celebrate that victim, confront the imagination with the ordeal of dying, remind one that a dancing skeleton freezing to death was once a living woman—but without the consolations of heroism. The living woman fades from memory as with pitiless inadequacy the human body fights its dreadful battle for survival.

The human body is the protagonist of *None of Us Will Return*, its limbs and organs struggling against impossible odds to retain their traditional functions. When survival is reduced to such an elementary level, the courage and intelligence which Camus honored as leading human virtues appear as luxuries. A gesture suffices to define a life—and a death. From the window of their barracks, the narrator and her friends see a pile of corpses dumped naked in the nearby snow. Suddenly one of the living sees the hand of one of the "corpses" move—she is still alive: "The fingers open slowly, the snow blossoms into a discolored sea anemone" (p. 23). But atrocity desensitizes compassion, eliminates the once clear border between life and death, makes the longing to die seem more of a virtue at times than the will to live. The narrator looks numbly at the spreading fingers and feels void of response: "I watch this corpse that moves and to which I am insensitive" (p. 23). Accustomed to wholeness, how is one to acknowledge a hand as the last vestige of a human being? Delbo substitutes parts of the body for the integrated self, merging them with nature until both image and idea of the human are threatened with extinction.

The pattern is repeated throughout *None of Us Will Return,* as Becker's conception of "creatureliness" is transformed into separate corporeal fragments that sometimes seem to have little relationship to each other. One day the women watch another prisoner straining to climb a slope down which she had slid to get some clean snow to wash her swollen lips. Her body is too weak to regain the road. The uncoordinated efforts of her limbs are like an agonizing ballet in slow motion, her fate the ultimate degradation of the human image under conditions of atrocity:

Her whole body was tensed, her jaws were tensed, her neck with its wrenched cartilage was tensed, all that remained of muscle on her bones was tensed. . . .

Now her hands clutched a crust of hardened snow, her feet without support sought a rough spot, a toehold. They kicked in thin air. Her legs were wrapped in rags. . . .

And her hand writhed toward us in a desperate appeal. Her hand falls back—a faded mauve star on the snow. Once fallen, it lost its wasted look, it softened, became once again something living and pitiable. The elbow props itself up, slips. The whole body slumps. . . .

We stood motionless. The will to struggle and resist, life, had taken refuge in a reduced part of the body, just the immediate vicinity of the heart. . . .

All the effort for a handful of snow which in her mouth is a handful of salt. Her hand drops, her neck bends. A fragile stalk that must break [pp. 28, 29, 31].

What inner image of human dignity can link the physical with the symbolic self in such an instance? Here "living" is merely physical exertion, while dying is the literal defeat of the body. Charlotte Delbo has captured that moment of atrocity when the victim has neither time nor space for transcendent longings, while the situation forbids even the minimum consolation which makes dying part of someone else's life. When the SS guard finally orders his dog to attack the woman, the witnesses stand paralyzed by dread, their own bodies numbed by a spectacle that mirrors the inhumanity of their condition: "The dog pounces on the woman, sinks its teeth into her throat. And we do not move, stuck in a viscous substance that prevents us from making even a gesture—as in a dream" (p. 33).

As I have tried to suggest, one of the qualities of the experience of atrocity is its hermetic nature; it is sealed in the moment of its occurrence, resisting efforts to establish it as part of continuous time. Survivors still recall the instant of flash in a blue sky that made Hiroshima a locus of atrocity, and record their difficulty returning to a "normal" world after their encounter with this unique form of death. Charlotte Delbo draws on the resources of her art to dramatize that problem for her contemporaries. Or rather, since the "drama of Auschwitz" suggests a sequence that is inconsistent with the episodic vignettes of her narrative, she uses language to petrify events and prevent their escape into the fluidity of time. Image first supports and then *becomes* idea. Describing the columns of women departing each morning for forced labor, the narrator says: "We advance. So numb that we seem to be only a chunk of cold that advances in one piece. Our legs move on as if they were not a part of us" (p. 36). Motion and sound, all those attributes that enable the human creature to assert its vitality and enter into communion with reality, are temporarily suspended as the victims tread the boundaries of another world, which coexists with the familiar one but defies all hope of wedding the two: "Fifteen thousand women stamp their feet and it makes no noise. The silence is solidified into cold. The light is immobile. We are in a setting in which time is abolished. We do not know if we exist, only ice. Light, dazzling snow, and us, in this ice, in this light, in this silence" (p. 37). One day literary archeologists will rediscover these diminished human mastodons, and wonder what ritual they were performing when time stopped and froze their woe for the future. It is a fanciful idea, but Charlotte Delbo writes as if she has some such distant moment in mind.[4]

Images confirm this notion, and much more: "We are embedded in a block of crystal beyond which, far off in our memories, we see the living" (p. 38). Just as one day *their* present will be part of the experience of *our* past, one so bizarre that it may seem inaccessible to us, so their past, obscured by inexpressible suffering, seems strange and incomprehensible to them. They are truly isolated in time as well as space, as their recollections of childhood, when adults warned them not to sit in the snow lest they catch cold, must contend with the tableau of a woman from their ranks who groans softly and lies down in the snow to die:

We watch without comprehending.

The light is still immobile, wounding, cold. It is the light of a dead star. And the vast frozen expanse, infinitely dazzling, is that of a dead planet.

Immobile in the ice in which we are caught fast, inert, unfeeling, we have lost all the senses of life. No one says: "I am hungry. I am thirsty. I am cold." Transported to another world, we are at the same time exposed to the breath of another life, to living death. In ice, in light, in silence [p. 38].

A truck glides noiselessly past the scene, jammed with women on their way to the gas chamber, and though one would expect it to disrupt this motionless ballet of futile pain, it becomes part of the tableau itself. The doomed victims cry out in terror, but in this sealed world there is no audience for their fear, only other victims: "Each woman is a materialized cry, a scream that is not heard" (p. 39). The truck drives by, more vehicles come and go, but their motion marks the indifference of that other universe, which exists in time and supports this timeless one while ignoring its features. Charlotte Delbo is herself the intermediary between the two, but in *None of Us Will Return,* at least, she offers no assurance that her reimagined account can establish a genuine bond.

Her style, employing the rhythms of music, also uses the visual energy of art, as if she would persuade us that a single medium were insufficient to convey the content of her vision. How does one hear terror? How does one see anguish? How does one describe the feelings of women on a journey to the gas chamber, or of the witnesses who must watch them? As fighting such death is a never-ending defeat for Dr. Rieux, who nonetheless commits his humanity to the struggle, so Charlotte Delbo attempts the impossible, as witness to the horror of the human condition when atrocity rules:

> We watch with eyes that cry out, that do not believe.
>
> Each face is inscribed with such precision in the icy light, on the blue of the sky, that it is marked there for eternity.
>
> For eternity, shaven heads squeezed together and bursting with cries, mouths twisted with cries that are not heard, hands waving in a mute cry.
>
> The screams remain inscribed on the blue of the sky [p. 39].

They are also etched on the imagination of the reader, engraved in the memory of survivors from the "other" world who remain incredulous to this portion of their past, compelled to depend on prose sculptures like Charlotte Delbo's for access to its truths. But "truths" is such a genteel word for the unredeemable humiliation of the body which these victims endured: "They screamed because they knew, but their vocal cords had ruptured in their throats" (p. 40). Is the very record of these living deaths a testament to an unabsorbable heritage, a reply to Freud's World War I caution, a confirmation that these generations, at least, are doomed by the history of their times to live psychologically beyond their means?

Suddenly it occurs to us that our premises may be reversed, that in this world of atrocity "inappropriate" may be the epithet for *survival,* and "appropriate" the proper term for death. "We have died to ourselves" (p. 41), says the narrator, as she and her companions lose their sense of the reality from which they have come: "We had yielded at once to the fantastic and we had forgotten the reflexes of the normal human being when confronting the outrageous" (p. 43). It is a principle of endurance which we may have inherited against our will, a point of view contrary to the "protest" that proves serviceable to Camus when the enemy is plague or the indifference of the universe. When the body is so vulnerable and its persecutors so concrete, "perception" and "consciousness" (as Améry would also insist) dissolve into "reflexes of the normal human being," protest turns abstract and the distressed self stands dazed and mute in the face of its own suffering and the suffering of others. If the women are indeed like so many "pitiable, defenseless insects" (p. 53), as the narrator concludes at one point, then perhaps the human image has been overvalued and they are more dispensable than their "normal" heritage has led them to believe.

Some of the literal survivors, as we shall see, never entirely recover from this palpable threat to the idea of the integrated self. Once wholeness has been displaced by fragmentation, the mind is scarred by a possibility that cannot be erased—like the keloids that marked the bodies of some Hiroshima survivors. Again these implications coalesce in a single vivid image in *None of Us Will Return,* as Charlotte Delbo seeks to illuminate atrocity's power to desanctify death and humble the concept of human dignity. One of their number, a woman with an artificial leg, has died, and while her body disappears amidst a "hayrick of corpses" that is food for rats while waiting transportation to the crematorium, her friends discern in the snow nearby her detached leg, "alive and sentient," a bizarre reminder of the flesh's transience and wood's ability to endure. "Alice had been dead for weeks while her artificial leg continued to lie on the snow. Then it snowed again. The leg was covered over. It reappeared in the mud. That leg in the

mud. Alice's leg—severed alive—in the mud" (p. 47). There
are moments when "facing death" undermines one's resolve
to stay alive: the emblem of Alice's leg is a stark contradiction to traditional ideas of the vitality of the body and spirit.

Of course, such inversion is offered as a quality of the
sealed world of Auschwitz. The universe outside cannot
penetrate the barricade of its gleaming barbed wire, whose
uncanny, mocking whiteness is one of Charlotte Delbo's
vividest images. Unlike the patients at Mann's Berghof, the
inmates here have no illusions about their fate, no opportunity
to risk, like Joachim, a "nobler" if more foolhardy end, no
dreams of a temporary respite in the flatlands below. Like
Hans Castorp, they realize that association with death is a
fulltime occupation, though for them visions of counter-
positions are forestalled by the immediacy of their experience. *We* may fit this experience into a larger perspective,
but they—this is perhaps its most distinctive feature—have no
way to use it. Pure atrocity cannot justify itself even in literature as a process of initiation for the initiate, because atrocity murders the future as it destroys hope for survival. The
painful paradox of its triumph is that it can exert its hold
over the survivor too, who like Charlotte Delbo brings with
her the memories of what has been killed. Thus the seal is
broken from *inside* rather than outside, and the soiled image
of man spills over the rim of this closed universe and stains
the terrain of the "normal" imagination that only reads
about its horrors.

Art breaks down these frontiers, bringing the "unthinkable"
to men who had confused it with only the "worst." Language
extends itself, as words convey the silence with which the
narrator and her friends greet another roundup for the gas
chamber: "Nothing heard these cries from the edge of terror.
The world stopped far short of here. The world that says: 'It
would be nice to take a walk.' Only our ears heard and we
were already no longer alive. We were waiting for our turn"
(p. 57). The knowledge that death will strike is offset by the
uncertainty of when and how, so that atrocity of its very nature prevents the preparation that might permit one to en-

dure. We endure the worst, but are always surprised by the unthinkable. For this reason, one will never move beyond atrocity until the unthinkable enters the deepest recesses of human consciousness. Long accustomed to sky, men finally learned to know the earth. Accustomed to earth, they must now learn to know the mud, the mud of the marshes about Auschwitz where the prisoners dig daily, until their bodies merge with the very soil they seek to exhume. Its density once more reduces movement to an agonizing slow-motion, as if the quicksand of primeval ooze were sucking the human creature back into the ancient slime from which his ancestors originally crept.

Nightmare displaces dream as a confirmation of this condition in *None of Us Will Return*. A section called "Night" begins with this macabre, spasmodic ballet of human limbs and organs in mortal combat with the unimaginable:

The octopi were strangling us with their viscous muscles and we freed an arm only to be choked by a tentacle that wrapped itself around our necks, squeezed the vertebrae, squeezed them until they snapped. The vertebrae, the trachea, the esophagus, the larynx, the pharynx and all the passages of the throat, squeezed them till they broke. We had to free our throats and in order to save ourselves from strangulation, we had to sacrifice our arms, our legs, our waists to the clasping intruding tentacles that multiplied endlessly, sprang up everywhere, so innumerable that we were tempted to give up the struggle and the exhausting vigilance. The tentacles unwound, unwound their threat. The threat hung poised a long moment and we were there hypnotized, incapable of beating a retreat in the face of this beast that was charging, coiling, clinging, crushing. We were about to succumb when we suddenly had the impression of waking up. They are not octopi, it is mud [p. 61].

The progress from nightmare to recognition, the connection between death threat and daily experience is not lighted by a gleam of hope; daylight brings no normality, only further waking nightmares. This monster is to an age of atrocity what the demon frozen in ice in the lowest depths of Dante's *Inferno* was to his Christian contemporaries, though Delbo's beast belongs to no heritage that acknowledges a difference between guilt and innocence, sin and redemption. Character succumbs to anatomy; crowded in restless sleep with her friends on a narrow wooden platform, the narrator merges with them and loses her definition of self: "Everything vanishes into a shadow in which the leg that is moving belongs to Lulu, the arm belongs to Yvonne, the head on my chest that presses on me is Viva's head, and awakened by the sensation that I am at the edge of the void, at the edge of the tier, on the verge of falling out into the corridor, I plunge again into another nightmare. . ." (p. 62).

Sleep suffocates the spirit instead of bringing refreshment, as death infiltrates moments of dream and waking. Night is more exhausting than day because the barracks, "peopled with coughs and rattles, with those who are dying alone" (p. 64), offer no respite from the omnipresence of death. If one dreams briefly of returning home to one's kitchen and discovering one's mother, one awakens to the groans of sleeping "larvae" whose blankets "are shrouds that cover them for they are dead, today or tomorrow, it is all the same, they are dead to a return to the kitchen where their mothers await them" (p. 63). Camus challenged his contemporaries to live within the limits of the possible; in Charlotte Delbo's universe, women are forced to *die* within those limits, when their lives are merely a reflection of their impending deaths and the imagination is left no room to breathe, the will little space to hope. The extremity of their ordeal is no reflection of the "normal" human condition, of course—but that is a principle source of their anguish. The mud, dogs, and shouts of their day pursue them into sleep and dream, so that some of them will be found dead when the others awake, victims of a life without refuge that still only hovers on the edge of the modern sensibility. But for those who inhabit that sealed universe, "each dead woman is as light and as heavy as the shadows of the night, light in that she is wasted and heavy with an accumulation of sufferings that no one will ever share" (p. 64).

Reverence for life is one of those phrases that traditionally supports the human spirit under stress. Atrocity undermines its force, leaving a vacuum into which pours a longing for death. In speaking of his torturers, Jean Améry had raised the possibility of a world where men bent on transcendence but disenchanted by the prospects of grace might logically turn to devil worship instead. A canopy of evil perversely offers more protection than does exposure to the void. So in Charlotte Delbo's world, a moment is reached when the hopelessness of atrocity induces the human will to accept the inversion of values with which atrocity threatens men and to regard death as the kind of bliss that one usually associates with love. In a unique sort of organic suicide, which has no resemblance to the intellectual or physical surrender of which Camus writes in *The Myth of Sisyphus,* Delbo's narrator admits death into her heart. It is neither the dying for love that achieves a climax in Wagner's *Liebestod* nor an acknowledgment of the fatal opposition between love and death that Hans Castorp discerns in his snow vision. For the moment, it answers with a melancholy negative Mann's question at the end of *The Magic Mountain* whether out of "this universal feast of death" love one day may mount:

My head is contracted, pinched, pinched till it hurts, and suddenly I feel something snap there in my heart. My heart breaks loose from my chest and from all that surrounds it and supports it. I feel a stone dropping within me, dropping with a thud. It is my heart. And a marvelous sense of well-being invades me. How comfortable it is to be rid of this fragile and demanding heart. One slips into a state of elation which must be that of happiness. Everything melts inside me, everything takes on the fluidity of happiness. I surrender and it is sweet to surrender to death, sweeter than surrendering to love and it is sweet to know that it is the end, the end of suffering and struggling, the end of asking the impossible of a heart that can bear no more. The giddiness lasts less than an instant, long enough to attain a bliss that we did not know existed [p. 73].

It is another *locus classicus* for the literature of atrocity, a literal reversal of Hans Castorp's resolution *not* to surrender to the temptations of death as he lay freezing in the snowstorm. (The narrator herself has been standing for hours in the cold, annihilated by the frost, lungs cracking in the icy wind.) But it is only a momentary impulse, though not because she has balanced the appeal of the blood-sacrifice against the human beauty of a golden age. She is prepared to accept death as the worst, but even in her ultimate despair she cannot accede to the unthinkable, that image of atrocity with which nothing in her heart, though wrenched from its mooring, can correspond—a corpse destined for the crematorium: "I want to die but not to be carried out on that little stretcher. Not to be carried out on that little stretcher with my feet dangling and my head dangling, naked under the ragged blanket. I do not want to be carried out on that little stretcher" (p. 76). Not death, with which she now feels kindred—"Those who painted it with a hideous face had never seen it," she confesses (p. 76)—but what follows, that final indignity to the human body, drives her to resist. A corporeal solidarity, far more diminished than Camus's idea of human communion, restores her equilibrium—a "forced solidarity of brain, of nerves, of bones and of every organ in the belly" (p. 76) that reawakens the heart, though not with a reverence for life in reaction against so humiliating a death. What is one to say of a universe where the last source of protest is concern for the fate of one's corpse?

Part of the explanation for this limited impulse to resist is the extraordinary sensation of some victims of atrocity of being dead while still alive. This is not a constant feeling, but when it comes we get a graphic image of how mass dying can impose a sense of nonbeing on the living. Thirst reduces the narrator to a numbed perception of her paralyzed vitality, as if the wellsprings of life had literally dried up inside her: "It is despair born of my inability to tell them of the anguish that has choked me, the feeling of being dead and knowing it" (p. 79). It is the moment of purest negation, when the parts of the body refuse to cooperate and one feels defeated by the inadequacies of one's "creatureliness": "My cheeks stick to my teeth, my tongue is hard, stiff, my jaws are blocked and still this feeling of being dead, of being dead and knowing it. And terror grows in my eyes" (p. 80). The triumph of atrocity means the end of all that is human. But its very presence, its alliance with terror, its power to infect the human organism with a feeling of being dead and knowing it, provides a grim metaphor for the altered consciousness of our era. To ignore Delbo's image is to falsify the nature of our reality, or at least that part of it which is the imperishable heritage from atrocity.

But to let that image obliterate all others, to assume that the "moment of purest negation" is the ultimate expression of human destiny, would be to mistake Charlotte Delbo's intention and to falsify the nature of reality in another way. Although life (and death) within the limits of the possible, beneath the shadow of atrocity, excludes summits, it does not automatically plunge experience into the craters of a permanent despair. *None of Us Will Return* summons the imagination to "see" the unthinkable as the base for all that follows, but recognizes the necessity of "the better" (if not "the best") for human survival. If the mood of annihilation dominates the first volume of Delbo's trilogy, conditions for enduring prevail in the second *(Une Connaissance inutile)*, while the quality of life after the "return" attracts most attention in the third *(Mesure de nos jours)*. But the existence of the "unthinkable" controls the tone of all three, so that progress through them does not represent a process of purification, as in Dante's *Commedia*, but a testament to the persistent influence of atrocity as the individual seeks renewal from that devastating moment which marked "the end of asking the impossible of a heart that can bear no more."

Only a spirit of community made survival possible to the imagination—though by no means certain—because planning for the "return" together gave substance to its details: "No one believes in the return when she is alone" (p. 115). As with Dr. Rieux in *The Plague*, the momentum in Delbo's volumes alternates between loneliness and solidarity, though there is never any question of one triumphing over the other. The narrator in *None of Us Will Return* is still so numbed by her experience, her senses so enveloped by the viscous "stench of diarrhea and carrion" (p. 124), that she cannot convey with dramatic conviction her intuition that return may be made possible by the presence of others. She states it, but the "memory" of hope, at the end of this volume, is silenced by the visage of death. Like a paralyzed skeleton herself, whose will has wilted in an atmosphere of timeless suffering, she cannot respond to the appeal of a dying neighbor. She concludes the first part of her narrative with words of unconsolable despair, illuminating the darkest bequest of atrocity: "None of us will return. None of us should have returned" (pp. 126–27).

A main theme of the first sequel is a rediscovery of the body, a renewal of the senses that restores to the human creature a feeling of being alive. Two remarkable episodes in *Une Connaissance inutile* evoke in painstaking detail this quintessential struggle between atrocity and the physical will to endure which takes place at a level so much more elementary than the intellectual. In the first, the narrator is at the point of total exhaustion because of a maddening thirst when only the promise of water at work in the fields the next day keeps her from collapsing immediately. Once again the essence of human suffering is conveyed through the afflicted parts of the body: "My lips were torn, my gums swollen, my tongue like a piece of wood. My swollen gums and tongue prevented me from closing my mouth, and I kept it open as if I were feeble-minded, pupils dilated and eyes wild."[5] Her friends, who for a time think her mad or blind, persuade a Polish woman worker, in exchange for a ration of bread, to leave a pail of drinking water in a secluded spot (since drinking during work was forbidden by the SS). The narrator throws herself on the water like a thirsty horse, her whole face plunged into the bucket so that she has to raise her nostrils to breathe, but without stopping drinking. It is a bizarre baptism, devoid of spiritual content, that restores physical existence to a desiccated body ready to surrender the last tokens of vitality.

It is neither a familiar nor a pretty image of deprivation, but it reminds us how atrocity has altered our idea of dignity and added some unforgettable portraits of *in*dignity to the gallery of human suffering. The mind plays no role in the body's revival, as the narrator slowly returns to the condition of sentience when the afflicted parts of her body begin to function normally:

Suddenly, I felt life returning in me. It was as if I had regained awareness of my blood circulating, my lungs breathing, of my heart beating. I was alive. Saliva returned to my mouth. The burning in my eyelids abated. Your eyes burn when your tear ducts are dried up. My ears heard again. I was alive [p. 48].

The abnormality of such tormenting thirst highlights the casual indifference with which one satisfies such needs under "normal" conditions. The narrator acidly concludes the episode with the observation that there are "people who say 'I am thirsty.' They go into a café and order a beer" (p. 49).

She might have said the same about people taking a bath, since in the other episode dramatizing the secular resurrection of the body, the narrator washes herself (in a brook) for the first time since her arrival at Auschwitz, a period of more than two months. The rehabilitation of flesh encrusted by the filth of atrocity is an essential preliminary step for anyone interested in rescuing the mind from memories of inappropriate death, though once more the first ritual does not guarantee the success of the second. But the bath rite is elaborate, a grotesque ballet of readjustment to life as the earlier frozen motion was an adaptation to death. The leader of the work detail had given the prisoners permission to wash, but might withdraw it at any moment, so that the narrator must struggle against time as well as dirt and the need to keep her meagre garments dry: "I went down carefully to the edge of the brook and considered how I should go about it, adapting and coordinating my gestures so as not to lose a second" (p. 58). Her decision to wash her face while her feet were in the water so that both might be cleaned together would sound comic if the proximity to death in Auschwitz did not make it seem so painful. Removing her stockings for the first time in seventy days, she finds they are stuck to her toes; she tugs and they come free, showing an odd design near the bottom. Only after inspecting her toes encrusted with dirt does she discover that the curious design is made by her toenails, which have adhered to her stockings and come off with them. "Naturally," she recollects, "I didn't have time to meditate on this detail" (p. 59). Later she learns that her toes had frozen (the lost toenails thus signify the partial victory of death even as she washes away some of its sting); the ritual is as much a reminder of what must be cleansed as of what will emerge underneath.

Thus she comments on her inability to revive memories of her sense of smell during those moments, as if the odor of liquid manure and decay which suffused her body were as normal to her as the process of bathing was to her readers. The shock of contact between the two crystallizes the extent to which atrocity is an ordeal of the body, transforming our normal expectations of physical existence: "On that day," the narrator recalls, "I took off my underpants stiffened by the remnants of dried diarrhea . . . and I was not sickened by the odor" (p. 60). Bizarre because of its rude simplicity, the horror of her past world bursts on the uninformed wonder of ours, where our reaction of disgust suddenly becomes a betrayal of her humanity and a rejection of her ordeal. Charlotte Delbo gathers the details of this purification rite into an overwhelming confrontation between woman and the fragility of her flesh, the "creatureliness" that shares ordure with perfume as her proper vestment, the one perhaps invented to conceal the other. At this very moment, rubbing her skin vigorously a piece at a time, the narrator ponders what she can think about while washing herself, and recalls the first (and last) shower she took, on the day of her arrival at Auschwitz. The link between "then" and "now" is a stunning commentary on man's fate under conditions of atrocity.

With a premonition of that fate, the narrator had taken from her belongings in the "disrobing" antechamber a small bottle of perfume which she had received in a package at her detention prison, and poured its entire contents over her body. Then in the shower she had avoided certain spots on her body, so as to preserve the pleasant odor as long as possible. The name of the perfume—*Orgueil* (Pride)—intensifies the symbolism of the gesture, as she seeks to clothe her naked flesh with an aroma of dignity as armor against the ordeal before her. The futility of that attempt is confirmed by her vigorous rubbing in the brook, where flesh is so obscured by layers of dirt that she must use a handful of sand to penetrate its sheath. The spectacle dispels all illusions of pride, shatters prior conceptions of dignity, and translates into stark visual terms our diminished image of the human. Leaving her face and back, the narrator searches for another part of the body to "purify," and chooses the thigh just above the knee: "The skin was growing a little lighter, turning red. Yes, truly, it seemed to me that it was turning lighter. I rubbed with all my strength, especially near the knee. But I had to rub somewhere else when I noticed tiny drops of blood forming. I had rubbed too hard and the sand was too coarse" (p. 64). The blood is an authentic sign of life, more genuine than perfume, an indication that beneath the humiliation of filth a human creature still exists. "I bleed, therefore I am," is an austere enough principle for an age of atrocity; but even more accurate, more consistent with this episode and with the idea that the condition of the body itself is somehow allied with our acceptance of life and of death, would be: "I smell clean; therefore I am."

In the imaginative (and literal) world of atrocity, preservation of the body is a paramount challenge to the individual. It explains Dr. Rieux's ambition to be a "healer," and it clarifies Hans Castorp's misguided devotion to his departed cousin—a trespass on the finality of death in order to restore Joachim's corporeal form. It also illuminates Kostoglotov's determination to preserve the vitality of his body at the risk of shortening its term. But a withering irony coexists with this impulse to physical survival, because the conditions making it possible simultaneously threaten a major purpose for wanting to survive—the desire to love. In the imaginative vision of the authors we have been examining, intimate contact with mass dying, with the intense experience we have called atrocity, begins to erode that relationship which previous generations have celebrated as the summit of human experience. Although Mann's *Magic Mountain* stands in the vestibule to the world of atrocity, the question it raises—whether love will one day rise from such slaughter—persists in the worlds of others. Rieux pays for his resistance to dying with the life of his wife (and his friend), though the logic of cause and effect is symbolic rather than rational. Kostoglotov cannot fulfill his love in the vicinity of so many other victims, while the indifference of those outside the hospital to the atmosphere of death inside again deflates the power of love to relieve the "knowledge and memories" of the survivors. And Charlotte Delbo, whose own husband was shot by the Gestapo after they had granted her a brief final interview with him, transforms this personal memory of love's defeat by atrocity into one of the most haunting themes of her trilogy.

The memory of love destroyed pursues her through the pages of her work, inspiring some of her most memorable lyrics and moving passages. The opening episode of *Une Connaissance inutile,* "Les Hommes" ("The Men"), sets the stage for this theme; even in transit prisons before Auschwitz, the men and women inhabit different worlds and their roles as defined by normal society have been permanently altered. Separation prevents the men from alleviating the suffering of the women; the women, who do not face execution (a perverse gallantry still seems to move their Nazi jailers in France), try from a distance to support the faltering spirits of the men. But the only means of communicating is a mutual deception: the women pretend not to know how fragile the men's lives are, and the men, in a last interview, tell their wives they are to be deported when they know they are about to be shot. How can love flourish in an atmosphere which violates all preconceptions of the human bond? The women return disarmed: "Their faces seemed suddenly stripped of every expression or convention, with that nakedness given by unexpected illumination or a terrible truth" (p. 16). And the attempt to pass the time in their cell by reciting poetry only reinforces the disruption between the romantic idea of love and the new mask which death has imposed on it. The lines are an ironic dirge to a dying platitude, the swan song to that kind of heroic resolution which once fostered for them the illusion of transcendence: "For nothing exalts/Like having loved a dead man or woman/It strengthens you for life/And you need no one else any more" (p. 17).

The narrator herself, whose husband had been executed some months earlier, already exhibits in her attitude the consequences of this large-scale, arbitrary form of inappropriate death. It cuts the cord that binds her to the common human tragedy, so that she cannot summon genuine feeling for those still alive: "I had an immense pity and an immense terror for them. Pity and terror in which I could not truly participate. Deep within me was a terrible indifference, indifference which comes from a heart in ashes. . . . I still had not found within me a prayer of forgiveness for the living" (p. 10). Since *Une Connaissance inutile* ends with a poem called "Prayer to the Living to Forgive Them for Being Alive," it would seem that Charlotte Delbo has used her further experience of atrocity in Auschwitz and other camps to liberate an artistic impulse to give form to her private anguish. We shall have to see whether it also restores the tragic sense which links pity and terror with the destiny of men and offers survivors an opportunity for catharsis.

Like Jean Améry, Charlotte Delbo discovered that atrocity introduced one to a reality indifferent to conventional responses—and conventional reasoning. She compares the situation of Auschwitz inmates after their return with the stories told by ex-prisoners of war, who spoke of the emptiness of *their* days while waiting to be released. "We couldn't describe the anguish of ours," says the narrator. "For those who were in Auschwitz, waiting was a path leading to death" (p. 89). To those who argued later that you could take everything away from a human being except the faculty of thought or imagination, she replied, again using the grim corporeal imagery that defines the victim of atrocity: "You don't know. You can make a human being into a skeleton bubbling with diarrhea, take away from him the time to think, the power to think. Imagining is the first luxury of an adequately nourished body, enjoying a minimum of free time, having at its disposal a nucleus for fashioning dreams. At Auschwitz, you didn't dream—you were delirious" (p. 90). The past, which normally furnishes substance for dreams, was to them unreal and incredible, an unraveled existence whose recollection could but intensify their pain. They could speak only of concrete and material things. "We had to dismiss everything that evoked grief or regret. We could not speak of love" (p. 91).

Yet these same women, removed from the proximity of immediate death and transferred to a laboratory in the vicinity of Auschwitz where they can use some of their scientific training, suddenly find the minimum time necessary for the imagination to breathe. They reconstruct from memory Molière's *Le Malade imaginaire,* mount a performance in the barracks, and for a brief space the imagination displaces reality, though reality hovers on the perimeters of their respite: "It was magnificent because for two hours, without the chimneys ceasing to pour forth smoke from human flesh, for two hours, we believed in [the imagination]" (p. 96). Later, Charlotte Delbo will face the challenge of deciding which approaches closer to the essence of human experience, the imagined reality of a Molière or the reimagined reality of Auschwitz. The very title of the Molière play—*Le Malade imaginaire*—crystallizes the problem, since the fancied invalids of art cast an irreverent comic light on the genuine maladies of the survivor. Molière's role in the drama of Auschwitz increases when a gypsy prisoner offers the narrator a copy of *Le Misanthrope* (its origin remains a mystery) in exchange for a portion of bread. She delights in the language of Célimène and Alceste, which offers her a momentary escape from the terrors of Auschwitz.

Molière belongs to the realm of her past, his art once having been a source of form in her existence. Auschwitz is her present, its spirit of disorder permeating her being. Survival and return raise the question that Charlotte Delbo weaves subtly throughout her narrative: will Molière (and the communicable order of art) or Auschwitz (and the inexpressible chaos of atrocity) determine the tone of her future? They represent contradictory worlds, though history, no respecter of contradictions, thrusts the survivor into the magnetic field of both. In the grip of atrocity, how much of "normality" dies, beyond the capacity to revive? Returned to life, how much of the past can one forget, supress, absorb, so that the human image can achieve a necessary reintegration? The enormity of the problem surfaces when the narrator and a few members of her group are suddenly transferred from Auschwitz to Ravensbrück, which requires a long train journey and a stop at the public station in Berlin. They hear a man (presumably an emigré laborer) speaking French, and excitedly identify themselves as Frenchwomen. His response is a disagreeable look and a muttered *"Merde!"* They are dumbfounded. "How is it possible? Some women in striped uniforms call out to him, and this free man doesn't even ask who they are or where they come from. We were from Auschwitz. Everyone should have known that. We had seen the gulf between the world and us, and we were much saddened by it" (p. 113).

The "useless knowledge" of the title radiates in many directions, but it cannot easily cross this gulf. The literal survivor partakes of both worlds, but the others only of one, and this establishes a permanent breach which first shocks and then grieves the naiveté of the survivors. The lesson is a hard one to learn; we get a hint of the difficulties from a conversation between two of the inmates when it becomes clear that their liberation is only a few days away. They speak of the first thing they will do when they are free:

"And you, what do you want?"
"Me? Nothing."
"Nothing?"
"No. Nothing. To believe in it. To be sure of it. To get used to it."
"You'll get used to it quickly enough."
"To get used to getting up late, going here and there, doing what I please. . . . No, that doesn't come back quickly."
"That's the least of your worries."
"You're right: we're not there yet" [p. 145] .

The substance of this dialogue is dramatically demonstrated to the narrator in a macabre episode during the night before their release. Each of the prisoners has received a Red Cross package containing "delicacies" that they had not seen or tasted for years—cigarettes, chocolate, butter, instant coffee. That night, when the others are asleep, the narrator resolves to make herself her first cup of coffee, a foretaste of the freedom she is about to regain. The ensuing ordeal becomes one more parable of the arduous journey from inappropriate death back to life within the limits of the possible—and of the folly of accelerating the journey by forgetting death's claims on the image of the human.

While her companions are sleeping, the narrator mixes herself a cup of coffee, inaugurating a ritual of expected pleasure comparable to the rite of drinking and bathing that she had described earlier. But it does not give her as much pleasure as she anticipated—the coffee is bitter. You have to get used to such tastes slowly, she concludes, confirming the previous dialogue. But her body rebels at this casual attempt to contact normality, with a ferocity that almost suggests a jealous need to preserve the "purity" of its suffering. The narrator tries to return to sleep: "Scarcely had I stretched out when I felt a strange sensation. I asked myself what was happening to me. My throat was knotted in agony. I was shaken by heartbeats so violent that the din swelled in my ears. . . . I was suffocating" (pp. 168-69). Panting, feeling faint, she staggers to the door of the dormitory, tears open the collar of her prison dress and—out falls her copy of Molière's *Le Misanthrope,* which she had hidden beneath her dress to prevent its discovery by the SS. It had suddenly begun to press tightly on her breast, impeding her breathing.

At this point Charlotte Delbo's art fuses with her account of a reimagined reality, for the details solicit interpretation as well as response. Just as the feigned illness of *Le Malade imaginaire* reminds one of the solemn anguish of the inmates, so the comic misanthropy of Molière's hero casts a lurid glow on the universe of atrocity from which the narrator is about to be released. No one escapes this realm of death unbranded:

"I leaned against the doorframe," says the narrator, "I held my heart in both hands to squeeze the wound together. . . . I tried to breathe in some air, and at each breath, I thought I was dying. The last night at Ravensbrück. My last night alone. I was going to die now that I knew *Le Misanthrope* by heart and didn't need it any more" (p. 169). She throws her copy of Molière at her feet and, when she arrives in freedom a few days later, she realizes that she has forgotten it.

But she has learned something about misanthropy, about death's injury to the heart, that will suffuse her own art with a somber mood that makes Molière's mordant wit seem mellow. Although her farewell to Molière is temporary, other farewells are more final. Death by atrocity dislocates the rhythm of arrival and departure, exodus and return, which in more normal times provides a consoling pattern for life's journey. Near the end of *Une Connaissance inutile,* as the expectation of liberation mounts, Charlotte Delbo introduces a brief chapter called "L'Adieu," in which the narrator recalls her last meeting with her husband in his cell several years earlier, just before his execution. This is what farewell to Auschwitz really means: the renewal of a memory which release will threaten with oblivion, the terror of parting when premature death triumphs over love. So the knowledge of love was "une connaissance inutile," and the acquaintance with death is another "connaissance inutile"—the double meaning of the title coalesces in this final encounter. It is a modern version of the Orpheus and Eurydice myth, though here Orpheus is not the agent of his loss, and Eurydice can appeal to no one to modify her fate. Atrocity deprives love and death of the ordering framework of myth, and thus of the possibility of transcendence.

Charlotte Delbo has one sanctuary for her pain, a lyric impulse that itself becomes a kind of transcendence as the language of verse distills experience into a potent and concentrated version of the ordeal of atrocity. Interspersed throughout her three volumes, juxtaposed with the prose vignettes, are groups of poems that condense her main themes into incantations of remorse, alienation, and inconsolable loss. They enable her to preserve the condition of her existence "then" even as she wrestles with the challenge of adjusting to her return to the familiar world "now." But the stakes are high and it is never clear whether winning is worth it:

I'm back from another world
to this world
that I didn't leave
and I don't know
which is real
tell me am I back
from that other world?
As for me
I'm still there
and I'm dying
back there
every day a bit more
I die again
the death of all those who died
and I no longer know what's real
in this world
from the other world-back-there
now
I don't know any more
when I'm dreaming
and when
I'm not dreaming.   [pp. 183-84]

If "the death of all those who died" is not merely a memory of past misfortune but an abiding presence, then one is left inhabiting an intermediate realm where dying and living merge and re-form, and for which few images exist to aid the imagination of those who would endure in such a realm. Perhaps the ordeal of atrocity is so private that generalizing myths which once distinguished between the world of life and the world of death are no longer possible; maybe "death-with-life"[6] is the unhappy heritage of the twentieth century. Certainly Charlotte Delbo does not, like Odysseus, keep the spirits of the dead from encroaching on her living person. Nor does she, like Aeneas, return from a visit to the underworld with a happy vision of the future.

The prospects for civilization beyond atrocity are not promising. Death is itself an earthly homeland, says Delbo, from which it is impossible to flee:

Then you'll know
you mustn't talk with death
it's a useless knowledge.
In a world
where those who think they are
are not living
all knowledge becomes useless
to whoever possesses the other
and to live
better know nothing
know nothing of life's value
to a young man about to die.

*

I've spoken with death
so
I know
that so many things we learned were useless
but I learned that at the price of suffering
so great
I wonder
if it was worth it.   [p. 185]

Atrocity thus undermines one base of classical tragedy: the knowledge gained through suffering that enabled earlier generations to balance misfortune with insight, if not joy. The work of Charlotte Delbo raises an issue that western civilization has yet to confront: whether we have moved beyond tragedy into a new kind of cultural atmosphere where the redeeming power of love approaches bankruptcy and the more solitary goal of the Socratic tradition, "Know thyself," has exhausted its charm and its value. The old atmosphere persists, as Delbo discovers when she returns to "this desert" of the normal world, swarming "with men and women in love/who love each other and shout it to each other/from one end of the earth to the other" (p. 187). But she is left dazed in its presence, silenced by the difference of her ordeal yet forced to renew her existence by the accident of having survived atrocity:

I'm back from life among the dead
and I thought
it would give me the right
to speak to the others
and when I found myself facing them
I had nothing to tell them
because
I'd learned
down there
that you can't talk to the others. [p. 188]

Odysseus and Aeneas did not need to earn that right, since they shared with their potential audience the same premises about death in the underworld. Nor were they transformed by their visit, which only brought them necessary information, prophecies about a future that ratified continuity with the past and human agency in shaping man's destiny in time. Delbo inherits none of these assurances. Instead of extending the range of human possibilities, her heritage shrinks them, insulating her from life in time and forcing her to "abandon" knowledge—or at least to make that resolution—in order to survive. The myth, the inner imagery to join the two worlds, is that there *is* no myth or imagery to join them. In her "Prayer to the Living to Forgive Them for Being Alive," which ends *Une Connaissance inutile,* she makes a desperate appeal to the figurative survivors to find a way of justifying their good fortune, although she imposes no penalty on them and has no formula for bringing together the two worlds which atrocity has separated. Her baffled, futile response to their luck is statement rather than judgment:

because it would be too stupid
finally
for so many to have died

and for you to live
without doing anything with your life.   [p. 190]

As for her own role, nothing from that "other world" prepares her to return to this one, but condemns her to a dream
of permanent dualism, seeking forgetfulness as she records
her memories, confirming a chasm in the very process of using
language to cross it:

I've come back
from beyond knowledge
now I need to unlearn
otherwise it's clear
I couldn't go on living

                    *

And then
better not to believe
all these stories
of people returning
you'd never sleep again
if ever you believed them
these specters returning
returning
who come back
not even able
to explain how.   [p. 191]

Mesure de nos jours (Measure of Our Days), the last volume
in Delbo's Auschwitz trilogy, is the story of how a few survivors "go on living" (and, ironically, dying) within the cir-
cumference of this twin reality, one part of which remains
literally unendurable even as they "learn" to adjust to the
other part. Unlike some of Lifton's Hiroshima survivors, they
do not retreat from their ordeal through psychic numbing; if
anything, most of them are more numb to life than to death,
which paradoxically now lies vividly *behind* them; they cannot heal their anxiety by preparing for it. Essentially, the
book is a series of monologues, first by the narrator, then
several of her former Auschwitz companions, whom she seeks
out years after the return to record their stories of "re-entry."

The cosmic metaphor is unusually appropriate, except that they have made a journey from one universe to another without benefit of a protective "heat-shield" or the acclaim that accompanies unique achievements. Instead of leaving the solitude of outer space, they return to the loneliness of a world no longer familiar. We are made uncomfortable by their disorientation, but even more so by the gradual recognition that this "world no longer familiar" is also our own.

The initial revelation is that their inherited reality cannot support traditional ideas of character, or of the self. The bond that joins human beings to one another is the common chain of values and assumptions that they share with each other. But the bonds which joined the narrator with her comrades in Auschwitz had nothing to do with traditional values and assumptions. As we have seen, their physical being was the axis of their daily ordeal. As the plane bringing them back to freedom approaches Paris, the narrator finds that she has no way to preserve the human substance of her friends and fellow survivors. They grow transparent and ghostlike, apparitions who are doomed to lose their form when living reality draws near, like the spirits of the dead whom Aeneas and Odysseus seek to embrace. After they land, the narrator begins to doubt her own existence: "I floated in the midst of this crowd which was gliding all around me. And suddenly, I felt that I was alone, alone in the hollow of an empty space, where there was no oxygen, where I had trouble breathing, where I was suffocating."[7] She searches for the companions who have not returned, more real than the welcoming throng, raising a crucial issue for her own future and for our understanding of it: "If I confuse the dead and the living, with whom do I belong myself?" (p. 11).

She responds by using the word *absente,* though this does not clarify the state of being absent while being present. The meaning of words and phrases—"my life before" and "my life after," for example—dissolves in a fog of confusion. "How was I to refamiliarize myself," she asks, "with a 'me' that had grown so 'detached' that I wasn't sure whether it had ever existed?" (p. 14). The measure of our days may be that we no longer *have* any measure for our days, other than the memory of atrocity, which serves no end in the reality to which the narrator has returned. For survival requires some form of transcendence, and the power to transcend the limitations of the unaccommodated self is precisely what the narrator has lost in the camps. She returns with a clarity of vision from "that" life to the obscurity of this one, and discovers that those who try to help her by asking questions speak a language different from her own:

Everything was false, faces and books, everything revealed its falsity to me and I was in despair at having lost all capacity for illusion or dream, all resilience to imagine or explain things. That's the part of me that died in Auschwitz. That's what made a ghost of me. What should one be interested in when falseness is exposed, when there's no more ambiguity, when there's nothing to guess at any more, neither in the faces of people nor in books? How can you live in a world without mystery? [p. 17].

The narrator and most of her companions never entirely lose this residual bitterness, born of the discovery that their ordeal has transformed *them,* but not the world to which they have returned. Unlike Camus's absurd hero, they have no imagined universe to direct their scorn against, only the faces of other men—and they understand the futility of such personal resentment. Unlike Kostoglotov, they cannot return to the exile from which they have come, though in a grotesque sense most of them now have no other reality but that to inhabit. Perhaps nothing remains but to tell their story, and as Charlotte Delbo introduces the voices of the other survivors, we get a multiple portrait of how atrocity has succeeded in disfiguring the image of the human.

One of them remembers awakening alone in a hotel room the day after repatriation, and reconstructs a singular Kafkan nightmare as she finds the telephone and the bell disconnected, then ventures timidly into endless corridors which she hesitates to explore for fear of getting lost. Nothing inside her connects with sights that earlier would have been familiar—doors of other rooms, carpeted floors, an elevator, staircases. She is totally isolated by the intensity of the experience she has just left, so that all she can wonder is where the "others" are, feeling lost in their absence. Finally a strange man appears in the corridor, and the ensuing dialogue is a parable of the distance separating the two worlds that determine her existence:

> "Where are you from?"
> "From Auschwitz."
> "I've come back from Mauthausen myself, but that's not what I was asking you. Where are you from? From what region?"
> "From Bordeaux" [p. 28].

Bordeaux exists in time and space; at Auschwitz, time stopped and space was hermetically sealed by gleaming barbed-wire fences which defined the frontiers of one's hope. Once one has known a daily reality where the condition of the body sustains or curtails life, how does one adjust to a life where the body is taken for granted and the reflective power of the mind is the essential monitor of reality? The survivor from Bordeaux cannot accustom herself to the "new" arrangement: "To be happy—is that a question we can ask ourselves? To convince myself, I repeat that we came back twenty years ago, although I don't believe it. I know it as we know that the earth turns—because we've learned it. You have to *think* about it to know it" (p. 41). But atrocity creates a breach in the chain of events, in what we normally call the history of an individual. Usually, reflection adds perspective to even the most abrupt and unmotivated episodes; retrospectively, Oedipus' fragmented career reveals a pattern, an interaction of chance with choice that permits him to discover cause at work in his fate, to link a particular past with a probable future. But when an improbable past like Auschwitz cuts the victim off from any future commensurate with such a past, character is left floating in an ambiguous fluid, resisting all efforts to dissolve it in the solvent of society. *Mesure de nos jours,* beyond its immediate theme, is a study of the difference between those who understand that inappropriate death casts a continuous shadow over our lives and those who manage to elude this unappealing contemporary truth.

Out of context, such a conclusion might sound melodramatic, but properly understood, it reflects what Freud foresaw near the beginning of our century: that mass dying under conditions of atrocity challenges the psychological coherence of our lives. The problem, for novelist as for psychologist and historian, is that modern man is condemned to live with the knowledge and memory of atrocities that contradict the foundations of his civilization. Charlotte Delbo's literal survivors, by their very presence, embody the problem, while urgently questioning the adequacy of that civilization. With one exception, they inhabit an intermediate realm where no myth or vision can make them mistress of their counter-positions. They cannot rehabilitate their lives because there is no niche in the present for the dying they have experienced. A new kind of "double" emerges, a split personality not tormented by inner psychological contradictions like so many of Dostoevsky's characters, but by the incompatibility of the former daily crisis of facing life and death with the superficial choices which comprise existence in normal society. Having watched the meaningless death of so many of their companions, they cannot adjust to a world where such atrocity does not form part of everyone's reality. One of the survivors, Mado, recalls the words of one who did not come back: "If we return, nothing will be the same" (p. 59). But everything is the same; other people live as if Auschwitz had never happened.

Mado is *not* the same, separated from the rest of the world, as she confesses, by a "mountain of corpses" (p. 59), whom she refuses to idealize as martyrs, since the drama that destroyed them lacked any vestige of tragic dignity. But in the absence of any larger framework to accommodate their deaths, she must carry that burden herself, fully conscious of how it erodes her personality. "To live in the past is not to live," she admits:

That's cutting yourself off from the living. But what do you do to regain their side, and not stay paralyzed on the other bank? We don't have a single thing to hold on to in the present. Sometimes I try to imagine how I would be if I were like everyone else, if I hadn't gone 'there.' I can't do it. I'm different. I speak and my voice sounds like another voice. My words come from outside of me. . . . They don't have the same meaning [p. 60].

Atrocity has transformed the meaning of language for Mado far beyond the euphemisms that brutal regimes often employ to conceal their infamies. "I'm afraid," "I'm hungry," "my friends," mean one thing to Mado and another to those around her who have not shared her experience. The difference has penetrated to the core of her being, so that she is conscious of a constant unwilled deception which she cannot alter: "It's as if there were two parts of me, one in a dream, the other somewhere else" (p. 57). Thus when she says that she is interested in her young son's future, she is immediately confronted by one of those deceptive words that no longer carries a pure resonance for the ear or mind. Auschwitz has so contaminated the meaning of the word "future," that even as she uses it she drifts back into the other world where fidelity to her comrades was all that had meaning for her. Their "future"—those who died—is now her "past," and it controls the "significant" portion of her life. The rest is mere gesture.

She resists the description *mort-vivant* or "living dead," preferring to distinguish between the genuine and the mechanical in her responses to reality. On the "outside," she accepts her husband's good intentions in wanting to help her forget what happened "there"; but on the "inside," she acknowledges the falsity of this relationship, since those who "know" realize that such wounds never heal, that the scars they leave inflict twinges of pain on the victim throughout her life. They inflict too a new kind of solitude, a dualism of character that provides the only way of living psychologically within one's means. But for Mado it makes love a necessary gesture, not a source of fulfillment. The death of others, her own potential death, has shifted the direction of her life from future to past, and the traditional notion of time as the guardian of possibility perishes in the change. People think that memories grow hazy, she protests, that time effaces everything. "There's the difference: for me, for us, time doesn't pass. I'm not living. I died at Auschwitz and no one sees it" (p. 66).

One of Mado's fellow survivors, Poupette, probes even more incisively the effects of atrocity on one's expectations of life. During the experience itself, the will has only one goal: to return. For those who endured the numbing torments described in *None of Us Will Return,* life beyond atrocity meant only that. But what she discovered was that no balance book existed to add up the credits due her from the debits of Auschwitz. The world had its own way of reckoning one's "earnings" in life—the commercial metaphor is hers—but no concept of justice to accept the principle that a human being could pay in her sum of misfortune, as it were, all at once. "Yes," Poupette admits bitterly, "since our return we had to go on learning, learning that you never pay all at once" (p. 135). Her marriage gone bad, her husband calling her unfit to care for her children, "abnormal" and "mad" as a result of her ordeal, she finds no imaginative crypt in which to bury her past, no open receptacle to contain it in the present. In a sense, she rediscovers the absurd universe, whose injustice negates the happiness she not only longs for but feels she deserves because of her suffering. Atrocity transforms metaphysical revolt, an intellectual attitude, into personal anguish. And Poupette realizes that nothing exists in reality to translate such private ordeals back into a reflection of the general human condition. Nothing can widen the scope of her search for consolation.

Thus the monologues of *Mesure de nos jours* are the perfect form to express the hermetic world of the survivors, a world they seek to break out of in vain. This is the same Poupette, one assumes, who earlier in the volume had spoken of having the luck to return from Auschwitz and being able to live afterward as if it had never been. It does not take her too long to learn the supreme self-deception of this view. There seems to be only one exception to this attitude, the survivor called Marie-Louise. Since coming back she appears to have adjusted to a happy country existence with her husband and daughter, and to a bourgeois content with her books, her possessions, and her garden. Yet beneath her reassuring flow of words runs an uneasy current that warns the wary reader to be on guard. Marie-Louise is the only one of the narrator's companions to have returned to Auschwitz to visit the site of her ordeal and show it to her husband. But in the telling, the experience seems almost frivolous, like revisiting the summer camp where you were a counselor as a teenager, or the neighborhood where you grew up as a child. Marie-Louise has forgotten which "bunk" she used to sleep in, and she and her husband (with whom, unlike Mado, she talks ceaselessly about her Auschwitz period) have argued about its location. The narrator, rather drily, immediately identifies it from memory with precision, but it is clear that she is not enjoying this account of their past. Marie-Louise's concern for details pays little homage to the horror behind them.

A kind of intellectual tourism is one way of responding to atrocity, another form of what Lifton called psychic numbing. Although Marie-Louise speaks less than any of the other survivors about her former anguish, her narrative, midway through *Mesure de nos jours,* is one of the most unsettling. There is something mournful about the "success" of her rehabilitation: atrocity *need not* penetrate the facade of middle-class respectability, which becomes a defense against its attempts to deface the image of the human. Ironically, one has the feeling that Marie-Louise has *betrayed* her heritage by "overcoming" its efforts to defeat her. She has amassed a library of works on the death camps, about which she proudly boasts: both she and her husband have read them all. She boasts further that her husband knows more about the death camps than she, so that sometimes it seems as if he had been there with her. (One should contrast this with Mado's melancholy question whether she would have a more meaningful life with her husband if he *had* been at Auschwitz with her, so that he could understand the sense of double-personality that afflicts her.) Marie-Louise and her husband attend all the commemorative ceremonies for survivors who did not return, "first, because it's an obligation, and then, because it always gives us pleasure to see the old comrades again" (p. 98). But even this rings with unintended insincerity, as if the ritual of reunion resembled nothing more than a periodic gathering of "graduates" from the "University of Auschwitz" to talk over old times.

Surely Charlotte Delbo includes this episode to emphasize one of the supreme paradoxes of atrocity: reintegration into normal society is possible only if one ignores the depths and clings to the surfaces of the experience. Marie-Louise's monologue begins: "You see, I have everything I want. I'm happy" (p. 83). The rest of the volume is so full of failure to achieve this condition that the momentum of the narrative forces us to consider her *abnormal.* When near the end of her section Marie-Louise begins to ask about their joint friends among the survivors—How is Carmen? How is Lulu? Do you ever see Cécile?—we have a numb feeling that she is about to begin celebrating the "good old days." And when she adds, "What a trio they were! They were game for anything" (p. 98), readers of *None of Us Will Return* recall more vividly what they were "prey" for, and wonder at the curious limitations of Marie-Louise's memory. Her husband is disappointed when the narrator refuses their invitation to spend the night: "That's a pity," he says. "You could have taken her for a walk in the woods. You could have shown her the place where you were arrested" (p. 99). Thus in the end is the beginning, but at the price of virtually excluding what came in between. The narrator quietly has the last word: "I left them on the threshold of their pretty house at the end of a lane that the fir trees made cool and gloomy" (p. 99).

By this time a pattern emerges from Charlotte Delbo's complex interweaving of themes in her account of the journey to, in, and back from the world of the death camps. Specters stalk the survivors, though unlike the ghost of Hamlet's father, they do not seek revenge: there *is* no ritual of vengeance to lay them to rest. The survivor's past is like a dormant infection in the bloodstream that periodically erupts without warning and without apparent cause, bringing symptoms that baffle medical diagnosis because the etiology of the disease is not recorded in textbooks. If the manifestations are often physical rather than psychological, this merely confirms the conviction of Jean Améry and others that the wounds of atrocity "disfigure" the body even more than the mind. "Know thyself" assumes a meaning that neither Socrates nor Saint Paul intended, that even the victim can only feel but not express, as if the body itself were trying to adopt a unique "character" to protest inarticulately against the indignities it has suffered.

The traditional notion of the body's "character" is outlined by Marceline's husband, who admits that deportation must have been a terrible experience but also holds that "human nature is gifted with an extraordinary plasticity, thanks to which the individual can adapt and readapt himself to everything, without the will even entering into play" (p. 182). You can't let yourself be crushed (*écraser*) by bad memories, he adds. But as Marceline points out, his theory of health founders on the fact of her body's fragility. Every year since her return, at about the same time, she is seized by a high fever that lasts for some days. Medicine doesn't help, while laboratory analyses and x-rays reveal nothing. "My malady has no name," she says:

I call it my typhus anniversary. After each attack, it takes several weeks for me to get back on my feet. I search for the cause, I try to determine what triggered the crisis—did it follow a shock, exhaustion, nervous irritation? No, not at all. It's inexplicable. It always begins in the same way: violent headache, upset stomach, quickly rising temperature. And so suddenly, without any preliminary symptom, without my feeling dejected or even sad the night before. . . [p. 184].

She sounds like a ripe candidate for psychoanalysis, one of those who has been forced by atrocity to live psychologically beyond her means. But the truth is more elementary and more complex (because so unfamiliar): even more than psychologically, Auschwitz has compelled her to live *physically* beyond her means, and although Charlotte Delbo does not swerve into the psychosomatic implications of this situation, Améry's account of torture sheds some light on it. To live within the limits of the possible after Auschwitz is to acknowledge the limitations of psychological responses to reality. The mystery of Marceline's annual fever is locked in those organs that were abused by atrocity. Since in Auschwitz the unaided mind was virtually powerless to resist the threats of death, all effort was concentrated in the body. Survival can no longer be idealized: lung resections in Mann, plague serum in Camus, radiation treatment in Solzhenitsyn, and inexplicable typhus anniversaries in Delbo carry literal as well as symbolic force, as attitudes toward life are more and more controlled by bodily reactions to the threat of death. It is no longer possible to dress man's "creatureliness" in the robes of an outmoded classical dignity.

Since atrocity attacks the body more than the mind, its victim naturally equates survival with ministering to the flesh. Except for the ghosts of the dead, the spirit vanishes from Charlotte Delbo's imaginative world, which is dominated by physical presence, solid sense-images flashing vividly across the screen of memory. In her Auschwitz trilogy, no intellectual resources add substance to the immediacy of the original experience. The inversion of the normal sequence of events, in which a human being moves from youth through life to age and death, reaches a denouement in the last volume's penultimate chapter, "The Funeral," when the narrator and several other survivors meet more than twenty years later to attend the funeral of one of their comrades from *là-bas.* One quickly gets the sense that dying has become anticlimactic for many of them as they gather, ironically, for a different kind of train voyage that will bring them to a "different" kind of death—a normal one. "I never weep at funerals anymore," says one. "It's lucky if you have a funeral" (p. 190). Beyond atrocity, death is no longer a culmination, and this in turn leads to some new definitions of self and a revised perspective on the individual's relation to his reality.

On their way to commemorate one death, their conversation inevitably turns to the common event that joins them all, the death they survived, and though they recall some of the past episodes in a lighthearted tone, the muted effect on their present lives is evident. "When I was 'there,' " says one,

"I used to dream of home; and since I've returned, I dream that I'm 'there'" (p. 201). But which is dream, and which is reality? This is the final issue Charlotte Delbo raises, a question which unsettles previous assumptions about the role of the "best," the "worst," and the "unthinkable" in our existence. As they compare nightmares, we see how a particular kind of reality has chosen *them*, beyond their power to reject it. The narrator's is typical, though it occurs, like Marceline's fever, only about once a year:

It's always the same theme. I'm in prison. They release me on parole, and in the evening I return as I promised, after having been tempted to run away all day, after having tried to lose my way. I never succeed, the road always leads back to prison. Always the same theme, though the setting is different. . . . The most terrifying is the camp. Imagine, leaving Auschwitz and returning there on your own? [pp. 199–200].

The innocent question affirms one of the most sinister consequences of atrocity: one may survive, but never escape it. Yet one cannot absorb it into a meaningful context, penetrate the source of the energy that links it to our lives. The moment of return is so horrible and oppressive, the narrator continues, that she wants to cry out, but can't: "Finally I cry out and that wakes me up. That's when I see the barbed wire, the watchtowers, the outline of the chimneys. I never see anything else. I always cry out before seeing more. It's inexplicable" (p. 200). These are precisely the words that Marceline used when describing her mysterious fever, so we are not surprised when someone asks the narrator at this point whether there is any news about Marceline. Her fever and the narrator's recurrent nightmare are twin manifestations of the impulse to renew contact with an elusive reality that hovers on the fringes of meaning in their lives. Either the individual interprets this reality and finds a place for it in imaginative projections of modern experience, or admits that atrocity comprises an inexplicable feature of that experience, fragmenting for our generation former notions of the integrated self. In her Auschwitz trilogy, Charlotte Delbo dramatizes both options, without presuming to judge their value.

The very confrontation with these options requires a re-trained sensibility, though one achieves it not without paying a price. Confrontation with atrocity, Delbo repeatedly suggests, brings with it a dislocation in the center of self which may never be repaired. In the train compartment she notices how her companions seem simultaneously to have changed completely, and not to have changed at all. Their appearance "then" is so etched on the memory that their appearance "now" is both real and deceptive. How strange, she muses:

Have I several faces too? It seems that each of us has one face—tired, worn, congealed—and underneath this damaged face another one—intelligent, mobile—the one that we remember. And a veneer covering both of them, a mask that serves as a pass key to use when we leave the house, go out into life, approach people, take part in all the things that are happening around us, a mask of courtesy... [p. 187].

Like Robert Jay Lifton, Charlotte Delbo recognizes the survivor's need to give form to her feelings, but she is far less hopeful about the possibility of achieving "a new sense of self and the world." One heritage of atrocity is a divided sense of the self, and given this division in the survivor, how is the outsider to participate in her experience so as to "share the guilt and the responsibility"?[8] Although Delbo answers Lifton's call for images adequate to the prospect of annihilation and premature death, her vision foresees no transfiguration of the self. The tone of her narrative makes such expectations sound futile and slightly ludicrous.

Living on two levels may be a symptom of our age, but not a solution to its problems. The narrator listens to one of her companions recall an episode when all of them stole some tomatoes from a greenhouse near Auschwitz—and cannot recall a single detail of the adventure! She has blocked it completely. That was the time, another reminds them, when the narrator was a little out of her head (from the thirst, presumably, that we examined earlier). What do you remember, she wonders, and what forget, in order to keep your sanity? Forgetting tomatoes—that's stupid. That's not a very important memory. And then her mind drifts back to those images which lie at the very heart of the experience of atrocity, the haunting recollection of dying under extreme conditions which reappears when all the veils accumulated between "then" and "now" have been stripped away:

Why not rather forget the stench of the smoke, the color of the smoke, the red and sooty flames that shot forth from the chimneys, writhing in the wind that sent their smell to us? Why not rather forget all the dead in the morning and all the dead in the evening, why not rather forget the corpses with their tormented eyes, their hands twisted like the claws of frozen birds. Why not rather forget thirst, hunger, cold, exhaustion, since it serves nothing to remember, and I can't give anyone an idea of what they were like . . . since I can't make them understand the difference between time there and time here, the time there which was empty and which was heavy with all those dead. . . [pp. 196-97].

Forget? The narrator has no choice. Does the contemporary imagination? We "cannot maintain our former attitude toward death," wrote Freud in 1915, "and have not yet discovered a new one."[9] But we now have ample literary evidence to help us understand what prompted Freud's remark, and a better basis for achieving some new insights, if not the new attitudes he called for.

Delbo's chapter ends before the friends arrive at the funeral. What meaning would it have had? As in Solzhenitsyn, terms like "arrival" and "departure," "future," "survival," and "death" itself have other meanings in the dictionary of atrocity.[10] Even the "train journey" (again made more emphatic by Solzhenitsyn) no longer speaks to a single dimension of reality, once the imagination has made itself receptive to the dual implications of this vocabulary. The ceremony of single burial is an inappropriate conclusion to a narrative whose burden has been the inadequacy of "our former attitudes toward death." If the reader's feelings hope to escape by the consolations of this familiar ritual, Charlotte Delbo shatters those expectations by ending her trilogy with a different kind of "adieu," a farewell to life (and love) beneath the shadow of an inappropriate death that refutes all hope and consolation. The last episode introduces a familiar theme, the separa-

tion of lovers, an essence of atrocity that both Camus and
Solzhenitsyn recognized and that Charlotte Delbo was forced
to enact in her own life.

When the last of the survivors we meet, Françoise, is taken
to her husband's cell to say good-bye just before his execution, we do not get an account of the parting, but of a
woman's mind in the process of contemplating it and its consequences. Atrocity destroys sentiment, substituting a much
harsher and unredeeming challenge: how to remake one's life
having survived it. *"Refaire sa vie,"* says Françoise bitterly,
"quelle expression . . ." (p. 211). The meaninglessness of her
husband's premature death, the absence of any form of transcendence, makes renewal of her own life impossible to her
imagination. How does one live with this knowledge? "I live
under reprieve" (*en sursis,* p. 210), she says, giving us a useful
definition of existence in an age of atrocity: life is a stay of
execution. Survival is a respite, not a triumph. Rieux faced
this lonely fact when the plague had abated; Kostoglotov
discovers it when he is released—temporarily?—from the
hospital; Françoise and most of her friends know it despite
their attempts to "keep in touch" with each other; what Hans
Castorp felt, with an instrument of death in his hands and a
song about death in his heart, we can only guess. For them
all, death is a companion, not a destiny, and once again we
are faced with a gloomy truth that cannot take us beyond
itself.

It is not a vision of grandeur; but neither is its desolation
complete. In one of the three brief poetic statements that
end her trilogy, Charlotte Delbo raises a simple appeal from
that part of her generation which knew atrocity, as well as
an epitaph to the literature that blossomed from its weeds:

I don't know
if you can still make
anything of me
But if you have the courage to try. . . .   [p. 212]

It is a humbled posture for the once proud human figure—but
atrocity does not venerate heritage. In this instance, as in the

others we have examined, it carries no resonance beyond its mortal audience. If Charlotte Delbo speaks in a voice more muted than the tone of our other authors, it is because the experience at the heart of her vision demands a more sustained austerity. From her pages the human image, scarred by atrocity, stares wearily forth, to acceptance and understanding, if not to love. We may not admire it, but we are compelled to recognize its haunting features as one more exemplary portrait of our time.

NOTES

Chapter 1: The Examined Death

1. Aleksandr I. Solzhenitsyn, *The Gulag Archipelago, 1918–1956: An Experiment in Literary Investigation, I–II*, trans. Thomas P. Whitney (New York: Harper & Row, 1973, 1974), p. 93.

2. "Camus at Stockholm: The Acceptance of the Nobel Prize," trans. Justin O'Brien, *The Atlantic Monthly*, Vol. 201 (May 1958), p. 34.

3. A. Alvarez, *The Savage God: A Study of Suicide* (New York: Random House, 1971), p. 262.

4. Ibid., p. 246.

5. Ibid., p. 251.

6. Edwin S. Schneidman, *Deaths of Man* (Baltimore: Penguin Books, 1974), p. 25.

7. Reprinted in Sigmund Freud, *Civilization, War and Death*, trans. E. Colburn Mayne, rev. Joan Riviere, ed. John Rickman, new and enlarged edition (London: The Hogarth Press, 1953), p. 1.

8. Ibid., p. 11, 14.

9. Ibid., pp. 15, 17–18, 16.

10. Ibid., p. 17.

11. Robert Jay Lifton and Eric Olson, *Living and Dying* (New York: Praeger, 1974), pp. 28, 32.

12. Ibid., p. 129.

13. Ibid., pp. 24, 142.

14. Ibid., p. 143.

15. Ibid., pp. 31, 37.

16. Elisabeth Kübler-Ross, *On Death and Dying* (New York: Macmillan, 1969), p. 9.

17. Ibid., p. 17.

18. Avery Weisman, *On Dying and Denying: A Psychiatric Study of Terminality* (New York: Behavioral Publications, 1972), pp. 16, 26.

19. Albert Camus, "Reflections on the Guillotine," in *Resistance, Rebellion, and Death*, trans. Justin O'Brien (New York: The Modern Library, 1960), p. 138.

20. Ibid., pp. 141, 138-39.

21. A remark by Robert Jay Lifton in his study of Hiroshima survivors suggests that the catastrophe of the A-bomb drove parents to more complex confrontations with inappropriate death than the conventional modes of pathos and the rhetoric of grief adopted by Gunther: "Children's deaths had particularly strong impact, whatever the circumstances. These aroused in parents a special kind of guilt associated with failure to carry out the most fundamental psychobiological tasks in caring for the young—giving life to them and maintaining it in them. Parents' later self-reproaches had more to do with these basic emotions than with the actual details of a child's death, which, in fact, they often reconstructed in a way that made them most culpable." See Lifton, *Death in Life: Survivors of Hiroshima* (New York: Random House, 1967), pp. 38-39.

22. John Gunther, *Death Be Not Proud: A Memoir* (New York: Harper and Row, Perennial Library Ed., 1965), p. 32.

23. Ibid., pp. 65-66.

24. Ibid., pp. 96, 38, 111.

25. Ibid., pp. 112, 113.

26. Lael Tucker Wertenbaker, *Death of a Man* (Boston: Beacon Press, 1957), p. 65.

27. Ibid., pp. 150, 16.

28. Ibid., p. 67.

29. Ibid., p. 71.

30. Ibid., p. 141.

31. Ibid., pp. 95, 144-45.

32. See Leo Tolstoy, *Childhood, Boyhood, Youth,* trans. Rosemary Edmonds, (Baltimore: Penguin Books, 1964), pp. 93-94.

33. Simone de Beavoir, *A Very Easy Death,* trans. Patrick O'Brien (New York: Warner Paperback Library, 1973) pp. 45, 48.

34. Ibid., pp. 24, 25, 51.

35. Ibid., pp. 108, 67.

36. Ibid., pp. 112, 68.

37. Ibid., p. 115.

38. Ibid., pp. 78, 79.

39. Ibid., pp. 113-14, 123.

Chapter 2: Dying Voices

1. Simone de Beauvoir, *A Very Easy Death,* p. 106.

2. *Letzte Briefe zum Tode Verurteilter: 1939-1945,* hrsg. von Pietro Malvezzi und Giovanni Pirelli (München: Deutscher Taschenbuch Verlag, 1962), pp. 30-31. Translation mine.

3. Ernest Becker, *The Denial of Death* (New York: The Free Press, 1973), pp. 155, 158.

4. *Letzte Briefe,* pp. 56, 57.

5. Becker, pp. 283-84.

6. *Letzte Briefe,* p. 254.

7. Ibid., p. 251.

8. Ibid., pp. 252, 253, 254.

9. Becker, p. 87.

10. Jean Améry, *Jenseits von Schuld und Sühne: Bewältigungsversuche eines Überwältigten* (München: Szczesny Verlag, 1966), p. 32. Translation mine.

11. Ibid., pp. 36–37.

12. Ibid., pp. 37, 38.

13. For an alternative view of human behavior in the concentration camps see Terrence Des Pres, *The Survivor: An Anatomy of Life in the Death Camps* (New York: Oxford University Press, 1976). My own investigations have taught me to speak of "survivors" rather than a prototype called "the survivor." Every response to the camp experience contains the seeds of its own contradiction.

14. Becker, pp. 165, 245.

15. Améry, p. 43.

16. Ibid., p. 49.

17. Ibid., pp. 52, 53.

18. Ibid., pp. 59, 60.

19. Ibid., p. 61.

20. Becker, p. 251.

21. Ibid., p. 250.

22. Ibid., pp. 226, 218.

23. Améry, p. 64.

24. *Wir Haben Es Gesehen: Augenzeugenberichte Über Terror und Judenverfolgung im Dritten Reich,* hrsg. von Gerard Schoenbrunner (Hamburg: Rütten & Loening Verlag, 1962), pp. 274, 275. Translation mine.

25. Ibid., p. 275.

26. Ibid., p. 275.

27. Ibid., pp. 275–76.

28. Ibid., p. 276.

29. Robert Jay Lifton, *Death in Life: Survivors of Hiroshima* (New York: Random House, 1967), pp. 225, 21.

30. Ibid., p. 278.

31. Ibid., p. 256.

32. Becker, p. 87.

33. Lifton, p. 522.

34. Ibid., pp. 325, 371.

35. Ibid., p. 486.

36. Ibid., p. 488.

37. Ibid., p. 499.

38. Freud, *Civilization, War and Death*, p. 17.

39. Lifton, p. 190.

Chapter 3: Thomas Mann and Death on the Mountain

1. Thomas Mann, "The Making of the Magic Mountain," in *The Magic Mountain,* trans. H.T. Lowe-Porter (New York: Alfred A. Knopf, 1927), pp. 720, 721.

2. Mann, *The Magic Mountain,* p. ix. Subsequent references to this volume will be cited in the text.

3. Becker, *The Denial of Death,* p. 226.

4. Herman Melville, *Moby Dick* (New York: Rinehart and Co., 1948), p. 420.

5. Translations of the French dialogue between Hans and Clavdia are mine.

6. Albert Camus, *Notebooks: 1942-1951,* trans. Justin O'Brien (New York: Alfred A. Knopf, 1966), pp. 19-20 (March 1942).

7. Ibid., p. 5 (Jan.-Feb. 1942).

8. Mark Twain, *Adventures of Huckleberry Finn* (Boston: Houghton Mifflin, 1958), pp. 69, 70.

9. Melville, *Moby Dick,* pp. 186, 192.

10. Ibid., p. 192.

11. Camus, *Notebooks: 1942-1951,* p. 65 (Feb. 10, 1943).

12. Borrowing a phrase from Naphta, Hans says of his vision that we "dream anonymously and communally, if each after his fashion" (p. 495). But in the novel Hans's "fashion" is unique enough to blur the communal sources of what he "sees" and to stress the individual quality of the adventure.

13.

Der Lindenbaum	*The Linden Tree*
Am Brunnen vor dem Tore	By the well before the gate
Da steht ein Lindenbaum.	There stands a linden tree;
Ich traümt' in seinem Schatten	In its shadows I dreamt
So manchen süssen Traum.	Many a sweet dream.
Ich schnitt in seine Rinde	In its bark I carved
So manches liebe Wort;	Many a word of love;
Es zog in Freud' und Leide	In joy as in sorrow
Zu ihm mich immer fort.	I felt ever drawn to it.
Ich musst' auch heute wandern	Today I had to wander
Vorbei in tiefer Nacht,	Past it at dead of night,
Da hab' ich noch im Dunkel	And even in the darkness
Die Augen zugemacht.	I closed my eyes.
Und seine Zweige rauschten	And its branches rustled,
Als riefen sie mir zu:	As if they were calling to me:
'Komm her zu mir, Geselle,	'Friend, come here to me,
Hier findst du deine Ruh!'	Here you will find rest!'
Die kalten Winde bliesen	The cold winds blew
Mir grad ins Angesicht,	Straight into my face,
Der Hut flog mir vom Kopfe,	My hat flew from my head,
Ich wendete mich nicht.	But I did not turn round.

Nun bin ich manche Stunde	Now I am many hours journey
Entfernt von jenem Ort,	Away from that place,
Und immer hör' ich's rauschen:	But I always hear the rustling:
Du fändest Ruhe dort!	'There you would find rest!'

[Translation mine.]

Chapter 4: Albert Camus and the Limits of the Possible

1. Albert Camus, *Notebooks: 1942–1951,* trans. Justin O'Brien (New York: Alfred A. Knopf, 1966), p. 159 (25 June, 1947).

2. According to Germaine Brée, Camus finished *The Stranger* in May 1940, just before the German invasion, and *The Myth of Sisyphus* in January 1941. See her *Camus,* rev. ed. (New York: Harcourt, Brace & World, 1964), pp. 35–36.

3. *Notebooks: 1942–1951,* p. 90 (November 1943).

4. Ibid., p. 207 (September, 1948).

5. Albert Camus, *Notebooks: 1935–1942,* trans. Philip Thody (New York: The Modern Library, 1963), p. 125 (April 1939).

6. Ibid., p. 139 (September 1939).

7. Ibid., pp. 140, 147 (September 1939).

8. Ibid., p. 149 (November 1939).

9. Albert Camus, *Lyrical and Critical Essays,* ed. Philip Thody, trans. Ellen Conroy Kennedy (New York: Alfred A. Knopf, 1969), pp. 50, 37, 13.

10. Ibid., pp. 39, 78, 76.

11. Ibid., pp. 103, 104–05.

12. Ibid., p. 101.

13. Albert Camus, *The Rebel: An Essay on Man in Revolt,* trans. Anthony Bower (New York: Vintage Books, 1958), pp. 3, 4.

14. Camus, *Lyrical and Critical Essays,* p. 130.

15. Ibid., pp. 134, 135.

16. Ibid., pp. 139, 140.

17. Ibid., pp. 141, 142.

18. Ibid., pp. 148, 153.

19. Ibid., p. 164.

20. Ibid., p. 168.

21. Ibid., p. 169.

22. Ibid., pp. 216, 218.

23. Ibid., pp. 230, 240–241.

24. Camus writes that he responded to this volume "with the personal upheaval so often described by others." See "Encounters with André Gide," in *Lyrical and Critical Essays,* p. 250.

25. Albert Camus, *A Happy Death,* trans. Richard Howard (New York: Alfred A Knopf, 1972), p. 139.

26. Ibid., p. 75.

27. Camus, *Lyrical and Critical Essays*, p. 199.

28. Camus, *A Happy Death*, p. 81.

29. Ibid., p. 141.

30. Ibid., p. 143.

31. Camus, *Lyrical and Critical Essays*, p. 277.

32. Camus, *A Happy Death*, pp. 143, 147, 149.

33. Ibid., p. 150.

34. Albert Camus, *Caligula & Three Other Plays*, trans. Stuart Gilbert (New York: Vintage Books, 1962), p. vi.

35. See *Caligula*, p. vi, and *The Myth of Sisyphus*, trans. Justin O'Brien (New York: Vintage Books, 1955), p. 78.

36. Camus, *Caligula*, p. 8.

37. Ibid., p. 8.

38. Ibid., pp. 17, 16.

39. Ibid., p. 44.

40. Ibid., pp. 73-74.

41. Camus, *The Myth of Sisyphus*, p. 90.

42. Camus, *Lyrical and Critical Essays*, p. 356.

43. Ibid., p. 356.

44. Camus, *Myth of Sisyphus*, pp. v, 73, 72, 69.

45. Ibid., pp. 11, 9, 10, 75.

46. Ibid., pp. 84, 52.

47. Ibid., pp. 85, 87.

48. Ibid., pp. 91, 90.

49. Germaine Brée alludes briefly to the resemblance between the trials of Meursault and Dmitri Karamazov. See her *Camus*, pp. 112-13, n. 1.

50. Albert Camus, *L'Etranger* (Paris: Editions Gallimard, 1957), pp. 77, 95. Translation mine. Subsequent references to *L'Etranger* will be included in the text.

51. Albert Camus, "Pessimism and Courage," in *Resistance, Rebellion, and Death*, trans. Justin O'Brien (New York: The Modern Library, 1960), p. 45.

52. Camus, "Letters to a German Friend," in *Resistance, Rebellion, and Death*, p. 10.

53. Quoted from an unpublished manuscript of 1952 in Germaine Brée, *Camus*, pp. 219-20.

54. Camus, *Resistance, Rebellion, and Death*, p. 24. Camus's quixotic distinctions in this passage bear an uncanny resemblance to some equally idealistic lines near the end of Woodrow Wilson's war message to Congress in 1917: "It will be all the easier for us to conduct ourselves as belligerents in a high spirit of right and fairness because we act without animus, not with emmity toward a people or with the desire to bring any injury or disadvantage upon them, but only in armed opposition to an irresponsible government which has thrown aside all considerations of humanity and of right and is running amuck." Quoted in *The World of Randolph Bourne*, ed. Lillian Schlissel (New York: E.P. Dutton, 1965), pp. 98-99. Even Camus seemed reluctant to confront the

full mutilating possibilities of atrocity. Perhaps this helps to explain why he chose a natural disease rather than human agents as the source of evil in *The Plague.*

55. Albert Camus, *The Plague,* trans. Stuart Gilbert (Baltimore: Penguin Books, 1960), p. 9. Subsequent references to *The Plague* will be included in the text.

56. Camus pays tribute to André Gide for teaching him how to give himself limits in art. Of Gide he says: "His conception of classicism as a romanticism brought under control is something I share." See Albert Camus, "Three Interviews," in *Lyrical and Critical Essays,* p. 353.

Chapter 5: Aleksandr Solzhenitsyn and the Journey Through Humiliation

1. Camus, *The Rebel,* p. 305.

2. Aleksandr I. Solzhenitsyn, *The Gulag Archipelago, 1918–1956: An Experiment in Literary Investigation, I–II,* trans. Thomas P. Whitney (New York: Harper & Row, 1974), p. 591.

3. Aleksandr I. Solzhenitsyn, *The Gulag Archipelago, 1918–1956: An Experiment in Literary Investigation, III–IV,* trans. Thomas P. Whitney (New York: Harper & Row, 1975), p. 208. Subsequent references to this volume will be cited as *GA Two* in the text.

4. Alexander Solzhenitsyn, *One Day in the Life of Ivan Denisovich,* trans. Max Hayward and Ronald Hingley (New York: Bantam Books, 1963), p. 4. Subsequent references to this volume will be cited in the text.

5. The situation among Charlotte Delbo and her comrades in Auschwitz, as we shall see, is somewhat different, since they are joined by a patriotic impulse that is unavailable to Solzhenitsyn's Soviet prisoners, who were of course arrested and deported by their own countrymen. In addition, Delbo and many of her friends were united by their allegiance to the French resistance movement. Nevertheless, survival of the body is still the crucial feature of their existence.

6. In Mann's post–World War II novel, *Doctor Faustus,* the history of the Third Reich *is* assimilated into the imaginative vision of the novel, where it becomes a vital gloss on the action.

7. Saul Bellow's *Herzog* is another contemporary work which fuses elements of history with imagined reality. Herzog spends much of his intellectual energy composing "letters" to prominent historical personalities of past and present. The coherence of his fictional life depends in part on his ability to organize their impact on twentieth-century civilization into meaningful patterns. Its incoherence, though, reflects the confusion which the events of modern history have imposed on the private intelligence.

8. Camus, *The Rebel,* p. 4.

9. Alexander Solzhenitsyn, *Cancer Ward,* trans. Nicholas Bethell and David Burg (New York: Bantam Books, 1969), p. 103. Subsequent references to this volume will be cited in the text.

10. Committee of State Security—the Soviet security police.

11. Camus, "On the Future of Tragedy," in *Lyrical and Critical Essays*, pp. 306, 307.

Chapter 6: Charlotte Delbo and A Heart of Ashes

1. Mann, *The Magic Mountain*, pp. 536–37.

2. Camus, *Notebooks: 1942–1951* (15 December 1942), p. 48.

3. Charlotte Delbo, *None of Us Will Return*, trans. John Githens (New York: Grove Press, 1968), p. 61. Subsequent references to this volume will be cited in the text.

4. The idea grows less fanciful with repetition. In his preface to the first Gulag volume, Solzhenitsyn writes:

> Decades go by, and the scars and sores of the past are healing over for good. In the course of this period some of the islands of the Archipelago have shuddered and dissolved and the polar sea of oblivion rolls over them. And someday in the future, this Archipelago, its air, and the bones of its inhabitants, frozen in a lens of ice, will be discovered by our descendants like some improbable salamander [*The Gulag Archipelago One*, p. x].

5. Charlotte Delbo, *Une Connaissance inutile* (Paris: Les Editions de Minuit, 1970), p. 43. Translation mine. Subsequent references to this volume will be cited in the text. As will be seen, the title has dual implications: "A Useless Knowledge" and "A Useless Acquaintance."

6. Since "death-in-life" and "living death" seem to imply priority for life, I have rejected them in favor of the less graceful "death-with-life," to suggest an equal emphasis on each.

7. Charlotte Delbo, *Mesure de nos jours* (Paris: Les Editions de Minuit, 1971), p. 10. Translation mine. Subsequent references to this volume will be cited in the text. The trilogy, which includes *Aucun de nous ne reviendra (None of Us Will Return)*, *Une Connaissance inutile*, and *Mesure de nos jours*, also appears under the general title of *Auschwitz et après*.

8. Lifton and Olson, *Living and Dying*, p. 142.

9. Freud, *Civilisation, War and Death*, pp. 17–18.

10. Solzhenitsyn argues in *The Gulag Archipelago Two* (p. 634) that the camp experience affected everyday speech in addition to inspiring a special slang idiom among the zeks: "Nadezhda Mandelstam speaks truly when she remarks that our life is so permeated with prison that simple meaningful words like 'they took,' or 'they put inside,' or 'he is inside,' or 'they let out,' are understood by everyone in our country in only one sense, even without a context."

INDEX